LLEWELLYN'S
2 0 1 7
HERBAL
A L M A N A C

Cover Design: Kevin R. Brown
Editing: Ed Day and Lauryn Heineman

Cover images:
iStockphoto.com/22814004, 22918495/© mart_m
iStockphoto.com/36660630/© mooozi
iStockphoto.com/23933332/© edge69

Interior Art: © Fiona King

You can order annuals and books from
New Worlds, Llewellyn's catalog. To request
a free copy, call 1-877-NEW WRLD toll-free
or visit www.llewellyn.com.

ISBN 978-0-7387-3761-4
Llewellyn Worldwide Ltd.
2143 Wooddale Drive
Woodbury, MN 55125-2989

Printed in the United States of America

Contents

Herb Crafts

Herb History, Myth, and Lore

Moon Signs, Phases, and Tables

Introduction to
Llewellyn's Herbal Almanac

More and more people are using herbs, growing and gathering them, and studying them for their enlivening and healing properties. Whether in the form of plant therapy, a dye garden, or a new favorite recipe, herbs can clearly enhance your life.

In the 2017 edition of the *Herbal Almanac*, we once again feature some of the most innovative and original thinkers and writers on herbs. We tap into the practical, historical, and enjoyable aspects of herbal knowledge—using herbs to help you reconnect with the earth, enhance your culinary creations, and heal your body and mind. The thirty-one articles in this almanac will teach you everything from growing a square-foot garden to the etymology of the herbs you might plant there. You'll also learn how to create cosmetics from natural ingredients, to grow a garden that's beneficial to bees, and to craft cordials and liqueurs. Enjoy!

Note: The old-fashioned remedies in this book are historical references used for teaching purposes only. The recipes are not for commercial use or profit. The contents are not meant to diagnose, treat, prescribe, or substitute consultation with a licensed health-care professional. Herbs, whether used internally or externally, should be introduced in small amounts to allow the body to adjust and to detect possible allergies. Please consult a standard reference source or an expert herbalist to learn more about the possible effects of certain herbs. You must take care not to replace regular medical treatment with the use of herbs. Herbal treatment is intended primarily to complement modern health care. Always seek professional help if you suffer from illness. Also, take care to read all warning labels before taking any herbs or starting on an extended herbal regimen. Always consult medical and herbal professionals before beginning any sort of medical treatment—this is particularly true for pregnant women. Herbs are powerful things; be sure you are using that power to achieve balance.

Llewellyn Worldwide does not participate in, endorse, or have any authority or responsibility concerning private business transactions between its authors and the public.

Growing
and
Gathering
Herbs

Unraveling the Tapestry of the Medieval Garden

☙ by Natalie Zaman ❧

Can you find the frog? He's hidden in the flowers and easy to miss. Most folks who visit the Unicorn Tapestry room in the Cloisters museum and gardens in New York and gaze at *The Unicorn in Captivity* have their eyes on the unicorn. He sits in a garden under a pomegranate tree, the juice from the overripe fruit dripping down his back. The surrounding landscape is lush and filled with a thousand flowers (*millefleur*) as well as a few insects and, of course, the frog. Each of the seven tapestries is ripe with symbolism (as was much of the medieval world). But look closely at the scenes before you: amid the hidden references is a picture of life in the Middle Ages, much of which was centered around gardening.

The garden plots of the Middle Ages were places where practicality, pleasure, superstition, science, and spirituality all existed comfortably side by side. Plants that fed and healed the body also brought comfort to the soul through religious symbolism or protection—real and imagined—through old wives' tales and folklore. Elements such as fishponds, dovecotes, and beehives were incorporated into their schemes for their produce as well as sufficiency; fishponds were water sources, the denizens of dovecotes provided fertilizer as well as feathers for pillows and bedding, and bees were a means of pollination.

The Middle Ages encompassed the period from about 500 to 1400 CE—that's nine hundred years of horticultural evolution. According to Marilyn Stokstad and Jerry Stannard, curators of the *Gardens of the Middle Ages* exhibit at the Spencer Museum of Art in Lawrence, Kansas, and Dumbarton Oaks in Washington, DC, five types of gardens could be found in medieval Europe: the *cloistered* gardens of religious orders; the *kitchen* gardens tended by all households, large and small; *herbariums*, devoted to medicinal and other practical herbs; and the *patrician* and *pleasure* gardens of the upper classes. Each one has its own unique wisdom to share with us.

The *Hortus Conclusus*

Executed in the eleventh century, the plan for the cathedral, abbey, and gardens of the monastery of St. Gall in Switzerland (never fully completed) is the only large-scale architectural drawing to survive the Middle Ages. In addition to an herbarium and kitchen garden, a block of space just to the right of the cathedral was set aside for a *hortus conclusus*—an enclosed contemplative garden.

For folks who followed the Christian faith, paradise was the ultimate garden from which man was expelled. In one sense the contemplative garden (sometimes called a cloister garden because it is surrounded by covered walkways or a wall of some kind) was an attempt to recapture paradise as a man-made "heaven on earth."

Meant to be an expression of the divine order, the contemplative garden was a place of prayer, meditation, and solitude, and it was instantly recognizable because of its symmetry. Divided into quadrants by intersecting paths, this space was planted simply, sometimes just with patches of turf or lawn with trees for shade and benches to sit. Life sustaining and spiritually cleansing, a water source sat at its center in the form of a fountain or wellhead, at the foot of which at least three symbolic (and fragrant) flowers could usually be found.

A rosary was literally a **rose** garden, but in the thirteenth century the word evolved to mean the "garden of prayers" devoted to the Virgin Mary, whose array of floral symbols included the rose. The Venerable Bede, medieval historian, linked the **lily** to Mary: the white petals symbolized the purity of her body, the golden center was the light of her soul, and its heavenly scent represented her divinity. Low to the ground, the **violet** can survive in a variety of climates. It has a lovely fragrance, though not a showy blossom. These "humble" traits earned it a place as yet another symbol of Mary, whose humility and gentle power were a comfort and inspiration to humankind.

Obviously, the Virgin Mary was an important figure in the lives of medieval European and British peoples, but not everyone had the resources to create a contemplative garden. A tradition that began in monasteries and convents and then spread to lay folk was the creation of the Mary Garden. These small plots were no more than simple collections of plants and herbs, both cultivated and wild, which were connected to Mary and different admirable aspects of her character. **Columbine** was Our Lady's shoes: this flower with its dove-shaped petals sprang up under Mary's feet when she walked to the house of her cousin Elizabeth to share the news of her pregnancy. **Foxglove** was Our Lady's gloves, and interestingly, these flowers were also known as fairy gloves or elf's gloves. **Forget-me-not** was Mary's eyes; **Lily of the valley**, Our Lady's tears. **Marigold** literally means Mary's gold—calendula, or pot marigold, was the first flower to be named for Mary. **Parsley** was Our Lady's little vine, and **St. John's wort** was Mary's glory.

No matter what faith you follow, you can create a devotional garden that is medieval in spirit. Set aside a space indoors or out; like the contemplative gardens of the monasteries, this will be a place of respite, so try to clear it of any clutter so you will not be distracted by outside thoughts when you visit. Choose up to four plants that appeal to you or instill a sense of peace and calm when you see or smell them. Install the plants in a quadrant-shaped plot, or, if yours is an indoor garden, use four small pots. Devotional gardens are highly personal; if you wish, incorporate statuary, stones, or other objects or images that hold meaning for you.

Pottage for Castle and Cottage

The most common medieval plots, kitchen gardens (also called cottage gardens) were dedicated to growing food. They could be as simple as a few rows of root and leafy vegetables and cooking herbs or they might be vast fields that yielded produce for a manor or religious house and all its occupants. The gardens of plain folk had no formal plan but were plots of "toft and croft." As villages were organized, land was given to peasants to tend and live upon. The toft was nearer to the road and usually where houses were built, while the croft behind was a small enclosed pasture—here, gardens were tended.

A variety of fruits, herbs and vegetables were grown in kitchen gardens, and people, especially commoners, depended on this produce for survival and not just for adding to a meal. In the Middle Ages, they were also multipurpose.

A **cabbage** was the common base for pottage, but the leaves were also used to dress wounds. **Onions** added flavor and substance to the stew and doubled as a digestive aid. Onion skins were boiled to make dye. Not to be eaten raw as they could "corrupt the blood," **leeks** were often substituted for garlic in other dishes but were a staple of pottage. Mixed with vinegar, frankincense, and rose oil, they were ingredients in ear drops. "**Rosemary** for remembrance," wrote Shakespeare, but this herb was a remedy for toothache, among other things, and a favorite flavoring for meats and vegetables.

The basic ingredients of pottage—a vegetable stew cooked in a pot that was eaten by most people of all classes throughout the British Isles and the Continent—are vegetables and herbs that are readily available and easy to grow today. Ingredients varied by region, and other foodstuffs could be added to the stew: oats to thicken, herbs to flavor, and meat to add heartiness. To make a basic pottage, chop up one head of cabbage, one large onion, and one large leek. Put the vegetables in a pot along with the rosemary and add between four and six cups of chicken or vegetable stock. Bring the mixture to a simmer and stir occasionally until the vegetables are soft.

The Many Hues of the Herbarium

Early in the ninth century a boy named Walafrid Strabo was sent to the Benedictine monastery of Reichenau in Germany, where he grew up, and eventually became abbot. In his poem *Hortolus* ("the little garden" in Latin), he described the monastery garden as it changed throughout the seasons and the plants—thirty of them—he tended there. Walafrid also kept a notebook on the meanings of plants and their uses based on folklore and his own experience growing, processing, and using them. The primary purpose of the herbarium was to grow and process medicinal plants, but, as with those found in the kitchen garden, many of these had multiple uses, including the making of inks and dyes.

Woad was used for lowering fevers and curing infectious disease, but it was better known for making blue dye and body paint. Creating blue dye with woad was a two step process: after the leaves were steeped, the acidity of the water had to be adjusted for the blue color to activate. In the Middle Ages, urine was added to the bath to ensure a vibrant blue hue. **Lady's bedstraw** yielded a bright yellow dye, but it was also incorporated into salves to heal burns. Other plants that produced yellow dye include betony, agrimony, southern wood, and chaste tree (also known as monk's pepper), the seeds of which were taken to suppress the libido, thus insuring chastity. Red dye was made by simmering **madder** roots. A brew of the leaves was a cure for jaundice.

Shaping the Patrician Garden

In orchard or garden, trees played an important role in medieval sustainability. Like most plants, trees—their bark, wood, leaves, and fruit—had multiple uses. For those who had the resources, a garden with trees could be more than just a means of cultivating necessary plants. Patrician plots were gardens of mixed use; practical herbs, vegetables and fruit trees were elevated to ornamental status. Space was often a commodity in the patrician garden, so trees were trained to grow against walls or form natural arbors and trellises under which visitors could find a bit of shade or privacy. Espaliering—pruning and training trees to grow in a specific shape—was employed to make the most of every square foot of space.

Symbolic of knowledge and the Garden of Eden, **apples** were enjoyed right off the tree, baked into fragrant desserts, and, of course, pressed into cider. **Pears** were the second most popular fruit after apples—and were often paired with apples in recipes as well as in the orchard. A treat with dual symbolism, you will find pears incorporated into medieval artworks depicting Mary and the infant Jesus as well as bawdy lines from poems and plays that tout the pear as a phallic symbol. Of the **medlar** tree's fruit, Chaucer wrote, "Til we be roten, ken we not be rype" (Until we're rotten, we're not ripe). Effective as an antidiarrheal, medlars can only be eaten when their flesh is as soft as paste from a process called "bletting." As unappetizing as it may look, a ripe medlar can taste like rich apple butter with hints of vanilla and cinnamon. One of the trees found in the orchard cemetery at St. Gall, the **quince's** golden, apple-like fruit ripen late in the autumn. (They're said to be the golden apples of Hesperides come to earth.) Usually eaten cooked rather than straight off the tree, quinces were also used to staunch bleeding in small wounds.

The Essence of the Pleasure Garden

Pleasure gardens were planted, obviously, for pleasure, incorporating nooks to sit and read in, tables to play games on, and private places for friends and lovers to meet. While most people had keen religious sensibilities, the pleasure garden was a monument to human nature and a place where love reigned. Pleasure gardens titillated the senses by design and so were filled with trees, plants, and flowers that had both sensual and symbolic value.

Fragrance was of just as much import as visual delight and innuendo. An ingredient in love charms, **lemon balm's** leaves are heavily fragrant with citrus. Its small white flowers are favorites of bees—servants of Venus, the goddess of love and beauty, as expressed in the hexagonal shape of a honeycomb cell. A natural insecticide, **mint's** strong fragrance ensured its place in the pleasure garden. Also associated with Venus, it's no surprise that it was used as a tooth whitener and breath freshener. Sweet scented and beautiful, **roses** were and are the flowers of love. Their essence was distilled into rosewater for cooking as well as cosmetic use. **Chamomile's** pretty, daisy-like flowers brightened up the borders of the pleasure garden and give off a sweet, apple-like scent. A draft of chamomile calms a nervous stomach, but folklore tells us that it also has the qualities of an aphrodisiac.

Stepping into the Tapestry

Changing times and building and land improvements have ensured that no medieval garden has survived intact. However, thanks to these re-creations, it is possible to step back in time and stop and smell the flowers.

- The Cloisters of the Ancient Spanish Monastery: www.spanishmonastery.com
- The Penn State Medieval Garden: www.psumedievalgarden.org
- St. Clare's Garden at Santa Clara University: http://www.scu.edu/stclaregarden/
- The Cloisters museum and gardens: http://www.metmuseum.org/visit/visit-the-cloisters

When you visit the Cloisters, match the plants in the gardens to the plants in the tapestry—and find the frog in the lower right hand corner of *The Unicorn in Captivity*.

Resources

Cavallo, Adolfo Salvatore. *The Unicorn Tapestries in The Metropolitan Museum of Art*. New Haven: Yale University Press, 1998.

Cosman, Madeleine Pelner. *Fabulous Feasts: Medieval Cookery and Ceremony*. New York: George Braziller, 1989.

Eberley, S. E. S. "Designing a Medieval Garden." Wyrtig, 2011. http://wyrtig.com/Resources/Online/Designing TheMedievalHerbGarden.htm.

Larkin, Deidre. "Rotten-ripe: The Meddlar Goes Soft." *The Medieval Garden Enclosed* (blog), November 14, 2008. http://blog.metmuseum.org/cloistersgardens/2008 /11/14/rotten-ripe-the-medlar-goes-soft/.

———. "The Golden Quince." *The Medieval Garden Enclosed*, October 27, 2008. http://blog.metmuseum.org/cloisters gardens/2008/10/27/the-golden-quince/.

"Mary Gardens." Fish Eaters. Accessed September 10, 2015.
http://www.fisheaters.com/marygardens.html.

Osborne, Cindy. "Mary Gardens." The Marian Library of the International Marian Research Institute. Last modified March 27, 2012. http://campus.udayton.edu/mary/resources/m_garden/AB-MG.html.

"Plants." The Penn State Medieval Garden. Accessed September 10, 2015. http://www.psumedievalgarden.com/search.html.

Stokstad, Marilyn, and Jerry Stannard. *Gardens of the Middle Ages*. Lawrence: The Spencer Museum of Art, University of Kansas Press, 1983.

"The Plan of St. Gall." Carolingian Culture at Reichenau and St. Gall. UCLA Digital Library, 2012. http://www.stgallplan.org/en/index_plan.html.

Natalie Zaman *is a regular contributor to various Llewellyn annual publications. She is the coauthor of the* Graven Images Oracle *deck (Galde Press) and writes the recurring feature* Wandering Witch *for* Witches & Pagans Magazine. *Her work has also appeared in* FATE, Sage Woman, *and* newWitch *magazines. When she's not on the road, she's chasing free-range hens in her self-sufficient and Pagan-friendly back garden. Find Natalie online at www.nataliezaman.blogspot.com or at www.broomstix.blogspot .com, a collection of crafts, stories, ritual, and art she curates for Pagan families.*

The Herbal Insectary

∼ by Jill Henderson ∼

Most gardeners grow herbs for their savory flavors and healing properties, but with a little extra planning, the herb garden can become a powerful insectary that attracts thousands of butterflies, beneficial insects, and pollinators right where gardeners need and can appreciate them the most.

What Is an Insectary?

Simply put, an insectary is a place to rear and keep live insects. As a gardener, I can't think of a better place to rear and keep live insects than in the garden, especially when those insects can help produce more fruit and vegetables by pollinating crops and feasting on truly destructive insects like cabbage worms, aphids, and bean beetles. Beneficial insects allow the gardener to reduce or eliminate their dependence on hard-core chemical and even organic insecticides by wreaking havoc on "bad bugs" that chew holes in leaves, spread viral diseases, disfigure fruits, and weaken or kill plants. Thankfully, the herbs and flowers that surround your garden can become a natural insectary that supports the life cycles of beneficial insects by providing them with food, shelter, and water.

You can probably find a few beneficials flitting about your herb garden on any given day, but if you really want to reap the benefits of these powerful natural insecticides, you'll want to learn a little more about them: what they like to eat, where they like to sleep and overwinter, and how they reproduce.

The first thing anyone thinking of encouraging the presence of beneficials needs to know is that one size does not fit all. You may have a few wasps, a handful of ladybugs, and a couple of praying mantises lurking in your garden, but that's just not enough to affect the bad bugs in any appreciable way. What you really need is an entire army of good bugs—one that is diversified, well fed, protected, and supported year-round. And if you want your army at the ready from the first signs of spring to the first frost in fall, you must be prepared to support your beneficials with everything they'll need to survive. In return, your army of good bugs will decimate the bad bugs year after year.

It's Dinnertime

The first and most important thing you'll need to do to attract adult beneficials is to provide them with a quality food source. For that, you'll need to know what they like to eat. For example, praying mantises and spiders feed primarily on other insects, while braconid wasps and hover flies eat only pollen and nectar. Beneficials such as ladybugs are true omnivores that feast on pollen and nectar when their insect prey is in short supply. The most important thing to remember is that if you provide adult beneficials with the right kinds of food, they will eventually produce hundreds of larvae, which are voracious eaters of other insects.

When it comes to providing food for your beneficials, herbs just can't be beat. Not only are they relatively care-free, but many herbs produce small clusters of flowers that beneficials find irresistible. The beneficials that don't eat pollen or nectar will prey on other insects attracted to the flowers. Of particular interest are herbs, vegetables, and flowering plants in the following plant families:

Carrot Family: Apiaceae (formerly Umbelliferae)
    Angelica (*Angelica archangelica*)
    Anise (*Pimpinella anisum*)
    Anise hyssop (*Agastache foeniculum*)
    Caraway (*Carum carvi*)
    Carrot (*Daucus carota* ssp. *sativus*)
    Celery (*Apium graveolens* var. *dulce*)
    Chervil (*Anthriscus cerefolium*)
    Cilantro/Coriander (*Coriandrum sativum*)
    Culantro/Mexican cilantro (*Eryngium foetidum*)
    Cumin (*Cuminum cyminum*)
    Dill (*Anethum graveolens*)
    Fennel (*Foeniculum vulgare*)
    Fenugreek (*Trigonella foenum-graecum*)
    Gotu kola/Centella (*Centella asiatica*)

Lovage (*Levisticum officinale*)

Parsley (*Petroselinum crispum*)

Parsnip (*Pastinaca sativa*)

Queen Anne's lace (*Daucus carota* var. *carota*)

Sweet cicely (*Myrrhis odorata*)

Mint Family: Lamiaceae (formerly Labiatae)

Basil (*Ocimum basilicum*)

Bee balm (*Monarda didyma*)

Bergamot (*Monarda fistulosa*)

Catnip / Catmint (*Nepeta* spp.)

Horehound (*Marrubium vulgare*)

Horsemint (*Monarda punctata*)

Hyssop (*Hyssopus officinalis*)

Korean Mint (*Agastache rugosa*)

Lavender (*Lavandula* spp.)

Lemon balm (*Melissa officinalis*)

Marjoram (*Origanum majorana*)

Mint (*Mentha* spp.)

Monarda (*Monarda* spp.)

Mountain mints (*Pycnanthemum* spp.)

Oregano (*Origanum vulgare*)

Penstemon (*Penstemon* spp.)

Rosemary (*Rosmarinus officinalis*)

Sage (*Salvia officinalis*)

Salvia (*Salvia* spp.)

Savory (*Satureja* spp.)

Thyme (*Thymus* spp.)

Aster Family: Asteraceae (formerly Compositae)

Calendula (*Calendula* spp.)

Coneflowers (*Echinacea* spp.)
Feverfew (*Chrysanthemum parthenium*)
Yarrow (*Achillea millefolium*)
Yellow coneflower (*Ratibida pinnata*)

Onion Family: Amaryllidaceae (formerly Lilliaceae)
Bunching onions, scallions (*Allium fistulosum*)
Common cooking onions (*Allium cepa*)
Garlic (*Allium sativum*)
Garlic chives (*Allium tuberosum*)
Leeks and elephant garlic (*Allium ampeloprasum*)
Onion chives (*Allium schoenoprasum*)
Potato or multiplier onions, shallots (*Allium cepa* var. *aggregatum*)
Walking onions (*Allium cepa* var. *proliferum*)

One look at this partial list of plants attractive to beneficial insects will tell you that many of the herbs that you already have in your herb garden are excellent candidates for the herbal insectary. Most culinary herbs are perennial in nature, which is why they are often grown in permanent beds outside of the vegetable garden. But annual herbs like dill and basil, grown primarily for their leaves and seeds, are often sown in the garden right alongside the carrots and the beans. I don't know any gardener who doesn't want to protect their annual herbs from hungry caterpillars and chewing insects, but some of the pests of annual herbs are beneficials in their own right. For example, many of the herbs in the carrot family are host plants for the larval stages of several species of swallowtail butterfly, which can quickly defoliate even large, healthy plants. The best way around this problem is to plant a plethora of annual herbs in the insectary—separate from those grown in the garden. Let the caterpillars eat the dill and fennel in the insectary, and if you don't want to kill them, move those found in the vegetable garden to the same plants in the insectary, where they can live out their lives as beneficials. And remember, if you plant extra annuals for the beneficial pollinators, you will also see an increase in beneficial, insect-eating adults like spiders and praying mantises.

The Perennial Insectary

Most gardeners grow herbs for the same reason they grow a vegetable garden—to reap a valuable harvest for the kitchen and herbal medicine chest. But when you grow herbs or any edible flowering plant specifically for beneficials, you will need to let them flower for an extended period of time. This can be a conundrum for herb gardeners because we have been taught that in order to obtain the highest quality product we must cut our herbs just before or just as they are beginning to bloom. However, this timing doesn't work out so well for beneficial insects, which rely on the early availability of the pollen and nectar that flowering herbs provide. If you have an established herb garden and don't have the space for a dedicated insectary, try harvesting some of your perennial herbs a few weeks before the plants begin to set flower buds. By harvesting earlier than normal, you will still get plenty of flavorful herbs for the kitchen, and in a few weeks the insects will have all the flowers they'll need to get them through the season.

On the other hand, if you have space in your yard near the vegetable garden, you might consider planting a mixture of herbs and flowers in a separate insectary bed. Better yet, plant an entire hedgerow of herbs and nectary plants and include a few early and late-flowering shrubs and trees such as crape myrtle, lilac, and fruit trees, too. As a perennial bed, the hedgerow can be mulched deeply to reduce weeding and watering chores. Use natural mulch such as bark, wood chips, or deciduous leaves, which provides many beneficials with the perfect shelter for hiding and resting during the heat of the day and for hibernating sites in the winter. In addition, the relatively undisturbed soil in the perennial insectary is crucial for many beneficials that spend some portion of their life underground, either to hibernate or to metamorphose into their adult forms.

With so many herbs that fill the requirements of beneficials in terms of food and shelter, you might be tempted to stop there. But wherever time and space allow, go ahead and add in as many flowering plants, shrubs, and trees as possible—the more the merrier! And don't overlook native species, which increase the overall biodiversity of your insectary. Indeed, one of the most important things you can do to support beneficials is to have a variety of plant species flowering throughout the growing season, particularly early in the spring and late into fall when beneficials need the nectar and pollen most.

One final consideration for the perennial insectary is water, which is crucial for good plant development and the survival of the beneficials living there. Insects don't need a lot of water, but they do need to have access to it in a form they can use. The easiest way to ensure that insects have available water is to shower or spray plants daily. The tiny droplets that catch on leaves and stems make excellent "watering holes" for your tiny guests. This works especially well if your sprinklers are set on a daily timer. You can even plant herbs and flowers with leaves that catch water and hold it for several hours. *Sedum* 'Autumn Joy' is a perfect example of a water-catching plant, and it doubles as a powerful fall nectary plant as well. If you don't water daily, consider adding a few "butterfly waterers," which all of the beneficials can use, around the garden. Start by burying several ceramic or glass pie plates to the bottom of their rims. Next, fill the pans with coarse sand and gravel. Fill the pans with just enough water to be level with the surface of the sand. Beneficials simply stand on the sand and suck up the water below. Be sure to fill the waterer several times a week, especially during the hot, dry summer months. Simply adding a little drinking water to your insectary can make a dramatic difference in the number of beneficials that will call it home.

Protect Your Assets

An insectary is a place for beneficials to find food, shelter and water, but they also need your protection—both inside the insectary and throughout your vegetable garden and orchard. Almost all pesticides used in season will kill good bugs and bad bugs without discretion. And don't think that just because you only use organic insecticides that your beneficials are safe from harm. After all, beneficials are insects, too.

If you feel that you absolutely must use some type of insecticide to control a pest in the garden, focus on those that do not have an immediate "knock-down" effect. Pyrethrum, pyrethrin (along with the synthetic pyrethroids), nicotine, and rotenone are all examples of extremely powerful organic insecticides that kill or permanently paralyze insects, including beneficials, on contact. The same is true for seemingly innocuous products like insecticidal soaps or lightweight horticultural oils meant to suffocate eggs, larvae, and scale-type insects. Use these products with caution and apply them only to the target pests early in the morning or late in the evening to avoid injuring beneficials, which are more active during the warmer daytime hours.

A few relatively safe insecticidal options are available to the organic gardener wanting to protect as many beneficials as possible. Pure neem oil used as directed (see product label) and applied with precision to foliage only (avoiding flowers whenever possible) is an excellent option because it only affects insects that eat the treated vegetation. Microbial insecticides are another organic option for treating insect pests while protecting beneficials. According to the Clemson University Cooperative Extension, microbial insecticides "comprised of a single species of microorganism may be active against a wide variety of insects or group of related insects (such as caterpillars) or they may be effective against only one or a few species. Most are very specific. Since there is such a narrow range of insects killed, they spare the beneficial insects almost entirely."

As a gardener, I know how difficult it is to resist the temptation to address pest issues in the garden with any one "magic bullet." Yet, in the twenty-five years I've been an organic gardener, I have had little difficulty handling pests without the use of any insecticides at all. Handpicking pesky hornworms, using spunbond polyester fabrics and screens to keep pests off target crops, using pheromone traps and scent deterrents, and interplanting vegetable and fruit crops with fragrant deterrent plants and herbs have always done the job well enough. And once my garden was free of indiscriminate insecticides, the beneficials arrived in droves and are now a permanent part of the landscape.

The Three Ps

Beneficial insects are generally recognized as being predators, parasites, or pollinators, but the truth is that many beneficials fill more than one role in the garden. Predators prey on bad bugs for food, while parasites lay their eggs in or on bad bugs, which the young larvae consume à la carte. Of course, pollinators can be any insect that moves pollen from flower to flower as it feeds or hunts, helping gardeners produce more fruits and vegetables.

And while each beneficial specializes in one of the three Ps, many fill multiple roles as they morph from larvae to adult. And since adults and larvae often look nothing like one another until their metamorphosis is complete, it is important to learn how to identify beneficials in all their forms. Remember that larvae are powerful predators, often consuming many more pests than the adults, and you don't want to accidentally kill them because you didn't recognize them. In fact, some beneficial insects actually look a lot like their pesky counterparts. For example, the spined soldier bug (*Podisus maculiventris*) looks an awful lot like a destructive stink bug because the two are related to one another. Yet, where the stink bug (and there are many) is a hard-to-control pest, the spined soldier bug is a beneficial eater of Colorado potato beetle and Mexican bean beetle larvae.

Use this short list of some of the more important beneficial insects to search for images of adult insects and their larvae that you may find in your garden and herbal insectary:

Braconid and ichneumonid wasps (Hymenoptera)

Damsel bugs (Heteroptera)

Earwigs (Dermaptera)

Ground beetles (Coleoptera)

Lacewings (Neuroptera)

Ladybugs (Coleoptera)

Mantids (Mantidae)

Mealybug destroyers (Coleoptera)

Minute pirate bugs (Heteroptera)

Soldier beetles (Coleoptera)

Spiders (Araneae)

Syrphid and hover flies (Diptera)

Tachinid flies (Diptera)

Trichogramma wasps (Hymenoptera)

Call It a Wrap

At the end of the season when your beneficials are calling it a wrap, ensure they hang around for next summer by providing them with the right environment for hibernation. Whenever possible, avoid removing spent vegetation in the insectary, and leave as many large clumps of dried ornamental grasses as you can. Sow cover crops in or near the insectary for added protection from harsh winter weather. And when pruning shrubs or trees, be sure to keep an eye out for the foam-like egg cases of praying mantises, which contain next year's brood. Also, when mowing the lawn for the last time, consider setting the blade just a little higher than normal. Long grass provides ample hiding places and allows beneficial weeds such as dandelion a chance to regenerate faster in early spring. Fall leaves make excellent mulch for garden beds as well as hidey-holes for ground-dwelling beneficials and their larvae. If you want to keep the yard tidy, pile up leaves of deciduous trees (but not fruit tree leaves, which should be removed and burned to prevent future leaf diseases), sticks, and cut grass into a pile near the insectary but hidden from view. These piles make great hibernation sites that will double as compost in the future.

Beneficial insects are a boon to gardeners and food producers everywhere. With the rising incidence of insecticide-resistant species and the decline of pollinators and other beneficial insects due to overuse of potent chemical insecticides, the herbal insectary may be one of the best investments you will ever make in the garden and, perhaps, the world.

Resource

Russ, Karen and Joey Williamson. "Less Toxic Insecticides." Clemson University Cooperative Extension. Last modified September 2015. http://www.clemson.edu/extension /hgic/pests/pesticide/hgic2770.html.

Jill Henderson is a self-taught herbalist and long-time contributor to Llewellyn's Herbal Almanac and writes for Acres USA magazine. Jill has written three books: The Healing Power of Kitchen Herbs, A Journey of Seasons: A Year in the Ozarks High Country, and The Garden Seed Saving Guide: Seed Saving for Everyone. She also writes and edits Show Me Oz (ShowMeOz .wordpress.com), a weekly blog filled with in-depth articles on gardening, seed saving, homesteading, wildcrafting, edible and medicinal plants, herbs, nature, and more. Jill and her husband, Dean, live in the Missouri Ozarks.

Gardening Square by Square

⇜ by Charlie Rainbow Wolf ⇝

You may have heard of square-foot gardening. It was pioneered by Mel Bartholomew several years ago, and it is based on the idea that huge plots of gardens can overwhelm many would-be gardeners. Square-foot gardening incorporates gardening with the seasons, companion planting, using trellising, and more to make the most of every inch of space possible. Now, the square-foot gardening method can be found taught in some schools and communities and even in international outreach programs as a means of teaching people how to become more self-sufficient, eat more healthily, and make the most of whatever space is available. Gardening doesn't

have to be full of rows and weeds. Square-foot gardening teaches that gardening can be enjoyable and bountiful without requiring a lot of time or hard work.

This method of gardening is adaptable for those who may have physical limitations that keep them from traditional gardening. The square-foot method can be employed in raised beds so that those in wheelchairs or those who cannot stoop to garden might enjoy the simple beauty of fresh produce. Because the plots are so manageable, watering and pest control are easier than in large beds too.

Very little equipment is required for this type of gardening. Once your soil is prepared, you'll need a spade, a trowel, and a watering can. That's it! No heavy duty tools, no tillers or cultivators or sprinklers (though you may want a wheelbarrow from time to time). The only exception to this is if you're breaking ground for a brand new plot; you'll likely want someone to rototill it for you, just to save you the backache of digging. However, consider this carefully because tilling exposes dormant weed seeds to the elements so that they can germinate, and it can also dig the grass back into your planting area. My husband and I learned that the hard way and ended up combining the square-foot method with lasagna gardening, adding layers of organic material.

Row by Row—No!

The square-foot method of gardening allows you to grow for your family needs without the size of your property dictating how much you can grow. You just have to be a bit diligent, plan a little bit, and learn a bit about the process to make it work. Once you start getting the hang of this, you should find that it's an easy method and that it can grow a lot of food in a little area. This method is called square-foot gardening because it's based on segments that are a mere twelve square inches in size. In theory, every square holds a different plant, but obviously some plants require more room than others. The basic plot consists of sixteen of these squares in a four-by-four grid, making a forty-eight-inch square. For some people, one plot will be enough; others may want a series of plots. It may be best to start with one or two and plant more once you've decided that you like it.

If you already have a garden bed tilled and ready to plant, it is easy to map out the forty-eight-inch plots and then, using string, break them down into twelve-inch squares. Try not to walk on the soil that you're going to plant. If you do, you'll compact it and make it harder for the growing plants to get the water and the air that they need. We have overcome this in the past by putting paving stones around the perimeter of the forty-eight-inch plots to separate them. Not only were we able to walk through the beds, but it looked very appealing too.

Going Up?

Many vining crops such as melons, squash, cucumbers, and tomatoes can be grown using the square-foot method. Obviously these plants can take up a lot of room. Zucchini, for example, will take up one full plot, so careful planning is needed to ensure you have enough room for the plants you want to grow. The other plants that sprawl and climb, like green beans and peas, can be grown up trellises in order to save space. This also eliminates bending the plants and keeps the harvest off the ground nicely. We've actually put up trellises for tomatoes on the south side of some of our forty-eight-inch plots, and as the tomatoes grow, they shade the kale and the brussels sprouts, helping prevent them from wilting under the hot summer sun.

In one area of the garden, we experimented with digging a trench just for a trellis. We used a sixteen-foot cattle panel cut in half and tied it to two steel fence posts. We made the trench eight feet long and one foot wide and placed the trellis along the north side of it. Last year we planted tomatoes there, and this year the cucumbers did very well there. While this is not proper square-foot gardening, it did work, and you might want to consider making a backdrop with your climbing vines.

We've also grown muskmelons in this way. As the fruit hung and started to get heavy, I put each melon in a muslin cradle tied to the cattle panel. The fabric was lightweight enough to allow the sun and the rain to reach the fruit, stretchy enough to allow the fruit to grow and expand, and strong enough to hold the fruit until it was ready for picking. I don't know that I'd want to try to grow a huge pumpkin or watermelon using this method, but the muskmelons did very well, and I would imagine small watermelons and pie pumpkins would do well also.

Companion Planting

Square-foot gardening lends itself to companion planting very easily. Companion planting is a way of combining and taking advantage of certain plants' unique qualities to benefit the entire garden. For example, pest-deterrent marigolds can be added for color as well as to protect the vegetables growing near them. Garlic, chives, and other members of the onion family will help deter deer, and nasturtiums will deter aphids. Because the forty-eight-inch plots are usually placed fairly close to each other, strategically placed garden companions on one plot will actually help the surrounding ones—not all plots have to be planted identically. In fact, it's probably best that they are not, for the sake of variety.

Rotation

Another reason to plant the plots differently is that it makes it easier to rotate the crops, which helps keep the soil healthy. When the same crops are planted in the same place, they deplete the soil of the same nutrients; rotating the crops helps give the soil a chance to reestablish itself and replaces other nutrients. Because different plants are often susceptible to different diseases, rotation decreases the disease-causing organisms' chance to thrive.

Rotation is easy with the square-foot method. As soon as one crop is finished, another one can be planted. Spring spinach can be followed by autumn cabbage, and then perhaps peas can be planted the following spring. Because you're only working with forty-eight inches at a time, you're far less likely to get overwhelmed by what goes where. The most important thing is to look after the soil, which should come easily as long as repetitive planting is avoided and the plants are well mulched. This feeds the soil in addition to helping keep the weeds away.

It's also possible to plant things at different times yet still keep the main crop in the twelve-inch square. For example, a flat Dutch cabbage will take up one square foot. However, the seedlings look very lost in there because they're tiny and will stay quite small for a few weeks. This gives you time to plant some spinach, chives, or radishes, which can then be harvested before the cabbage crowds them out.

Positioning

My dad grew his vegetable garden at the back of our property, out of plain sight and hidden by my mum's flower beds. I just assumed that was how it was done, but once I had a garden of my own, I did some rethinking. It never made sense to me to have the vegetable gardens away from the house, so I started companion planting things along the drive and just outside the door, where it was easier to keep control of them. The plants were in full view, and with them growing so close to the house, it seemed easier to keep them looking nice or to nip out of the kitchen door and grab a few leeks for supper. I still have my main garden right outside my kitchen door so that I don't have to go far to get the fresh produce when I'm preparing a meal. Both attractive and functional, the herbs are grown right in with the plots, tucked in where there is space.

We're lucky that the bulk of our property is sunny and faces south, so positioning the beds wasn't difficult. In order for your forty-eight-inch plots to be successful, you'll want to take into consideration the amount of sunlight versus shade the plot receives. You don't have to put your plots side by side, either. Some with plants that need heat to flourish, like tomatoes and cucumbers, could catch the warmth of the sun, while others, housing leafy greens like kale, could rest in more shaded areas. Remember, you have some control over the soil condition and the water, but you'll have little control over the sunlight. The morning and afternoon sun are more intense than the late afternoon and evening sun, so plan accordingly.

If you have trees in your garden, remember that they grow! This may seem obvious, but what is a sunny position now may be a shady one in five years' time. You can always have the trees trimmed, of course, but you may want to think about this when planning your plots, or consider eventually converting these plots for shade-loving plants in years to come.

What and Where Do I Plant?

The first answer to this is plant what you want to eat. There's little point stocking up on home-grown tomatoes if you can't stand them! Look for plants that are fairly easy to grow or that you like to eat or look at. Flowers are an agreeable addition to this method of gardening. A good start—particularly if you're just going to try this method with one plot as an experiment—is to look at what you regularly buy from the supermarket, what you've successfully grown in the past (if indeed you have), and what is local. For example, everyone around here seems to grow sweet corn. We're not particularly keen on it, so there's no point in growing it; we can barter with friends for it if we feel we want some.

You're also going to have to decide how much time you want to invest in your garden. This is a simple and low-maintenance method, sure, but it's not maintenance free. It is logical that the more plots you have, the more time you're going to spend in your garden. If you're fairly new to gardening, it makes sense to try things that are easy and in season. Those who are more experienced may want to rise to the challenge of growing things a bit more atypical.

Now it's time to consider just how much room each plant is going to take. Remember, you're not planting in rows: if you've been used to sprinkling the seeds in rows, leaving a gap between the rows, and then thinning out the seedlings as they become established, you're going to have to alter your thinking. Contemplate the space-to-plant ratio carefully. Earlier I touched on putting smaller plants around the larger plants when they're young, but there are other ways of utilizing space. For example,onions can be planted with only three inches between each plant, so you can get sixteen onions in one twelve-inch square. Cabbage, on the other hand, will take up that whole area, so you will only have room for one mature cabbage per each foot. Is it starting make sense, yet?

Some plants are going to need more than a square foot in which to grow. Particular varieties of cabbage, bush beans, or aubergines might need extra space, so you'd measure out an eighteen-inch square for them. This means you could get four of them in your forty-eight-inch plot and have room along two sides for some smaller companions. One zucchini, with its huge leaves, needs a plot all to itself! While it's absolutely fine to grow these plants in the square-foot garden, keep in mind that bigger doesn't always mean better. There are other varieties of summer squash that vine and can be trained up a trellis so that you've got the best of both worlds: compact space and fresh produce. If the sunlight doesn't reach the soil, the undesirable plants are less likely to germinate and grow underneath the canopy of leaves. You may find (as we did) that the smaller plants, placed closer together, not only yield well but also help to keep down the weeds.

Ready, Set, Grow!

Of course, what you grow is entirely up to you, and everyone's going to have their favorites. I've listed some of my easy success stories below, along with their basic requirements for space and planting season. While these provide a general rule of thumb, read the seed packets and plant according to your own climate zone.

Aubergine: (Eggplant—we planted 'Rosa Bianca'.) 1 plant per 12-inch square. Plant in spring.

Beets: (We planted 'Bull's Blood'.) 16 beets per 12-inch square. Plant in spring, summer or fall.

Broccoli: (We planted purple sprouting broccoli.) 1 plant per 12-inch square. Plant in spring or fall.

Brussels Sprouts: (We planted 'Nautic'.) Allow 18 inches per plant.

Cabbage: (We planted 'Early Flat Dutch'.) 1 plant per 12-inch square. Plant in spring or the fall.

Cauliflower: (We planted 'Veronica'.) 1 plant per 12-inch square. Plant in spring or fall.

Kohlrabi: (We planted 'Delicacy White' and 'Delicacy Purplc'.) 4 plants per 12-inch square. Plant in spring or fall.

Peppers: (We've planted all colors with success all around, from the 'California Wonder' green pepper to the highly amusing red Peter pepper—*Capsicum annuum* var. *annuum*.) 1 plant per 12-inch square. Plant in spring.

Tomatoes, cucumber, squash, and **melons** are best grown up trellises, as mentioned above. If you would rather cage your tomatoes, allow 4 cages per 48-inch square. Growing basil near the tomatoes will help to bring out the flavor.

I'm sure I haven't yet touched on your favorite veggies, so now it's time for you to experiment! It's only soil, so don't be afraid to get your hands dirty. If you're uncertain how to start, then prepare your beds and buy seedlings from garden centers. You've got little to lose—but if you find that you enjoy this low-cost, low-care gardening method, then you've got a bountiful harvest to gain!

Suggested Reading

Bartholomew, Mel. *Square Foot Gardening: A New Way to Garden in Less Space with Less Work.* Emmaus, PA: Rodale, 1981.

Jabbour, Niki. *The Year-Round Vegetable Gardener: How to Grow Your Own Food 365 Days a Year No Matter Where You Live.* North Adams, MA: Storey Publishing, 2011.

Madigan, Carleen, ed. *The Backyard Homestead.* North Adams, MA: Storey Publishing, 2009.

Lanza, Patricia. *Lasagna Gardening: A New Layering System for Bountiful Gardens: No Digging, No Tilling, No Weeding, No Kidding!* Emmaus, PA: Rodale, 1998.

Louis, Joy. *Ultimate Gardening Book: 5 Gardening Books in 1; Square Foot Gardening, Container Gardening, Urban Homesteading, Straw Bale Gardening, Vertical Gardening.* CreateSpace Independent Publishing Platform, 2011.

Riotte, Louise. *Carrots Love Tomatoes: Secrets of Companion Planting for Successful Gardening.* Rev. ed. Pownal, VT: Storey Publishing, 1998.

Warren, Spring. *Quarteracre Farm: How I Kept the Patio, Lost the Lawn, and Fed My Family for a Year.* Berkeley: Seal Press, 2011.

Charlie Rainbow Wolf *is happiest when she is creating something, especially if it can be made from items that others have cast aside. Pottery, writing, knitting, astrology, and tarot are her deepest interests, but she happily confesses that she's easily distracted because life offers so many wonderful things to explore. She is an advocate of organic gardening and cooking and lives in the Midwest with her husband and special-needs Great Danes. Visit www.charlierainbow.com.*

The Oriental Poppy

⚘ by Estha K. V. McNevin ⚘

The splash of perennial color that poppy flowers can bring to any garden is transformative, especially when placed in those pesky barren spots that we keep meaning to do something about. Horticulturalists have sculpted some of the great scenes of rural cottage romance with the dreamy splendor and regal petal scale of the Oriental poppy, *Papaver orientale*, of the crepe-paper flower family (Papaveraceae). So beloved is the poppy throughout history that we find well-documented cultivation records and early evidence of selective seed preservation that dates back to Persian antiquity.

Nowadays, we celebrate a medley of poppies featuring remarkable double rosettes and stunning colors ranging from 'Bonfire' red and the yellow of the California poppy, to a Basque salmon pink color and the Iceland poppy's snow-queen white. Yet, this elegant ballerina of the rural oasis is often linked to a darker cousin, *Papaver somniferum*, the great scarlet poppy. Known more for its use in highly regulated pharmaceutical cultivation, the wild child of the Papaveraceae family is the original poppy from which the culinary seeds and all other poppy strains have been derived for domestic use.

Origins

First cultivated in Asia Minor by the Sumerians sometime around 4000 BCE, poppy was prized as a nutty spice. The seeds are still cherished for their refined alkaline flavor that enhances and tenderizes fish, poultry, and other meats. Poppy also adds a satisfying crunchy texture to dishes and has a calming effect following the meal. Used in baked goods to enliven sandwich breads, poppy seeds provide an excellent source of fiber. They release linoleic acid as they are digested, soothing intestinal discomfort and cramps associated with both malnourishment and constipation.

The fragile poppy flower gives way to a large blue or green stock topped with a seedpod. Its contents offer a host of antioxidant benefits as a source of flora latex, and the seeds are rich in iron, copper, calcium, potassium, magnesium and zinc. Poppy seeds are also an excellent source of B-complex vitamins and oleic acid. Still widely used in Eurasian pastries and Central Asian roasted dishes, poppy seeds are a Caspian mountain specialty that have become beloved the world over.

Poppy tea was a traditional herbal pain reliever in historical Mesopotamia, the Indus Valley, and China, but the pods utilized in the brew were not cultivated for trade in the West until around 300 BCE, when they were brought to Egypt from Anatolia. The poppy is frequently depicted in the art, literature, and textile motifs of the classical world. The bright flowers are pared in myth and legend with other symbols of allegory and fantasy, frequently relating to dreamland adventures and visionary out-of-body worlds. Poppy is an essential flower in the gardenscape of every verdant "fairy world" allotment, often brimming along orchard walls beside Siberian iris or skirting a nicotina border with baby's breath in a kaleidoscope of otherworldly fragrance and color.

Indeed, the scent and toxicology of the poppy is steeped in our somewhat obscure allegories of recreational hallucination. This was masterfully evidenced by L. Frank Baum, who employed the poppy to pop-cult acclaim in his 1900 novel, *The Wonderful Wizard of Oz*, when he wrote that the traveling group finds a "great meadow of poppies. . . . Their odor is so powerful that anyone who breathes it falls asleep. . . . So presently [Dorothy's] eyes grew heavy and she felt she must sit down to rest and to sleep." Sieving the myth from the reality takes little more than a trip to a local seed store, where domesticated varieties are clearly labeled to differentiate *Papaver orientale* from urban legend.

Numerous law enforcement agencies, including the United States Drug Enforcement Agency (USDEA) and the UN Office on Drugs and Crime, list two varieties of poppy as Class A Schedule I and II drugs. Storing the seeds of *Papaver bracteatum* or *Papaver somniferum* as well as growing the plants is illegal in the United States and many other countries. Currently, only large-scale pharmaceutical corporations are licensed, exclusively by governmental contract, to legally grow the plant, produce stocks and pods, and extract thebaine from poppies for use in medical-grade narcotic opiates including morphine, methadone, heroin, oxycodone, and codeine. International medical-grade trade of thebaine is restricted to a handful of approved and stringently regulated countries: Turkey, India, Spain, France, Poland, Hungary, and Austria. Afghanistan and Pakistan are not approved legal suppliers of thebaine or its derivative opiates, nor are they reliable countries of origin from which to purchase the innocuous *Papaver orientale*.

Poppy Propagation

Poppies must be planted in wide, well-spaced rows, and should be thinned on a weekly basis throughout the growing season. Plants should not be allowed to ground-sprawl at leisure or they will take over quickly. Disperse poppies carefully in garden beds and rows by variety, preventing cross-pollination. Take precaution when selecting flowers to cut for arrangements or display: select only the most verdant blooms so that cutting back the heads will result in a second flowering. More fragile varieties will either die back or go dormant for the rest of the season if they are pruned early, neglectfully starved of nutrients, or overwatered.

The flowers and bulbs will suffer if there is less than two feet of soil between each plant. This fussy need for nutrients is due in part to this flower's reliance on humus-rich soil and calcium to produce its large seed pods. Poppies planted closer together than two feet will compete for nutrients, often choking each other to death. As a result, plants will produce much smaller flowers and dwarfed seed bulbs, yielding considerably less-reliable seeds. Attentive pruning, however, will prevent this.

The stocks of the poppy grow between two and three feet in height, and a single plant will easily spread between two and four feet in a loose, light loam bed of finely sifted soil. Cuttings last longer when taken on their very first day of flowering, between four and six in the morning, which is when the buds teasingly reveal the shade of the poppy yet to unfold in the morning light. These can be refrigerated at 58 degrees Fahrenheit for up to three days to delay blooming or placed in warm water for a dramatic unfolding display at the luncheon, dinner, or dessert table.

Full sun–loving perennials, poppy flowers begin to open in early summer and will bloom until late autumn if carefully sown in two-week increments throughout the first season. This will create a wave of blooms that travel throughout the garden as each grouped set begins to mature. Flowers vary in size from a modest three or four inches, as in North American dwarf varieties like California's *Stylomecon heterophylla,* to the eight-inch varieties like the Persian *Papaver bracteatum.* The latter is selected for size and narcotic potency, being highly regulated and exclusively grown for the production of controlled opiates.

Papaver orientale will tolerate light shade but really loves the warm sunshine. It is often paired with textured, light-loving shrubs like gardenia and witch hazel, whimsical border choices cherished in cottage gardens. For a bushy ground cover, Oriental poppies can be tucked with nearby neighbors such as catmint, hosta, Siberian iris, or cottage pinks, all of which help to set a lavishly perfumed scene into which the poppies can boldly flower.

To train them along a bed, plant complementary orna-mental grasses like blue fescue, quaking grass, pampas grass, or feather reed grass. These will help new shoots refrain from spreading. Nearby roughage will also encourage self-sowing, helping a controlled patch of *Papaver orientale* to become pro-foundly lusher, effortlessly presenting large vivid flowers each year. Fillers also serve to improve water drainage by thriving in the gaps of more dramatic bloomers. This keeps a garden bed looking full and tidy even as foliage blooms and wilts.

Unless you resow in rounds, poppies will burst into color, flourish, and die back within a matter of days. Timing a bed for this explosion of color is what some gardeners live for, and *Papaver orientale* very rarely disappoints because the seeds ger-minate easily. Once established, perennial poppies are quite hardy and have reliably long lives.

Transplanting

Maintaining a patch of poppies can supply a gardener with all-natural gifts for friends and family. Dividing any overgrown patches is a must at the end of each season. This is easily done by digging up root clusters and separating them into eight-inch clumps with garden sheers or a sharp spade.

Repot or reposition the transplants in well-drained and sunny areas of the garden for the best results. Always give transplants plenty of room to expand. Be sure to water them generously every other day to help the poppies settle. Give the plants extra nutrients every five weeks by adding a bit of liquid tomato feed and one tablespoon of molasses to a gal-lon of water. If you apply this mixture throughout the small bed religiously, it will improve the health, scent, and size of the blossoms.

Prevent shock in lower autumn temperatures by mulching or otherwise nestling all perennials and any transplants so they are comfortably insulated for the winter season. Poppies will not survive being transplanted into differing soil or temperature conditions, so it's best to pick new locations with great care: dig them out with a wider girth of soil, providing some of the old soil along with newly sifted, soft loam to safeguard success.

Cultivation

Prepare a well-drained bed with eight inches of hand-sifted loose loam soil. This should consist of one part old soil, two parts humus-rich compost, and one part composted raw pine sawdust. Using your finger, trace a seeding line in the areas of the bed designated for *Papaver orientale*. Carefully pour the seeds into a seed injector and place one seed every two feet along the row. Gently mist twice a day until germinated seeds sprout and produce folded or twisted leaves.

The variegated leaves of many strains of poppy will produce fine hairs that are exceedingly fragile. Body heat and the oils transferred from our touch will inhibit leaf, stem, and bud growth. Overfondling or excessive pruning will introduce disease and blight. As the foliage spreads and budding shoots are sent up, delicately trimming back molting leaves becomes essential for full flower growth. Once bulbs flower, the stalks can be removed to encourage a second round of flowering. Otherwise, the seed bulb will begin to mature, exhausting the plant of nutrients in an effort to produce millions of seeds. After the stalks are cut in late summer and autumn, the foliage will die back as the plant begins its dormancy for winter.

Harvest

The seed bulbs, stalks, and seeds are harvested when a series of small apertures appear just below the sepal star on the stigmal tip of the seed bulb. The pips (another name for the poppy's seeds) will rattle inside the pod when they are ready to be harvested. If left to dehydrate inside of the pods, the seeds will yield a better flavor for culinary use and be more viable in the garden when resown. If letting the seeds wander, be warned that they will easily scatter on the wind.

Large varieties like *Papaver rhoeas*, the field poppy, reseed themselves effortlessly and will create their own wild poppy oasis if not thinned back and weeded away from other beds and the garden pathway. Thebaine, codeine, and papaverine are found in trace amounts in all poppy seeds. These are essential alkaloid compounds found concentrated in opium. When refined pharmacologically, they are the compounds used to create our many medicinal opiate derivatives. The seeds are very micronutrient-rich and beneficial to the body. Used to calm nerves, treat intestinal disorders, and relieve pain, poppy seeds are a favored ingredient in curative oils and holistic teas.

To harvest, diligently collect the seed bulbs when they begin to dry; the bulbs should rattle when shaken. Seeds can be scattered in a bed and tucked in for winter, or they may be resown in the spring. To preserve poppy seeds for long-term storage, open the brittle pods and scatter the kernels onto a small, flat piece of cardboard. Allow them to fully dehydrate for seventy-two hours in a cool, dark, dry place; afterward bag and freeze the seeds for ideal germination results.

Like many other foothills perennials, poppy does best in areas that experience a hard winter frost (but there are also a few annual varieties to choose from). They prefer oak and pine mulch for insulation and in some areas will begin to produce spring shoots as early as February if covered nightly from frost. Poppies are not only hardy perennials, but they also add a touch of whimsy to the garden. They are heavy producers of pollen, making them a real hotspot for bumblebees and butterflies. The vivid colors and fragile crinkled petals capture the imagination and help to round out the rising architectural features of a traditional cottage garden, making growing them a horticultural habit that is very difficult to break.

A hardy and brimming bed of poppies will take time to develop, and we all meet with some measure of reform when learning Mother Nature's rules of thumb. I watered my first poppies to death, in a manic fear that record-high temperatures one summer would suffocate them. I harvested my second attempt too soon, putting the plants into a drooping shock and producing utterly unreliable, immature seeds. My third and final attempt was a success, and I call her Goldilocks: she's decided to reseed every bed in my garden now that she's found just the right spot.

Selected Resources

Baum, L. Frank. *The Wonderful Wizard of Oz*. Chicago: George M. Hill Company, 1900.

Burnie, Geoffrey. *The Practical Gardener's Encyclopedia*. San Francisco: Fog City Press, 2000.

Griffin, Judith. *Mother Nature's Herbal: A Complete Guide for Experiencing the Beauty, Knowledge & Synergy of Everything That Grows*. Woodbury, MN: Llewellyn, 2008.

Kowalchik, Claire, William H. Hylton, and Anna Carr. *Rodale's Illustrated Encyclopedia of Herbs*. Emmaus, PA: Rodale, 1987.

McDonough, Kate. "Clay Pot Cooking, an Ancient Cooking Method with Modern Results." The City Cook. Accessed August 15, 2016. http://www.thecitycook.com/articles /2012-10-03-the-essential-kitchen-clay-pot-cooking.

McGee, Harold. *On Food and Cooking: The Science and Lore of the Kitchen*. New York: Scribner, 2004.

"Opium Poppy: Legal Status." Erowid. Accessed August 15, 2016. https://www.erowid.org/plants/poppy/poppy_law.shtml.

Robuchon, Joël, and Prosper Montagné. *Larousse Gastronomique*. New York: Clarkson Potter, 2001.

Rudrappa, Umesh. "Poppy." Nutrition-and-you.com. Last modified August 15, 2009. www.nutrition-and-you.com /poppy-seeds.html.

Estha K. V. McNevin *(Missoula, Montana) is a priestess and ceremonial oracle of Opus Aima Obscuræ, a nonprofit Pagan Temple Haus. She has served the Pagan community since 2003 as an Eastern Hellenistic officiate, lecturer, freelance author, artist, and poet. Estha studies and teaches courses on ancient and modern Pagan history, multicultural metaphysical theory, ritual technique, international cuisine, organic gardening, herbal craft, alchemy, and occult symbolism. In addition to hosting public rituals for the sabbats, Estha organizes annual philanthropic fund-raisers, full moon spell-crafting ceremonies, and women's divination rituals for each dark moon. To learn more, please explore www.facebook.com/opus aimaobscurae.*

Natural Pest Control for the Garden

⇜ by Melanie Marquis ⇝

When insects and other pests are eating up your garden's bounty by the bushel, what's an earth-loving gardener to do? Chemical pesticides are harmful to soil, plants, animals, and humans alike. These toxic formulations can seep deep down into the earth or wash away in the rain, poisoning both land and water. Fortunately, there are many ways to get rid of garden pests naturally, using nothing more than common sense and a few common ingredients.

Keep It Clean

The most essential key to natural pest control is to maintain a clean and healthy garden. Diseased, damaged, or otherwise weak plants make easy prey for garden pests, attracting undesirables by the droves and rendering healthy plants vulnerable to attack. Check regularly for weak links and rid your garden of all but the healthiest specimens. If you've been working with diseased or insect-ridden plants, clean your gardening tools and gloves before moving on to healthy areas of the garden. You'll also want to clean out any weeds, fallen dried plant matter, sticks, or other debris that would otherwise provide prime habitat for unwanted insects and other critters. The neater your garden, the less appealing it will be to plant-eating insects who prefer a dwelling place with plenty of nooks and crannies in which to hide. Keep your plants well spaced and be sure to minimize any standing water. By watering early in the day rather than at evening or night, you'll give the foliage and soil a chance to dry in the sunlight, thereby deterring slugs and bugs who prefer damp conditions.

Mix It Up

Mixed plantings are another effective way to minimize insect damage to your garden. Like humans, many insects have favorite foods they crave. When you happen to have a large swath of this favorite food in your garden, the bugs just can't resist and will quickly establish themselves in large numbers. By mixing your plants—some spinach here, some squash there rather than consecutive rows of single varieties—you make your garden less attractive to insects searching for the ideal place to set up shop. Rotating crops from season to season is also helpful. Many insects spend the winter snuggled deep within the garden soil, ready to reemerge alongside their favorite food source come spring. If they find a completely different crop than what they're used to feasting on, they're more likely to relocate.

Take the Team Approach

Getting rid of harmful insects in your garden can be quite a challenge, but you don't have to fight the battle alone. Attract beneficial insects that will eat the unwanted insects, and all you have to do is sit back and let nature take its course. To combat a caterpillar problem, try enlisting the help of ichneumon wasps, chalcids, or brachonids. Attract them with the flowers of Queen Anne's lace, carrots, or parsley. Hoverflies and lacewings are very effective against aphids. They can be lured to the garden with asters or goldenrod. Ladybugs will eat a variety of plant-destroying insects including aphids, whiteflies, and mites. Try planting daisies or yarrow to attract them, or simply order a batch from a gardening shop.

If you have an infestation of beetles, cutworms, or root weevils, try populating your garden with nematodes. You can purchase their eggs, which come on small pieces of a spongy material that is moistened with water and mixed into the soil. If you really want to pull out the big guns, try a praying mantis. Those big fellows will eat nearly any insect, making them an ideal choice when you're not really sure what sort of bugs you're dealing with, or when you're having issues with multiple insects. Obtain praying mantis eggs through your gardening supplier, then place them in your garden to hatch and grow into hungry adults.

In addition to beneficial insects, you might also employ a small squad of ducks, chickens, or other birds to help weed out unwanted pests. Ducks love to feast on slugs and bugs alike, while chickens will make short work of grasshoppers.

Even wild birds like sparrows and robins will gobble up large quantities of garden intruders. Place feeders and nesting materials near the garden to attract them.

Hand-to-Hand Combat

Though a bit tedious and potentially time consuming, hand-picking and physically removing harmful pests from your garden is a viable and effective option. Wear some gloves and go out in the early morning armed with a flat piece of cardboard. Place the cardboard under each plant and give the plant a gentle shake. Any insects clinging on to the foliage will lose their grip and plummet onto the cardboard below. You can then relocate the bugs, or dump them into a bucket of soapy water. To reduce a slug population, go out in the evening or nighttime armed with a flashlight. When you find a slug, pick it off and toss it into a pail. You can relocate the slugs or destroy them in seconds with a hefty sprinkling of salt—not a very nice action, decidedly, but they *are* eating up the fruits of your labors, after all.

Solid Barriers for a Solid Defense

One of the most effective means of garden pest control is also one of the most straightforward. Physical barriers keep bugs at bay by literally sealing them out, leaving them with no chance to sink their mandibles into your precious plants. One such barrier that many gardeners find highly useful is the floating row cover. Made of a porous, lightweight fabric that's sold in wide strips by the foot, floating row covers lie over your plants like a blanket, expanding outward as your plants grow larger. Sunlight and water can penetrate the floating row cover just fine, but bugs stay out. There are other barrier-type deterrents you might try, as well. To protect single plant sprouts from insect damage, try slitting an empty toilet paper tube vertically down the middle and cutting off a small piece that you can fit around the young plant like a protective collar. Just be sure it's low enough that it doesn't limit the plant's access to sunlight. As a slug deterrent, wrap a couple inches of copper wire around your plants about two inches above the base. They won't be able to crawl over it and will be forced to turn around.

Sticky Traps

Covered with a tar-like substance and painted in various bug-specific colors, sticky traps lure insects, which then become immobilized on the sticky surface. You can simply hang up strips of flypaper, or if you're more ambitious, you might make your own custom or super-sized versions. You can prop a large, rectangular piece of wood against a garden fence to create a very large sticky trap, or you could go for quantity and create several smaller rectangles out of wood or heavy cardboard that can then be spaced around the area. Paint the wood or cardboard yellow to attract whiteflies, aphids, fruit flies, or midges. If flea beetles or cucumber beetles are your targets, paint the boards white. For flower thrips, use light blue. When apple maggots are a problem, red is the color of choice, only you'll want to use a spherical shape rather than a rectangle. An apple-sized ball will do fine. Cover the traps with clear plastic wrap, then coat the plastic wrap with Tree Tanglefoot paste or any other sticky substance that's moisture-resistant. You may have to recoat the traps after heavy rains. Once the trap catches its victims, you can peel away the plastic wrap, dispose of it, and replace it to catch the next intruders.

All-Natural Bug Sprays

Though insecticidal sprays (even all-natural, nontoxic ones) can be harmful to your garden if used in large doses, they do work, and quickly. The trouble is they harm the good insects as well as the bad ones, and some formulas can wilt plants if left on too long in the sun or if used in too-high concentrations. Use sprays in moderation, and only as a last resort when other methods fail. You'll want to spray the insects directly, as these sprays do not work through residual contact.

To get rid of soft-bodied insects like aphids, mites, and mealy bugs, mix one tablespoon of vegetable oil and one tablespoon of dishwashing liquid into a quart of water. Shake well, then spray the plant from the bottom up and from the top down wherever you see the insects. For heartier insects, try adding a couple tablespoons of hot pepper sauce or cayenne pepper to the mix. Let the concoction rest overnight, then shake vigorously before spraying onto bugs. After applying the spray, rinse your plants with a good watering. Since these recipes only work through direct contact, there is no reason to leave that icky stuff sitting on your plants all day.

Taking On the Four-Legged and the Furry

Not all garden pests are creepy-crawlies. Depending on where you live, you may get a variety of rodents, gophers, and even deer in your garden, all trying to gobble up your beautiful crops. Fortunately, there are plenty of effective and cruelty-free ways to repel these creatures. For starters, be sure to secure all open food sources, such as the compost bin. Your garden delights are temptation enough as it is without you leaving other tasty snacks lying around. Then you'll want to install in the garden some offensive aromas that will send the beasts packing. For mice or rats, soak rags or cotton balls in peppermint oil and tuck under eaves and in rock borders near the garden space. To repel gophers or deer, human hair is the thing. Save some clippings from your next haircut or obtain some from a barbershop, then place large handfuls into nylon, mesh, or cheesecloth bags. For deer, hang the hair from trees and bushes. For gophers, tuck the sacks down into their holes. You might also try hanging a bar of heavily scented soap near your garden, as the strong odor will repel a variety of sensitive-nosed creatures.

Learning to Live with Nature's Balance

As every experienced gardener knows, you will have to put up with a few unwanted critters here and there. We share the earth with so many creatures great and small, and it's unrealistic to expect these instinct-driven organisms to respect our notions of personal ownership when it comes to the tasty treats springing up in our backyard gardens.

Despite your best efforts, some of your plants are likely to be nibbled. Instead of getting irritated, expect it and plan for it by planting extra—more than you will need so that there will be plenty to share. Insects and other garden pests need to eat too, after all! By practicing natural pest control and respecting nature's balance, you'll be able to keep your garden healthy and thriving with minimal headache and minimal harm to the earth.

Melanie Marquis *is a lifelong practitioner of magick, the founder of United Witches global coven, and a local coordinator for the Pagan*

Pride Project in Denver, Colorado, where she currently resides. The author of numerous articles and several books (including The Witch's Bag of Tricks, A Witch's World of Magick, Beltane, and Lughnasadh), she's written for many national and international Pagan publications. She is the coauthor of Witchy Mama and the cocreator of the Modern Spellcaster's Tarot. An avid crafter, cook, folk artist, and tarot reader, she offers a line of customized magickal housewares as well as private tarot consultations by appointment. Connect with her online at www.melaniemarquis.com or at www.facebook.com/melaniemarquisauthor.

For the Bees

⤛ by James Kambos ⤜

A s I write this article, I'm in my herb garden and it's June. Or, as writer James Whitcomb Riley put it, we're "knee-deep in June." I know what he means. The garden is brimming with early summer lushness as summer settles over the Appalachian hills I call home. The lemon thyme is cascading over rocks, a hummingbird flashes like a jewel with wings among the monarda, and the basil is doing nicely. And on this warm, sunny June afternoon I also see one of the world's most beneficial insects, the honeybee, quietly going about its business. This frequently under-appreciated insect is the world's most important pollinator, helping sustain life as we know it.

As I watch these industrious insects buzz from my cone-flowers to the slender spikes of my blue speedwell, I'm reminded of a disturbing news report I heard recently. It seems that once again over the past year, the honeybee population has taken a sharp decline. Bees are responsible for pollinating about 80 percent of the food crops we eat. The bee is also the only insect in the world that produces a food that humans eat, which is, of course, honey. Other bee products we use are bee pollen and wax. As you can see, any drop in the honeybee population should be taken seriously.

Some food crops depend on animals or wind for successful pollination. But the majority of food crops such as apples, cherries, cucumbers, melons, peaches, and pumpkins depend heavily on honeybees for pollination. I don't know about you, but I'm not willing to give up peach cobbler or pumpkin pie!

As herbalists and herb gardeners we can help create a safe haven for honeybees and other types of bees, such as bumblebees. By planting nectar-rich producing herbs and other methods, your herb garden can become a bee sanctuary. To begin, let's take a look at the history of the honeybee and why its population has declined.

Bee History

There are about 20,000 known species of bees. For the purposes of this article, we'll be concentrating on the honeybee, *Apis mellifera*. Within this species there are different nationalities of *Apis mellifera* depending on their place of origin. To keep things simple I'll just refer to them as honeybees.

The honeybee we know today originated in Eastern Asia at least 125 million years ago. It began as a wasp-like insect that ate smaller insects and was a cavity-nesting bee. It's unclear exactly when these early bees switched to a diet of nectar and pollen.

Eventually, honeybees spread to Africa and the Near East. Humans learned early how important bees were. Honey was collected by our early ancestors, and ancient Egyptians used honey in their embalming process. The ancient Minoan civilization on the Greek island of Crete associated the bee with the Goddess and created the feminine name *Melissa*, meaning "bee," as well as gold jewelry in the shape of bees.

Bees were introduced to North America in the 1600s. Commercial beekeepers today breed bees for honey production and to pollinate crops.

Threats to the Honeybee Population

In recent years the honeybee population has declined at an alarming rate, and in some instances the causes remain a mystery. Here are some known, possible causes:

Colony collapse disorder (CCD): This happens when worker bees in a colony leave behind the queen, honey, and immature bees. The reason for their disappearance is still unknown. The hive can't survive without them; as a result, it dies.

Varroa mites: These are an external parasite that sucks blood from honeybees. Unchecked they can wipe out a colony.

Pesticides and herbicides: Many of these are toxic to bees, birds, and other beneficial insects and plants. In some instances these products may not kill the bees directly, but instead they may kill plants that honeybees feed on.

Loss of habitat: As cities, highways, and suburbs grow, the honeybees' natural habitat and food sources shrink. This is one area in which the home herb gardener can help our honeybee population.

The Herbs and the Bees

Bees need three things to survive: pollen, nectar, and water. Pollen, produced on the anthers of flowers, provides protein. Nectar, the sugary solution, serves as a carbohydrate and provides energy. Many herbs are an excellent source of pollen and nectar, and we can provide water in a bird bath, fountain, or pond.

When selecting herbs for bees, remember to let them flower. As herbalists, we frequently cut back herbs to use the foliage, but to help feed the bees, let some of your herbs flower. Also keep color in mind. Bees see colors in the blue color spectrum and seem to be most attracted to blue, blue-violet, white, and yellow. Although the experts say honeybees avoid red, I've observed them on my red monarda and pink coneflowers.

What follows is a selection of some herbs that are known to attract honeybees to the garden and have been, in my experience, dependable performers. By spreading your flower-blooming period over the growing season, you'll encourage the bees to keep visiting your garden. The blooming seasons for some of these herbs may overlap.

Spring/Early Summer

Allium: These tall flowers grow from bulbs planted in the fall and bloom in late spring. The flower heads, usually blue-violet or white, are round and stand on sturdy stems 2–3 feet tall. Rabbits and deer don't like them, but honeybees do.

Betony: Sometimes called "woolly" betony, this old medicinal herb is now grown as an ornamental and bee plant. It stands about 18 inches tall. The leaves are deeply crinkled, and the pink flowers bloom in May/early June.

Catmint: The blue, small, tubular-shaped flowers bloom in May/June along stems about 18 inches tall. The bees find them irresistible.

Chive: The fluffy, pink-purple flowers bloom in early spring and may be one of the first flowers available to bees.

Crocus: Blooming in very early spring, this bulb is a bee magnet. Plant large amounts of blue and white crocus in the fall. Since they only reach about 3 inches tall, I plant them in the front of the border of my garden.

Dandelion: Many people think of dandelions as weeds and are determined to kill them. Don't. Dandelions are a valuable bee herb. I'd rather help the bees than have a perfect lawn.

Summer

Borage: This is an annual herb with fuzzy foliage. Stems are 18 inches tall and are topped with vivid blue, star-shaped flowers. Bees are crazy for them, and they bloom in June.

Coneflower: Also known as echinacea, both the pink and white varieties are popular with honeybees. Usually reaching 2–3 feet high, they bloom in June and July.

Daisy: Not only are bees drawn to all varieties of daisies, the flat shape of the flower makes it a convenient landing pad for honeybees. I have daisies that bloom in June to late summer.

Lavender: I know it's hard to keep from cutting lavender flower stems for drying, but the blue-violet flowers are a bee favorite. My lavender reaches its peak in June.

Monarda: Also known as bee balm, monarda is a mint, and like all mints it draws honeybees. The shaggy flower heads can be white, violet, or red. Standing 3–4 feet tall, it's a show-stopper in any bee garden. Bloom time is June–July.

Sage: All sages, including Russian sage, attract honeybees. Most sages bloom in June to late summer and range in height from 18 inches to 4 feet.

Thyme: This culinary herb and ground cover is a treat for bees. I've found English and lemon thyme to be the best.

Veronica: This bee herb is also known as speedwell. Its slender 2–3 foot spikes are topped with small blue, white, or pink flowers. I have several clumps of blue veronica in my herb border. They're usually covered with honeybees in June to July.

Late Summer/Fall

Aster: Blue, purple, and white asters will carry your bee garden almost up to the first frost. Easy to grow, they range from 18 inches to 4 feet tall.

Goldenrod: This herb can become weedy, but if any grows in a wild area of your property, leave it alone. Blooming in August through September, goldenrod serves as a late-season feast that ensures enough honey for the bees to survive the winter.

Some Final Thoughts

As you plan your honeybee herb garden here are some things to remember: Plant herbs of the same variety in groups of three if possible, in a sunny area. If your herb garden is only a terrace, then plant containers of small growing herbs such as chives or thyme. Remember to provide a water source. Please don't use toxic weed and pest controls—let the birds help control destructive insects. In lawns, allow honeybee favorites like dandelion and white clover to grow.

Let your herb garden go a little wild, and the honeybees will reward you with their presence.

James Kambos *has raised herbs for many years, and his garden has been included on local garden tours. He's a writer and an artist from Ohio.*

The Winter Herb Garden: Bringing Your Outside Herbs In

❧ by Jill Henderson ❧

Just because winter is knocking on your door doesn't mean gardening season has to be over. In fact, while you're out readying the herb garden for the big chill, why not take a few minutes to pack up a bit of that summer sunshine for the dreary days ahead? And with just a little planning, many of the herbs in your outdoor garden can easily be brought indoors for a flavorful harvest all winter long!

All you will need in order to bring your outside herbs inside is a few pots, a little potting soil, and one or two relatively warm and sunny windowsills on which to perch them. And while an indoor herb garden will likely produce less than those

from the garden in the summer, winter-grown herbs are ever-useful, flavorful, and oh so beautiful.

Dig It

Whether you start a few annuals from seed or take cuttings from some of your perennial herbs from the garden, growing herbs indoors couldn't be easier or more rewarding. Simply pick several of your favorite herbs from the garden, and using a sharp spade, dig up a small clump and repot it. If the plant is woody, like rosemary or tarragon, you can take one or more stem cuttings and root them in a pot. I do this every year with rosemary, since it regularly dies during the cold, wet winters of the Ozarks. By spring, I have a nice large plant to put back in the herb garden.

Perennials such as bay, lemon verbena, rosemary, tarragon, winter savory, thyme, salad burnet, chervil, oregano, garlic, onion chives, marjoram, sage, and mint all thrive indoors when given the right conditions. Keep in mind that compact varieties tend to grow better in pots than standard varieties, so use those if you have them.

If your herbal wish list is like mine, you might want to go ahead and add English mint (*Mentha spicata*), Greek oregano (*Origanum vulgare* ssp. *hirtum*), Cuban oregano (*Plectranthus amboinicus*), 'Grolau' chives (*Allium schoenoprasum* 'Grolau'), and creeping savory (*Satureja repandra*) to next year's roster. Or better yet, get them started indoors this winter and transplant them to the garden come spring. That way you'll have the crucial "pot" varieties ready to go when fall rolls around again.

Also, don't overlook some of the more decorative edible herb varieties as possible candidates for indoor growing.

Golden and 'Berggarten' sage, trailing rosemary, and variegated thyme are not just beautiful, they are deliciously edible, too. And while the leaves of ginger and turmeric are truly inedible, all make very pretty houseplants that are easy to care for. As a bonus, you can harvest a few baby rhizomes from your pots and, come spring, return them to the garden for fall harvest.

Sow Some Seed, Too

Although this article is about bringing outside herbs inside, that doesn't mean annuals should be left out. Some annuals can be potted up and brought indoors without so much as a hiccup. Basil, for example, is amazingly resilient. But in general, if you want annuals as a part of your indoor winter landscape you should go ahead and start them fresh from seed in late fall. By the time winter rolls around, they will be ready and waiting for that sunny windowsill.

True cilantro (*Coriandrum sativum*) makes a very pretty and flavorful indoor herb. As you probably already know, a pinch goes a long way in salads, on sandwiches, and as a flavorful garnish for Mexican dishes and salsa. And while it's pretty easy to grow cilantro indoors, there are a few things to consider. First of all, cilantro is day-length sensitive and tries to bolt as days shorten. It has long taproots and will need a deeper pot than most other herbs, and it is incredibly slow to rebound after being cut. To get around these problems, you'll need a pot twelve inches deep to accommodate the roots, and you'll need to reseed a fresh pot every couple of weeks for a continuous harvest. I strongly suggest trying pot cilantro '99057' (*Coriandrum sativum* '99057') for winter cultivation, as it is the first true cilantro bred specifically for pot culture.

If growing cilantro leaf doesn't sound appealing or doable in your space, consider trying cilantro sprouts, which are easy, nutritious, compact, and absolutely delicious. And if you are one of the few people who find the taste of true cilantro a bit on the soapy side, check out Vietnamese coriander (*Polygonum odoratum*), which is not actually related to true cilantro but can be used in similar ways and grows much better indoors.

In fact, many herbs have specific cultivars that have been bred to be more productive in pots than standard garden varieties. Most people wouldn't dare think of growing celery indoors, but 'Zwolsche Krul' is a compact variety of leaf celery just perfect for the indoor herb garden. Dill is another herb that many herb enthusiasts find difficult to grow indoors because, like cilantro, it has a long delicate taproot and is too big and lanky for window cultivation. However, if you have a hankering for fresh dill leaf, try growing 'Fernleaf' dill. This little wonder grows only eighteen inches tall and resists bolting—perfect for winter conditions. For herbs like basil, which tend to grow very large, consider 'Spicy Globe', which is smaller, spicier, and has a more compact habit than traditional varieties do. It also grows at relatively low temperatures of 65 to 70 degrees Fahrenheit—a boon to winter gardeners everywhere.

Before you decide to grow an herb indoors, just remember that members of the parsley family have long, delicate taproots that are easily injured when transplanted. Therefore, instead of digging up existing plants, you will need to sow the seeds of parsley, dill, and celery directly into the pot in which they will grow all winter.

Pot 'Em Up!

Whether you want to bring in a small division of mature perennial herbs such as sage or rosemary, or some new seedlings of annual herbs like basil and parsley, the first step is to ready those plants for life indoors. Start by selecting sturdy plastic, ceramic, or terra-cotta pots big enough to allow plenty of room for new root growth. This is particularly important if you plan on growing more than one herb per pot or for herbs with long taproots, such as those in the parsley family.

Unglazed terra-cotta pots work great for indoor plants, especially for gardeners who tend to overwater. The porous nature of the clay allows the pot to breathe and transfers excess water away from plant roots. On the other hand, clay pots tend to dry out too quickly in the relatively low humidity found in most homes during the winter months. I've worked around both scenarios by fitting clay pots into slightly larger plastic pots without drain holes. This way I get the benefit of the breathability of clay with a plastic pot to catch any excess water.

Soil Isn't Always Dirt

Once you have your pots all lined up, you'll need to fill them with quality soil that will feed your herbs and regulate air and water circulation. Of course, you can use just about any kind of commercial potting soil for growing herbs indoors, but keep a few things in mind before you buy. Quality potting soils or mixes should be light and fluffy, hold moisture but drain well, and firmly anchor the plant while still allowing the roots room to grow. Cheap potting soil often contains poorly draining sedge peat, sand, and dirt that can make it too heavy to drain well. Bonnie Plants recommends potting mixes that contain "aged bark (or composted forest products), perlite, vermiculite, lime, sphagnum peat moss (not sedge peat), and a wetting agent (helps soil stay uniformly moist). Other ingredients might be gypsum, peat humus, and compost." That covers just about everything except the fertilizer, which I recommend you avoid as a built-in part of the potting mix. Fertilize with soluble organic products made specifically for herbs or simply drench the soil with diluted fish emulsion once a month.

And no matter how wonderful your garden soil might be, it's best not to use it for growing herbs indoors. Garden soil is very heavy for small containers, and more often than not it will either drain poorly or shrink from the sides of the pot and allow the water to run out too quickly. Garden soil also tends to harden after watering, reducing air flow and stunting roots. It's also chock-full of potential pests and diseases just waiting for an opportune moment to strike. If you're into making your own potting soil, try mixing a blend of 70 percent potting soil or sterile compost, 20 percent perlite, and 10 percent sharp sand together in a large bucket. This mixture will allow excellent air circulation, drainage, and moisture retention. Just keep in mind that herbs generally prefer a soil pH between 6.0 and 7.0. Herbs such as rosemary, thyme, marjoram, lemon balm, and cilantro prefer a pH of around 6.0. For herbs that prefer a higher pH, add one teaspoon of lime for each six-inch pot and adjust upwards for larger pots.

Let the Light Shine

Plentiful, high-quality light is a major aspect of growing herbs indoors. Before you plant or pot up your herbs, take a close look at how much light your plants will receive each day from natural sources, such as windows. Herbs need around five hours of direct sunlight each day. If your windowsill doesn't get that much light, you will need to provide some form of artificial light, which can be as simple as fluorescent tubes or as high-tech as multispectrum grow lights. For the home gardener, standard fluorescent lights are both effective and affordable.

Start by selecting a baffle that has space for at least two light tubes. Place a "warm" light tube on one side and a "cool" light tube on the other. This provides a color spectrum wide enough to produce healthy plants when combined with natural sunlight. It is important to ensure that this artificial light spans the entire growing area evenly or plants on the outer edges will suffer. Experts suggest leaving fluorescent lights on fourteen hours a day and adjusting them to hang between six and eight inches from the tips of the plants. A plug-in switch timer is a big help when it comes to turning the lights on and off.

Because plants will always lean toward natural sunlight regardless of the quality of an artificial source, it is necessary to turn your pots regularly. For young seedlings, you might need to turn each pot one-quarter of a turn at least once a day and sometimes as often as twice a day, depending on how much natural light they receive. Just be sure to turn the pots in the same direction each time.

Reverse Hardening Off

One of the most important steps to preparing potted herbs for life indoors is a process akin to the spring ritual of hardening off, only in reverse. Rather than acclimating herbs to more and more sunlight, as is done with spring seedlings, herbs that will be moved indoors need to be acclimated to less and less light if they are to thrive in the relatively low-light conditions inside your home.

Leaves use sunlight to generate food essential for the plants' survival. To do this in the most efficient manner, many plants produce specific leaf shapes in order to capture various levels of light. In response to very bright sunlight, plants will often generate long, thick, and narrow "high-light" leaves. These are leaves that receive abundant sunlight and do not need to be as efficient at producing food. On the other hand, "low-light" leaves are thinner and wider in order to make the most food possible with less sunlight. Therefore, when the intensity of light is suddenly reduced, as in winter or indoors, plants must respond by growing more low-light leaves. If they cannot produce these new leaves quickly enough, they will either flounder in the struggle to produce enough food or die.

Rosemary is notorious for being difficult to grow indoors, and the biggest contributing factor to this is its inability to respond quickly to changes in light intensity. Therefore, to prevent low-light shock, pot up woody herbs like rosemary and sage as much as six weeks before the first frost in your area and move them to shadier and shadier locations in two-week increments. I call this reverse hardening off. During this adjustment period, herbs will have time to grow many new low-light leaves and will burst with new growth when given a bright windowsill indoors.

Let It Rain

Indoor plants need water just as much as outdoor plants— the challenge lies in knowing how much water is enough and how much is too much. Garden soil is deep and can usually hold moisture for long periods of time; potting soil generally dries out much quicker. If this is your first time growing indoors, start by checking your plants every day to get a feel for how long each watering lasts. Water should be provided when the soil is almost but not quite completely dry. This may be once a week or once every several days, depending on relative humidity, growth rate, and soil type used. When the soil is at its optimum moisture level, it should feel like a well-wrung sponge. But don't rely solely on the appearance or feel of surface soil, as it often feels dry to the touch. The simplest way to test the moisture near the root zone is to plunge a finger into the soil to the second knuckle. Otherwise, a moisture meter is an easy and accurate way to test for moisture down in the root zone, where it counts.

When it comes to water, consistency pays in dividends. Pick one day a week to be watering day and stick to it. Once every seven to ten days is usually sufficient for indoor plants. Water deeply and thoroughly until the water runs out of the bottom of the pot. If you have shallow saucers underneath your pots, be sure to drain them after about thirty minutes. Standing water may lead to root rot, mold, and diseases.

On the other hand, plants growing in dry indoor air welcome humidity around their leaves. Create a moister environment for your plants by placing them on shallow trays filled with smooth pea gravel and water. If you grow herbs on gravel trays, you can forgo the saucers under the pots and let the water that runs from the drainage holes renew the water in the trays. Otherwise a small humidifier can be placed near the plants and used regularly to combat dry, indoor conditions common during the winter months.

I have talked to gardeners who swear by showering their indoor plants once a month in the bathtub. Using the showerhead and lukewarm water, the "rain" treatment should last for five to ten minutes. Afterwards, the plants are allowed to drain for several hours before being put back on their stands. This procedure accomplishes several things. First, it gives the plants a deep and thorough watering, which helps remove toxic salts excreted by the plant from the soil. Second, it rinses dust from the foliage, allowing more light to reach food producing plant cells. Last but not least, showering your plants creates a penetrating humidity that stimulates leaves to uptake moisture and nutrients, which is why this is an excellent time to apply a light foliar feeding of liquid kelp.

Resource

"You Must Use a Good Potting Mix." Bonnie Plants. Accessed December 15, 2015. https://bonnieplants.com /library/you-must-use-a-good-potting-mix/.

Jill Henderson is *a self-taught herbalist, author, mixed-media artist, and world traveler, with a penchant for wild edible and medicinal plants, culinary herbs, and nature ecology. She is a long-time contributor to* Llewellyn's Herbal Almanac *and writes for* Acres USA *magazine. Jill has written three books:* The Healing Power of Kitchen Herbs, A Journey of Seasons: A Year in the Ozarks High Country *and* The Garden Seed Saving Guide: Seed Saving for Everyone. *She also writes and edits* Show Me Oz *(Show MeOz.wordpress.com), a weekly blog filled with in-depth articles on gardening, seed saving, homesteading, wild-crafting, edible and medicinal plants, herbs, nature, and more. Jill and her husband, Dean, live, love, and write in the heart of the Missouri Ozarks.*

Culinary
Herbs

Eat Your Weedies

by Lupa

When I was a kid growing up in rural Missouri, my lawn was full of dandelions, chicory, clover, broadleaf plantain, and other hardy little plants. Wherever I moved in the United States, I found many familiar faces in the greenery around me. And some of these plants became early totems of mine, teaching me ways of connecting with the land I lived on.

What I didn't realize at the time was that these were also invasive species, not native to this country. They'd been transplanted by Europeans who arrived over the centuries; some were deliberately planted, while others hitched a ride in animal feed and other goods. Regardless, they put their roots down in new soil and became as much a part of the landscape as native plants, if not more so.

Today we often consider them to be weeds, since they grow in places where they aren't wanted, like gardens and sidewalks. The bigger problem is that some of them out-compete native species and cause problems in the ecosystems they've invaded. Here in Oregon, Himalayan blackberry is one incredibly pernicious example; it grows by spreading thick, thorny canes across wide areas and is very difficult to get rid of once it's settled in. It shoves other plants out of the way, and many acres of disturbed land have become completely covered in nothing but blackberry thicket, leaving little room for most of the wildlife that normally lives there.

Many efforts have been made to eradicate invasive plant species and reintroduce native ones. You can take part in this work as well—and in some really creative ways!

Edible Invasives

Many of the plants that have been introduced to the United States have long been considered edibles in Europe, even if they've largely fallen out of fashion in the face of modern agriculture. Some of them have flavors that may be considered strong or bitter by many standards, hence why they aren't grown on massive scales. Still, they often have plenty of vitamins and other nutrients, and if you're going to pick them out of your garden anyway, you may as well eat them!

Please be aware that not all parts of a given plant are safe to eat. Additionally, older leaves of some plants may be too tough and bitter to eat even with lots of cooking. Avoid eating plants that grow along roadways or other sources of pollution.

Wild Greens Salad

This is best made in late spring and early summer when there's still some rain. Pick a mixture of edible leaves. My salads usually include dandelion (*Taraxacum officianale*), bedstraw or cleavers (*Galium aparine*), popweed or bittercress (*Cardamine oligosperma*), broadleaf plantain (*Plantago major*), and the flowers of white clover (*Trifolium repens*) and red clover (*Trifolium pratense*), along with a small amount of creeping wood sorrel (*Oxalis corniculata*) or Bermuda buttercup (*Oxalis pes-caprae*). You don't want to eat a lot of oxalis in one sitting, as it has a lot of oxalic acid (which is also found in spinach, chives, and other common garden plants), and too much can be toxic. Wash the plants thoroughly, then toss in a bowl. You can add more conventional vegetables to cut the strong flavors if you like, or add in cut-up fruit and berries for sweetness.

An alternate use for these greens is ingredients in soup. Simply toss them in a pot with your favorite type of stock (I prefer chicken or mushroom) and whatever soup fixings you like, and cook thoroughly but not to the point of utter mushiness. Cooking will dull the flavors of the greens a bit and will neutralize oxalic acid, but the soup will still taste different from one made with more conventional vegetables like carrots and onions.

Fried Dandelions

Want a surprisingly tasty treat for a light dessert? Pick as many yellow dandelion flowers as you can find. Wash them, remove any remaining insects hiding in the petals, and pat dry. Then remove as many of the sepals (the green, petal-like things just under the yellow flower itself) as you can. Do this quickly, as the flowers will soon start to close, and you want them open for the next part. Now stir a few eggs together, and then pour some flour in a separate bowl. (I like instant pancake batter for this.) Dredge the flowers in the egg and then the flour, and fry in oil in a skillet, turning over halfway. You only need to fry them a couple of minutes, until browned. Set them on a paper towel to absorb extra oil, then serve while still hot.

I like to put a little clover honey on mine and serve them with fresh white clover flowers. However, you can also use them to jazz up some vanilla ice cream, and the honey and clover are also a nice addition here.

Weedy Crafts

Don't want to actually eat the weeds, or have some that you really shouldn't consume? You can still make some awesome projects with them! Who knew your backyard could be a craft store with lots of freebies for the taking?

Weedy Paper

This is a two-for-one deal—you can get rid of weeds and scrap paper. First, pick a bunch of weeds and press them between the pages of a few heavy books until they're dry. This may take a few weeks depending on how thick they are. Next, get some paper out of your recycling bin and tear it up into little pieces; it doesn't have to be primarily white paper, though the more ink on the paper the more blue- or gray-tinted your end product will end up being.

Get an old blender that you don't intend to use for food anymore, or buy one from a thrift store or yard sale. Add ½ cup of paper scraps to 2 cups of water in the blender, and blend for 30 seconds or until the paper is reduced to pulp.

Pour it into a larger container, like a plastic storage bin. Blend a few more batches until the bin has at least a few inches of pulp in it. Add some food coloring to dye the paper, if you like; green is a nice choice. Toss your dried weeds in at this point—you can reserve a few particularly nice ones for more deliberate placing later.

For the next part, you may wish to have a specialized screen and mold set for making small rectangles of paper; it should come with instructions on how to use it. The short version is this: dip the screen mold into the pulp, lift it up, and then gently shake it up and down and side to side to get the pulp evenly distributed. If you have any especially nice dried plants, carefully press them onto the surface of the pulp. Press the mold pulp-down on an old bath towel, and sponge away water that oozes up through the screen. You may have to do this a few times to get out as much extra water as possible. Carefully pull the mold away from the paper, and leave it to dry for a few days.

The paper will become thinner as you make more sheets. You can either choose to add more blended paper to your pulp mix or to make several thicknesses of paper out of one batch.

Ivy Wreath

English ivy is a lovely plant, but like Himalayan blackberry it can take over many acres of wild land in just a few years and is difficult to eradicate. Thankfully, its vines lend themselves well to weaving! Let's say you have a big pile of ivy you just pulled. Start by untangling a few of the longer vines from the rest. Strip the leaves off, and put them in the pages of a few heavy books to dry.

Now, take one of your vines and coil it up into a circle as though it were a garden hose. You can make it as large or small as you like, though if you haven't woven a wreath before, you may wish to keep it 1 foot or less in diameter so that it's easier to manage. Once you have a circle that's about 3 or 4 vines thick, take the rest of the vine (or a new one if you've run out) and start winding it around the circle like candy striping. You want to wind it tightly, leaving about ½ inch between stripes at the most, but be careful not to break the vine. Once you reach the end of a vine, tuck it in between a couple of the vines in your initial circle or under a couple of the stripes. Keep winding new vines around the wreath in this candy-stripe fashion until it reaches the desired thickness—or try winding a new vine in the opposite direction!

When you're at the end of your last vine, tuck it into the wreath securely. If you're worried about it coming out, take the wire from an old twist tie that's been stripped of paper and use that to secure the end in place. Then leave the wreath in a cool, dry place to dry for a few weeks. You may notice that it shrinks a bit as it dries; that's normal. If your wrapping wasn't tight enough, the wreath may feel a little loose. You can wrap it with a bit of decorative yarn or ribbon to help it stay together.

Now get the ivy leaves that you've dried. Using a hot glue gun or tacky craft glue, attach the leaves to the wreath however you like. You can also add other decorations, in order to include other dried invasive plants.

Doing Your Homework

My experience has been entirely in the United States, and so the examples I've given are from there. However, there are invasive species all over the world. Many of them are European in origin, though this is not universally true.

If you want to find out more about invasive plant species in your area, contact your local wildlife, forestry, or other nature-oriented commission. You can also ask any local environmental organizations and plant nurseries; even if they can't help you, they may be able to point you in the right direction. Once you've positively identified a plant, you should research it further to make sure it's safe to eat and handle. *Please do not ever eat any wild plant that you cannot 100% identify as edible!* Be cautious when eating a plant for the first time, as you may experience an upset stomach or other adverse effects if you are allergic or otherwise sensitive.

Suggested Reading

This essay should not be your only source on eating wild plants; please refer to the resources below when doing research.

Websites

The US Department of Agriculture has a website to help identify invasive species of all sorts (http://www.invasivespecies info.gov/resources/identify.shtml). Also check out their state-by-state database of invasive and noxious species (http:// plants.usda.gov/java/noxiousDriver). These are both great sites if you like the idea of saving the planet by eating invasive species: http://eattheinvaders.org/ and http://invasivore .org/.

Books

Many books on foraging wild plants include some that are invasive in theUnited States and elsewhere. Even if there aren't any of your local invaders in there, the books are still great resources for how to find and make use of supposedly "undesirable" wild plants. Here are a couple of favorites:

Thayer, Samuel. *Nature's Garden: A Guide to Identifying, Harvesting, and Preparing Wild Edible Plants.* Bruce, WI: Forager's Harvest, 2010.

Zachos, Ellen. *Backyard Foraging: 65 Familiar Plants You Didn't Know You Could Eat.* North Adams, MA: Story Publishing, 2013.

Lupa *is an author, artist, nature nerd, and wannabe polymath living in Portland, Oregon. She is the author of several books on totemism and nature spirituality, including* Nature Spirituality From the Ground Up: Connect with Totems in Your Ecosystem *(Llewellyn, 2016), and is the creator of the Tarot of Bones. Her primary website is http://www.thegreenwolf.com, and she can be contacted with questions or commentary at lupa.greenwolf@gmail .com.*

Beverage Craft: Cordials, Safts, Shrubs, and More

❧ by Susan Pesznecker ❧

Cordial craft is a gorgeous bit of magic in the kitchen—one of those sleights of hand that impresses your guests even as you give a secret smile. For all their elegance, home-made beverages are easy to make and satisfying to enjoy. They're also sustainable—a great way to use fruit when extra abounds and might be a bit too ripe for eating. With a little time and a few simple tools, you can fill your larder with an array of cordials, shrubs, safts, and other treats. And whether you're finishing a holiday feast, sitting around a campfire with friends, or picnicking on a sunny beach, the perfect libation will always add to the occasion.

Your Ingredients

Any herbal workings should begin with the best ingredients, and beverages are no exception. I only use organic produce when crafting, and the more local, the better. Explore your local farmer's market or green grocer. Many such purveyors will allow you to order ahead or buy by the crate, which saves a tremendous amount of money. Even better: grow or pick your own ingredients.

The recipes given here all rely on sugar. I prefer plain white sugar because it's clean, chemically stable, and works consistently and reliably. Raw (turbinado) sugar can be used interchangeably with white sugar. If you want to use brown sugar, honey, agave nectar, or another sweetener, it will probably work, but you'll have to do some experimenting. I don't recommend trying these recipes with sugar substitute. The syruping and fermentation processes are chemical reactions involving sugar and also may (as in the case of fruit cordials or infused alcohols) rely on sugar as a preservative. I recommend making a small (one-fourth size or smaller) batch as a test—that way, you won't waste a lot of ingredients if it doesn't work the first time.

If your recipe calls for vinegar, use a high-quality apple cider vinegar—homemade or organic if you can find it. If a recipe calls for alcohol, the general rule is to only use alcohol you would be willing to drink. In other words, if it isn't drinkable by itself, it's not going to do anything good for your recipe. For "clear" alcohol, I prefer a good-quality vodka, but Everclear will work too. I've found that asking liquor store owners for recommendations is really helpful; they'll point out choices that are high in quality and taste but not necessarily at the top end, pricewise. Saving money is good!

What Is an Infusion?

Beverage crafting begins with a little history of the most basic herbal preparation: the infusion. The simplest and most ancient form of potion is the infusion, created by steeping or soaking a mixture of plant materials in some sort of liquid. If you've ever had a cup of tea, you've had an herbal infusion. In an infusion, the liquid extracts the active constituents from the solid material. This liquid, called the "menstruum" or solvent, can consist of a number of different liquids, including water, oil, drinkable alcohol, or honey. The remaining solid material is known as the "marc."

An infusion containing one ingredient is traditionally called a simple, while an infusion with two or more ingredients is often called a brew or potion. An infusion with primarily medicinal qualities is frequently referred to as a tisane, while a philter (or philtre) is a brew historically described as a love potion. Infusions designed to fill the user with health and vigor are called tonics or elixirs, while those that remove toxins from the system are said to be cleansing or detoxifying.

Infusions are quick and easy to create and can be made with ingredients most of us have on hand. They're flexible and offer an almost infinite variety of tastes and effects, as you'll see in the descriptions to come. As you read on, keep in mind that even the most elegantly crafted cordials and liqueurs come from the same homely, infused beginnings.

What Are Cordials and Liqueurs?

A cordial is an alcohol-based infusion made with fruit pulp and juice. In contrast, liqueurs may or may not include fruit but use herbs, barks, flowers, roots, seeds, and sometimes cream. Both cordials and liqueurs can include spices and flavorings and are traditionally consumed in small amounts after the evening meal. They may also be used as flavor accents or as ingredients in other recipes.

Cordials and liqueurs are the offspring of medieval herbal remedies, whose makers found that high percentages of alcohol or sugar could preserve and prolong the life of any infusion. Cordials then were believed to be invigorating, stimulating, and even aphrodisiacal. Folks who consumed a volume of cordial or liqueur were noted to have a temporarily elevated mood, followed by somnolence (sleep!) and inevitably one heck of a hangover. Some of these beverages were both elegant and precious. The Royal Usquebaugh was fortified with flecks of gold leaf, echoing the alchemical *aurum potabile,* "drinkable gold." *Usquebaugh* comes from a Celtic word meaning "lifewater," with the golden flecks symbolizing the power of the sun. The French liqueur known as Green Chartreuse, still made today, is a natural infusion of more than 130 plants and herbs and is felt to have strong tonic and healthful benefits, in addition to a pleasing—if acquired—taste.

Homemade cordials are simple blends of fruit, sugar, and alcohol left to infuse for several weeks before bottling. Most cordials have an alcohol content between 15 and 30 percent (8 to 15 proof). The alcohol content of liqueurs tends to be somewhat higher.

Making Fruit Cordials

Cordial craft is a matter of time, patience, and good ingredients. You'll need 1-quart glass canning (mason) jars, fresh fruit, sugar, and good-quality alcohol. Wash the jars and lids in hot water and air dry or put through a dishwasher cycle. Rinse the fruit, drain on towels, and crush or chop as directed.

It is very important to measure all ingredients and have everything ready to go before beginning. In the cooking world, this is known as *mise en place* ("putting in place"). It helps you stay organized and ensures you don't forget any ingredients.

Begin by preparing your fruit (see proportions below) and measuring ingredients. Spoon the fruit into a 1-quart glass mason jar; a canning funnel will help avoid mess. Add sugar and slowly fill with vodka, stirring with a table knife as you fill to eliminate air pockets. Leave an inch of headspace. Screw on the lid and shake well. Leave the jar sitting on your kitchen counter—out of direct sunlight—and shake vigorously twice a day. The sugar will take a couple of days to dissolve fully, so don't be worried if it remains visible for a bit.

Your cordial will be ready in 3 to 4 weeks; the finished brew will have a rich, deep color and flavor. Strain it through a fine sieve or cheesecloth into a clean bowl, then pour the liquid into a decorative bottle or decanter. Store in the refrigerator, bringing to room temperature before drinking. It is best consumed within a few weeks but is drinkable for at least a year, although you may note that the alcohol contents rises and the drink becomes sharper as it ages.

Cane Berry Cordials

2 cups crushed cane berries

¾ cup sugar

Vodka—about 1 cup, or as much as is needed to fill the quart mason jar

Stone Fruit Cordials

Same as above, but finely chop or pulverize the fruit, which can include cherries or juicy strawberries.

Cranberry Cordials

2 cups finely chopped or pulverized cranberries

1 cup sugar

Vodka—about 1 cup, or as much as is needed to fill the quart mason jar

Age for 4 to 6 weeks. This cordial makes a gorgeous holiday drink. Rum may be used for a portion of the alcohol.

Some cordials include brandy or other spirits. For a brandied cherry cordial, follow the above stone fruit recipe but use ¼ cup brandy and ¾ cup vodka. Cover tightly; shake every 2 days and age for 2 to 3 months. Experimenting with your favorite mixtures is part of the fun in cordial crafting.

You can use herbs and spices to flavor your cordials too. For best results, go organic and work with whole spices rather than powdered: star anise, whole allspice, cinnamon sticks, whole cloves, sliced or candied ginger, cardamom pods, and so forth. Using whole spices makes it easier to retrieve the material and makes it easier to control the flavor.

Try not to open your in-process cordials any more than you need to, for opening may introduce germs and molds from the air. On the other hand, do take a tiny taste—using a clean spoon—every week or so. Learning how the taste changes and evolves is part of your work as a budding cordial crafter.

Serve your cordials in a fine decanter for the perfect toast or aperitif. Stir a spoonful into your favorite vinaigrette, pour over ice cream, or concoct a delicious adult milkshake. A bit of raspberry or cherry cordial stirred into a rich mug of hot chocolate is deliciously wicked!

The Vinegar Shrub

Shrubs are the cordial's grandmother, combining fruit and sugar with vinegar for a splendidly sharp, refreshing drink that's perfect in hot weather. Shrubs are also called "drinking vinegar" and are all the rage in modern upscale restaurants.

For a raspberry shrub, wash and crush ripe raspberries and add 1 part apple cider vinegar to 6 parts crushed berries. If needed, add a bit of extra vinegar so that the fruit is covered with vinegar. Mix well, cover, and set aside, undisturbed, for 4 to 5 days. Then skim off any foam and strain through a sieve or cheesecloth, discarding the solid berries (the marc). Measure the juice and add 1 part sugar to 2 parts juice. Boil the juice in a large saucepan until the shrub is reduced to a syrupy consistency and pour into clean jars. Store the shrub in the refrigerator for up to a year or freeze for longer storage.

The above recipe will work for just about any fruit—the juicier, the better. For tart fruits, use 1½ parts sugar for the final boiling. For super sweet fruits, use less sugar.

To serve your shrub, spoon two or three tablespoonfuls over a glass of chopped ice. Top with water, sparkling water, seltzer, ginger ale, or other soda-type beverages and stir. If you have a home soda machine, your shrubs will be a great way to flavor the homemade bubbly beverage.

Cordials, Fruit Syrups, and Safts

In Aussie-speak, a cordial is an alcohol-free fruit syrup that's mixed with sparkling water or soda before drinking. This refreshing drink is served at meals and consumed by the tumbler. Sweden's "saft" is much like the Australian cordial in that it involves an alcohol-free mixture of sugar and fruit juice, but saft is a cooked, reduced mixture.

To make a fruit syrup, you must first create a simple syrup, which is made by boiling 1 part water and 1 part sugar until the sugar dissolves. Allow to cool, then combine 1 part fruit juice with 1 part simple syrup; add lemon juice (or finely grated peel) and other whole spices if desired. Bottle in clean 1-quart mason jars and refrigerate for up to one week, or freeze for longer storage. To use this as an Australian cordial, mix 1 part fruit syrup with 10 parts sparkling beverage and serve over ice.

To make saft, crush 4 cups fresh berries (or include stone fruit for up to half the volume). Combine crushed fruit with a 1-inch piece of peeled, sliced fresh ginger and 2 cups water in a saucepan. Bring to a simmer and cook until fruit is soft, about 10 minutes. Strain the mixture into a second saucepan, pressing gently. Discard the fruit. Add 1½ cups sugar to the strained liquid. Bring to a simmer and cook until the liquid reduces to a light syrup, about 15 minutes. Cool and pour into clean bottles; refrigerate for 3 months or freeze for longer periods. To serve, pour ¼ cup (4 tablespoons) saft into an 8 to 10 ounce tumbler, add ice, and fill with soda or ginger ale. Of course, you could also include an ounce of your favorite alcoholic beverage too.

A Few More Treats

Interested in more? Infused waters are an easy way to replace sweet beverages in one's daily diet. Simply fill a pint or quart mason jar with slices or small pieces of ripe fruit (berries and citrus are especially good), add water, and allow to infuse for a few hours in the refrigerator. The results are beautiful, tasty, and healthful.

Looking for something more exotic? A search through old cookbooks will uncover the English *bragget*, a boiled, fermented cordial of beer, honey, peppercorns, cinnamon, cloves, and mace. *Claretum* was another English concoction of claret wine and honey, boiled down to a syrup and strained to clarity. You might discover *aqua mirabilis*—"wonderful water"—a richly spiced wine using whole spices and sliced fruits, not unlike the Spanish sangria. Ireland's ancient *aqua composita* combines anise, molasses, dates, and cloves to make a rich, spicy cordial.

Explore a hearth full of liquid experiments: may you sip well!

Susan Pesznecker *is a writer, college English teacher, nurse, practicing herbalist, and hearth Pagan/Druid living in northwestern Oregon. Sue holds a master's degree in professional writing and loves to read, watch the stars, camp with her wonderpoodle, and work in her own biodynamic garden. She is cofounder of the Druid Grove of Two Coasts and the online Ars Viarum Magicarum, a magical conservatory and community (www.magicalconservatory.com). Sue has authored* Yule, The Magickal Retreat, *and* Crafting Magick with Pen and Ink *(all Llewellyn), and is a regular contributor to the Llewellyn annuals. Visit her at www.susanpesznecker.com and www.facebook.com/SusanMoonwriterPesznecker.*

Cranberry Ketchup: Sweet and Sassy

⇜ by Doreen Shababy ⇝

The brilliant red fruit we call the cranberry may be small in size, but it's big in flavor. Sometimes called "craneberry," as the flower is said to resemble a crane's head, the North American *Vaccinium macrocarpon* grows on a trailing, vine-like shrub that rarely reaches over ten inches in height; it is part of the larger heath family, Ericaceae. This native to New England (especially Cape Cod) and the Great Lakes region of Canada was widely traded amongst native peoples of the region. It was often dried and combined with venison and melted fat to make pemmican, a fruit-and-meat jerky of sorts, which I call the original energy bar. Cranberries are also native to Europe

and Scandinavia, as well as northern Russia, and claim the jewel-like lingonberry as immediate relative and the popular blueberry and mountain huckleberry as cousins. They were successfully cultivated in Massachusetts starting around 1816, and a healthy bog can produce up to 20,000 pounds per acre. They are enjoyed all year round as a dried fruit (usually sweetened), but they make their biggest impact at harvest feasts and the American Thanksgiving. Cranberries can last up to a year frozen whole, making them very convenient for all sorts of recipes. Unsweetened cranberries and their juice offer a myriad of health benefits: they include polyphenols, which are associated with antitumor activity; they are used as a preventative for urinary tract infections; they have antioxidant flavonoids; and they contain salicylic acid, which reduces swelling. Food should always be our first medicine.

Let's Eat!

Here is a splendid cranberry condiment that can be prepared a week in advance of serving. Naturally, this can accompany your roast turkey dinner, but perhaps you will be persuaded to try it in these other, not-so-traditional dishes. Please choose all-natural and organic ingredients whenever possible.

First, the ketchup. Not so incidentally, the word "ketchup" does not traditionally or specifically refer to the popular tomato ketchup/catsup/ke-tsiap (from a Chinese dialect meaning "sauce of brined fish") with which we are familiar; it has also been prepared using mushrooms, lemons, apples, walnuts, and even anchovies and oysters. Ketchups first originated in the kitchens of Southeast Asian countries, including Malaya (modern-day Malaysia), Java, and China. Ketchup is simply a table sauce for enhancing the flavor of other foods.

Cranberry Ketchup

This recipe is a major component of the ones that follow. If you like more cloves or less ginger or want to add some peppercorns or a few raisins, give it a try. (You have my blessing.)

For the spice bag:

1 cinnamon stick (3–4 inches)

6 allspice berries

4 whole cloves

1 dried chile pepper

1-inch piece fresh ginger root

For the ketchup:

2 tablespoons butter

1 cup coarsely chopped red onion

1 teaspoon orange zest

1 teaspoon lemon zest

½ cup apple cider vinegar

12 ounce package fresh or frozen whole cranberries

2 cups water

Pinch salt

1 cup natural sugar or brown sugar, or to taste

1 tablespoon fresh orange juice

1 tablespoon fresh lemon juice

Take the spices and tie them in a little cheesecloth bag so they don't get loose. Set aside.

In a large heavy saucepan, melt butter over medium-low heat, add onion and citrus zest, and sauté for about 10 minutes or until onion is soft but not browned. Add vinegar, cranberries, water, salt, and spice bag. Turn heat to medium-high and bring mixture to a boil. Cook until berries pop (about 10 minutes) then remove from heat. Cool to room temperature and remove spice bag.

Pour berry mixture into a food processor or blender, and puree until smooth; return to pan. Add sugar, then bring mixture to a boil. Reduce heat to low and then simmer, stirring occasionally to keep from sticking, for about 1 hour or until thickened. Remove from heat and stir in citrus juices.

Store in a tightly covered glass jar in refrigerator, where it will keep for up to 1 week. Makes about 3 cups.

Pucker Up and Try Something New

Cranberries are known to be astringent—they make your mouth turn inside out—but when sweetened they become tangy, and their acidic nature helps make rich foods more digestible. What follows are several suggestions using cranberry ketchup that are (mostly) simple to prepare and certainly appealing even to the not-so-adventurous types.

Oven Fries

 6 baking potatoes or sweet potatoes

 Olive oil to coat

 Salt and pepper to season

 Cranberry ketchup

Heat oven to 400°F for baking potatoes or 350°F for sweet potatoes. Wash and peel potatoes, then dry on a towel. Cutting lengthwise, carefully slice potatoes into quarters or sixths (depending on their size) and place in a large bowl.

Drizzle just enough olive oil to coat the potatoes with a light film, then sprinkle with salt and pepper. Arrange on a baking sheet and place in oven. Bake about 1 hour or until easily pierced with a knife tip.

Serve hot from the oven with cranberry ketchup for dipping. Makes about 4 servings.

Spinach Salad

This next recipe (more like guidelines, really) puts a bit of a spin on so-called traditional spinach salad in that it's not drenched with bacon fat and vinegar, which I don't miss at all. But fear not, there is still bacon! And speaking of spin, do use your salad spinner, if you have one, for washing the spinach.

½ cup cranberry ketchup

2 tablespoons cider vinegar

1 bag (10 ounces) fresh spinach, washed and dried

1 large apple, thinly sliced

½ cup cubed sharp cheddar cheese (about 2 ounces)

½ cup pecan halves, toasted

6 slices bacon, fried crisp and crumbled

In a small bowl, mix the cranberry ketchup with the vinegar. Set aside; this will be the salad dressing. (You might want to double this if you like a lot of dressing.)

Distribute the spinach into four individual salad bowls. Arrange the apple slices and cheese in each bowl, then drizzle about 2 tablespoons salad dressing over each. Sprinkle the pecans and bacon over each salad and serve. Add remaining dressing as desired.

Makes 4 salads.

Saucy Sausages

This is easy-peasy to put together for a pot-luck. Simply cut up 2 pounds of your favorite smoked sausages into 1-inch lengths and brown in a skillet to render fat. Drain and place sausage in a slow cooker. Pour in cranberry ketchup to cover, cover with lid, and cook on high for 2 to 3 hours until hot and bubbly. Serve.

Makes 4 to 6 servings.

Shrimp Cocktail

- 1 pound cooked and cleaned large shrimp, cut into bite-sized pieces
- 1 stalk (rib) celery, diced
- ¼ cup frozen corn kernels, rinsed to thaw
- 1 cup (or more) cranberry ketchup
- Crusty bread for serving

In a mixing bowl, combine the shrimp, celery and corn with enough cranberry ketchup to make a moist but not drippy combo. Chill until ready to serve with the bread.

Makes 4 shrimp cocktails.

Cranberry Cream Cheese Spread

Delicious and a snap to prepare. Mix ½ cup cranberry ketchup with 8 ounces softened cream cheese in a bowl, then spoon into a pretty bowl or crock for serving. Spread on whole grain crackers. (Try and walk away from this one.)

Turkey Burgers

Everyone has their favorite way to make a hamburger. For turkey burgers, I like to season the meat with plenty of salt and pepper, a pinch of garlic powder, and finely chopped water chestnuts. Since ground turkey is fairly lean, cooking the burger in a skillet helps keep its shape and prevents it from falling through the grates of a barbecue grill (speaking from experience). If you have an electric, fancy-schmancy burger maker, by all means use it, especially if it enhances caramelization (i.e., flavor). Make your turkey burger according to your favorite method, and use cranberry ketchup for the condiment, with thinly sliced red onion and crisp lettuce or sprouts to garnish. Hold the mustard!

Turkey Cranberry Wraps

The hardest part about making any kind of wrap is not over-filling the tortilla so that when you actually roll it up, you can do so without squishing out the filling. Here are simple and simply delicious instructions for making a turkey cranberry wrap.

Gently warm a large flour tortilla over a burner or skillet to soften; remove from heat before it gets dry. Spread cream cheese all over the tortilla, except for a bit of an edge on one side. Spread some cranberry ketchup on the cream cheese—enough to really amp up the flavor. Next, layer on a few pieces of thinly sliced turkey, a few clover or alfalfa sprouts (washed and dried), and finally a sprinkle of pumpkin seeds (pepitas).

Start rolling on the opposite side of the plain edge, tucking firmly and evenly; don't worry about folding in the ends, since this is not a burrito. Roll it up all the way, then slice diagonally in the middle. Serve with purple heirloom potato chips for a fabulous lunch.

Oven-Glazed Barbecue Chicken

This final recipe, for oven-glazed barbecue chicken, is a bit more complicated but only on the surface. (And the aroma in your house will be heavenly torture.) I recommend serving the chicken with a lemony cabbage and apple slaw (no mayonnaise), a side of rice studded with dried cranberries and pistachios, and a cold, refreshing lager or crisp hard cider. Reservations suggested!

1 large (4–6 pound) chicken, cut up into pieces

Salt and pepper to season

Cranberry ketchup

Heat oven to 400°F. Season the chicken with salt and plenty of pepper, then place it skin-side up in a shallow glass baking dish. (You might need to use two pans to avoid crowding the pieces: you don't want them to steam.) Bake for 15 minutes, then reduce heat to 350°F. Turn the pieces over and roast for another 15 minutes.

Now that the chicken has released some of its fat, pour off the fat and turn the chicken again to skin-side up. Spoon a bit of cranberry ketchup onto each piece. Roast for 15 minutes.

Spoon more sauce over the chicken. Roast again for 15 minutes. Now, turn the heat up again to 400°F, dabble with sauce once more, and roast for a final 15 minutes. (That's 1 hour and 15 minutes total, or until done. If you use a smaller chicken, it will probably only take 1 hour, and you should baste it more often.) Serve piping hot from the oven with plenty of napkins.

Makes 4 servings of chicken.

Hungry for More?

Here are some additional ideas for using cranberry ketchup: as a glaze for pork roast or slow-cooked pork for shredding, as a finishing glaze for grilled salmon, poured over a baked brie wheel, on a ham and swiss cheese sandwich, next to succotash, or as dipping sauce for elk steak kabobs.

I hope I have provided you with plenty of inspiration for making cranberry ketchup. It doesn't take unusual equipment or boiling kettles of water to "put up" in mason jars because it is quick and easy to prepare, and you don't have to make a gallon. I have never tried freezing it, but I imagine it would keep for about two months this way. In any case, it won't last long enough to worry about leftovers.

Doreen Shababy *is the author of* The Wild & Weedy Apothecary. *She lives in northern Idaho and has surrounded herself with herbs and wild plants for decades, making and selling herbal remedies and concocting fabulousness in the kitchen. Doreen is fascinated with food history and has lately been involved with organic, gluten-free baking. She practices various and spontaneous forms of energy work, including Reiki and Source Connection, and she loves working with tarot and other oracle cards. Please visit her at www .doreenshababy.com and www.wildnweedy.com.*

The Secret Ingredient

⮞ by Alice DeVille ⮜

Sought-after recipes derive their
success from mouth-watering
ingredients that tantalize a diner's
taste buds. Every dish you savor has
a flavor profile that sends a sensory
message to your palate acknowledg-
ing that what you are eating is either
a fantastic winner or a disappointing
dud. Expert cooks find a way to elevate bland or boring foods to show-
stopping heights. What's the secret?
The combination of cooking technique and special seasoning in the
recipe adds life and enjoyment to the
main components of the dish. Foods
need balance, which calls for the
right combination of salt, searing,
zing, and sugar to temper the herbs
and spices. Often a dish just needs a

dash of lemon or sprinkling of herbs to bring it to a unified state after blending all the ingredients. The skillful use of herbs and spices is the secret to flavorful recipes.

When I was in elementary school, a neighbor on our street earned the reputation of making the best brownies in town. She baked and shared her goodies willingly so that many of the residents got to taste these beauties that were known as "Mary's Brownies." The word got out and neighbors traded notes when they received a treasured plate of them. Tasters swore she used mint in those gems, but my guess is that it could have been lemon thyme. Eager to duplicate the deliciousness without having to wait for the generosity of Mary's next baking spree, the neighborhood women asked for the recipe so they could make their own batches. Mary blew them off time and again. The women were relentless and kept asking.

Finally, after a number of years—by this time I was married and never thought the recipe would see the light of day—Mary caved and gave the women her famous recipe. Even the most accomplished of these passionate bakers could not get their batches of brownies to taste the same as Mary's. One day the women got together to share their experiences and to compare ingredients in the recipe she shared. They discovered that not one copy of the recipe had the same information. Mary had the last laugh.

The Truth About Secret Ingredients

The ingredients in a recipe aren't the only secrets—techniques and products used in preparation also count, and integrity rules when you share a recipe. Those fluffy pancakes you flip on the griddle flop if you forget to tell others that you added two tablespoons of baking powder to the mix. Herbs and spices can make the ultimate taste difference in culinary masterpieces and are meant to enhance flavor rather than shock your taste buds.

When you prepare recipes that include herbs, be sure to specify whether you are using them in fresh or dried form. The dried version is usually three times more potent than the fresh and can overpower the palate if used incorrectly. For example, using oregano with a heavy hand ruins a dish, so use it in proportion to the nature of the dish—a little goes a long way. Provide specific instructions when using hot peppers, such as habaneros, in your spicy recipes. Let others know that you have either removed the seeds or left them in before adding to the mix, as the seeds hold intense heat. An unexpected high level of capsaicin leaves the diner with a scorched tongue.

Appetizer Secrets

Sometimes the secret ingredient actually lies in how you prepare a dish. I make a very simple recipe for baked artichoke dip that I found in a magazine many years ago and have shared it with anyone who has requested it over the years. It has five ingredients, takes only 20 minutes to assemble, and tastes divine. Here is the recipe:

Baked Artichoke Dip

    1 cup grated parmesan cheese (grate your own)

    1 cup mayonnaise (not low-fat)

    1 garlic clove, mashed well

    1 14-ounce can artichoke hearts, well-drained and
       chopped

1 heaping tablespoon of finely chopped herbs of your
   choice for the topping

Combine the first 4 ingredients in a bowl; then pour into an ungreased 1-quart baking dish and bake until firm and lightly browned at 350°F for 25 minutes. Remove from oven and top with herbs. I recommend a combination of finely chopped parsley, chives, and dill. Serve with crackers, bagel chips, or vegetables, or as a side serving with your main course.

Surprisingly, more than half the cooks who prepare this recipe get different results. They think I omitted one or more ingredients (definitely not my style) and want to know the secret. When I ask how it differs from mine, they usually say theirs is mushy, separates, has a less intense taste, or does not brown. Texture differences mean that something is off balance, so I know their preparation technique is the culprit. Over the years I have added extra detail to the recipe above to help steer cooks in the right direction.

Here are things I discovered that make this recipe fall apart: Many cooks do not want to grate the cheese and buy the grated supermarket version to save time. Not all parmesan is created equal: brands differ in quality and taste. If you grate cheese on a grater that is better used for zesting rather than on a box grater or in a food processor, you are going to have cheese with a very airy and watery consistency that really does not equal a cup, so you will probably have a mixture that starts separating. Adding the right amount of cheese gives the dish a light brown and slightly crusty top. Some cooks admit they use low-fat or fat-free mayonnaise, which breaks down and adds to the mushy consistency. Also, when I say the artichokes have to be well-drained, I mean they have to be squeezed intensely to rid them of any excess water. Drain them the first time before you remove them from the can; then do a fine chop and drain them at least one more time to make sure they don't add water to the dish. This same principle applies if you are making quiches or pies calling for well-drained, thawed frozen spinach.

Topping the final product with herbs unifies the dish, bringing all the strong and the subtle flavors together rather than overpowering them. A sprinkle of herbs is a unifier, but a handful will stop the show and overpower the main dish.

Main Dish Secrets

The following recipe makes an abundance of tomato sauce and works well with your favorite pastas. Enrich the taste of the sauce by adding cooked meats such as sausage, meatballs (see the next recipe), spare ribs, or a pork chop that you have cooked ahead of time and set aside. If you prefer, you can cook some of the meat in the sauce pot before you add the vegetables as instructed below. This recipe yields 2½ gallons of sauce. Divide into portions and freeze the leftover sauce in containers for future meals. You might even fill a pint container for topping pizza or making chicken or eggplant parmesan.

Robust Red Tomato Sauce

    2 tablespoons olive oil

    1 medium onion, diced

    ½ green pepper, cut in quarters

    1 clove garlic, minced

    1 teaspoon butter

    2 28-ounce cans crushed tomatoes

Meat of your choice (optional)

1 28-ounce can tomato puree

1 28-ounce can tomato sauce

1 28-ounce can San Marzano tomatoes (or add another can of puree instead)

1 14.5 ounce can diced tomatoes

1 tablespoon tomato paste

1 heaping tablespoon brown sugar

2 teaspoons salt

1 teaspoon black pepper

¼ teaspoon crushed red pepper

½ cup low-fat chicken broth

½ cup red wine (Cabernet or Burgundy)

1 ounce chunk of rind from parmesan, asiago, or Locatelli Pecorino Romano cheese (black skin removed)

3 leaves of sweet basil, torn (or 1 teaspoon dried)

Begin by heating the olive oil in the biggest heavy sauce pot you own. Then add the diced onion and green pepper chunks and sauté lightly for up to 5 minutes. Add the minced garlic clove and the teaspoon of butter and sauté another 2 minutes. Add the crushed tomatoes and stir. Then add any cooked meats you may be using to flavor the sauce. I add 12 to 16 meatballs, 6 to 8 Italian sausage links (sweet or hot pork seasoned with fennel) cut in half, and a few pork spare ribs or 1 to 2 pork chops cut in half. Then add the puree, tomato sauce, San Marzano tomatoes, diced tomatoes, and tomato paste and stir. Add brown sugar, salt (I use iodized, sea salt, or kosher salt—usually a mix of two), black pepper, crushed red peppers, and chicken broth. Stir well and bring to a boil, stirring occasionally. Add the red wine and cheese rind; boil, then lower the heat and simmer for 1 hour.

Taste for seasoning at this time. Add sweet basil and more salt if necessary, and cook for another 1½ hours, stirring occasionally. Remove from heat and let cool for at least 30 minutes.

Butter, chicken broth, and red wine are three ingredients that bring the flavors together. Sweet basil hits a high note, and the cheese rind adds flavor fullness. San Marzano tomatoes, the main attraction, are thicker with fewer seeds and taste much sweeter than other tomato types. I like to mix tomato types because of the expensive price of San Marzanos, and sauce recipes work better with a variety of tomato textures. Canned tomatoes often come with basil added, but I prefer to add my own fresh sweet basil, the perfect tomato-sauce enhancer. Some cooks like to add oregano, though it can be very overpowering in a dish. This is often because cooks don't usually buy it fresh and use way too much of the dried version for seasoning sauces or pizza and bread dishes. I find that oregano leaves a bitter aftertaste, so I do not use it in any of my tomato sauce recipes. The longer it cooks the more bitter it becomes.

Heavenly Meatballs

The meatball recipe that follows is sure to win raves from your guests and pairs well with the sauce. They are firm yet tender and very flavorful if you follow the instructions and use ground meat with the correct fat content. Be sure to remove the meat from the refrigerator up to an hour before you are going to mix the meatballs. I usually double the recipe because this one yields 14 to 18 average size meatballs, and I need more for the large quantity of sauce in the previous recipe, intended for several meals.

1 medium onion, finely chopped

2 crushed garlic cloves

4 slices of dense Italian or other white bread (crust optional)

½–¾ cup heavy cream

1 cup grated parmesan cheese

1 teaspoon salt

½ teaspoon ground black pepper

2 pounds ground beef (80% lean / 20% fat or 85% / 15%) or 50% beef, 25% pork, 25% veal

1 beef bouillon cube, crushed

½ cup finely chopped parsley leaves, no stems

¾ cup plain breadcrumbs (seasoned if you prefer)

2 eggs, beaten

½ cup low-fat chicken broth

Cook the onion until lightly browned for 7 to 10 minutes. Add the garlic and cook for 1 minute. Set aside.

Spread the Italian bread slices in a large pasta-serving bowl. Pour ½ cup cream over them and allow it to soak in; add more cream if necessary. Sprinkle the parsley over the bread, and add ½ cup of the grated parmesan cheese, ¼ teaspoon salt, and ¼ teaspoon black pepper. Let sit for at least 30 minutes, until bread softens and absorbs the cream. (Your kitchen will smell heavenly.)

Tear the soaked bread in pieces using two forks. Spread ground meat on top of the bread mixture and then distribute the remaining cheese, salt, pepper, bouillon cube, and onion and garlic mixture over the meat; add the breadcrumbs and eggs and mix together with your hands, incorporating all ingredients. The mixture will be firm; add the chicken broth, and depending on mixture consistency, add the rest of the cream. Be sure the mixture is not too wet or your meatballs will fall apart. Shape into 14 to 18 oval or round meatballs. Cover a large-rimmed baking sheet with aluminum foil, insert a lightly greased rack in the center, and place the meatballs on the rack. Bake in an oven at 350°F for 1 hour, until browned. Add the meatballs to your sauce, or let cool and place in freezer bags for use in other meals.

What items hold the secret to these tasty meatballs? If you said cream, parmesan cheese, parsley, the bouillon cube, chicken broth, and meat texture you are correct. Sprinkling parsley in particular over the bread adds a wonderful vibrant taste to the meatballs, though I don't add the stems directly to tomato sauce when I'm cooking because of their potency; I recommend using it in a bouquet garni or with other seasoning combos like herbes de Provence, which you place in a net bag in the sauce but remove and discard when the dish is done. I use Italian flat-leaf parsley with its more robust flavor enhancers for the meatballs rather than curly parsley, which adds little flavor and is mainly used as a garnish.

Breakfast Pairings

Create a new taste sensation and elevate a classic breakfast dish by substituting key ingredients in favorite recipes with a couple of new pairings. The following egg recipe shows versatility.

Scrambled Eggs Three Ways

    4 large eggs

    3 tablespoons whole or low-fat milk

    3 tablespoons heavy cream or half and half

    ½ teaspoon salt

    ¼ teaspoon black pepper

    2 tablespoons butter

    ½ cup grated havarti cheese

    Large sprig of fresh dill, finely chopped

In a medium bowl, beat eggs until fluffy. Add milk, cream, salt, and pepper and whisk again. Heat a heavy skillet on medium and melt butter. Add eggs and let them set a bit before stirring and letting uncooked eggs run against the sides. As they firm up, push them to center. Add cheese and let it melt slightly before topping with dill. Makes 3 servings.

Dill is often paired with egg dishes as well as cheese, pickles, and pickled foods. It is tangy, and both its fresh leaves and its seeds are used in cooking. I find the seeds more bitter or intense, so I use the fronds when pairing with eggs. Dill can also be paired with yogurt dishes, cucumber salads, and fish like salmon, fresh trout, or orange roughy.

One variation of this dish uses the same base recipe but substitutes sharp cheddar cheese for the havarti and ½ teaspoon finely minced chives for the dill. Another version adds ½ cup of finely chopped ham to the eggs and substitutes nutty-flavored, coarsely grated jarlsburg cheese for the havarti; garnish with thyme leaves—a pungent, slightly minty, and lemony herb. Serve with an English muffin or your favorite toast. The herb and cheese combos and the ham are the secrets to flavorful egg entrées.

Avocado on Toast

    2 slices of bread

    1 avocado

    2 tablespoons lemon juice

    ¼ teaspoon salt

    ⅛ teaspoon pepper

    ½ teaspoon minced parsley

    2 tablespoons shredded monterey jack or sharp cheddar cheese

    3 arugula leaves

For a tasty breakfast treat, start with a crusty loaf of whole grain bread that has a variety of seeds on top, like sunflower, flax, or poppy seeds. Select bread that is of moderate density to enjoy the crunch in every bite of your sandwich, and toast two slices. Mash the flesh of 1 ripe avocado with a fork or avocado masher; then add 2 tablespoons of fresh lemon juice. Add salt, pepper, and minced parsley (to taste). Mix together and spread on toast, then top with 2 tablespoons of monterey jack or sharp cheddar cheese and 3 arugula leaves.

Turn this dish into a lunch by adding ½ teaspoon of finely minced onion to the avocado base before spreading on toast. Delicious!

The secret ingredients in this recipe are the bread (for texture), parsley, and peppery arugula leaves. Many shoppers buy cilantro when they are shopping for Italian flat-leaf parsley because the two herbs look similar, but their dishes do not taste the way they intended, especially if they are people for whom cilantro tastes soapy. Most chefs use parsley as a substitute for cilantro as well. The use of arugula leaves on the toast is simply to garnish, like lettuce. However, the leaves are small and tender, low in calories, and add a peppery, spicy bite to the taste. Restaurants everywhere are using it in salads, as a sandwich garnish, and in seafood and pasta dishes.

Alice DeVille *recently relocated to the Tampa Bay, Florida, area and is known internationally as an astrologer, consultant, and writer. She works with clients, offering a variety of options for managing life changes. Alice prepares food from a variety of cuisines and enjoys creating new recipes, hosting parties, and organizing holiday feasts. Her work appears in diverse media outlets and websites, including Oprah .com, StarIQ.com, Astral Hearts, The Meta Arts, and sites with popular and famous quotations. Alice's Llewellyn material on relationships appeared in Sarah Ban Breathnach's* Something More, *on Oprah. com, and in* Through God's Eyes *by Phil Bolsta. She is available for writing books and articles for publishers, newspapers, or magazines and conducting workshops, lectures, and radio or TV interviews. Contact Alice at DeVilleAA@aol.com or alice.deville27@gmail.com, or visit her website, www.astrologyondemand.com.*

Pocket Poor, Flavor Rich: Substitutes for Herbs and Spices

❧ by JD Hortwort ❧

Today when I inventory my kitchen to make a grocery list, I open the spice cabinet and see a world at my fingertips—Hungarian paprika, Indonesian clove, Jamaican ginger, Indian black pepper. The worth of a good cook can be tallied, in part, by his or her spice cabinet.

It's funny to think back on my mother's spice cabinet. If memory serves, there was rubbed sage, a small assortment of cake spices like clove and cinnamon, and a bottle of hot sauce that was used so little it tended to separate into a muddy, red layer of pepper juice topped with a translucent layer of vinegar.

We used a fair amount of salt, but that old metal box of ground

black pepper would last for months—and that was in a large family of two adults and nine kids! As small as Mama's spice inventory was, Grandma's was smaller. She had sugar, salt, and black pepper. The sugar was for baking. Salt went into the pot during cooking. Pepper was added, sparingly, at the dinner table. Her prized cooking ingredients were tiny bottles of flavorings for her delicious pound cakes.

She delighted in surprising us on Sundays with different flavors of this Southern classic. One week it might be peppermint. The next week it could be lemon or cinnamon. But these ingredients were metered out sparingly. Cooking extracts were expensive items, usually bought from the Rawleigh distributor, a modern-day tinker who came around periodically with suitcases full of pungent ointments, liniments, and flavored extracts. Like many in their day, my grandparents and parents made the best of what they could get. It wasn't always as much as they liked, and sometimes they had to make do with substitutes—but they had their tricks and secrets to compensate.

The Start of a Love Affair

Throughout history, wars were fought over nutmeg. America was discovered by people seeking a shorter, easier route to exotic eastern lands of spice (among other commodities). If people were able to experience exotic spices, they generally wanted more. Anything to extend the shelf life of meat or add some zest to an otherwise bland, boiled menu was certainly appreciated. Of course, there were also the real and imagined health benefits of these mysterious ingredients from far-off lands.

But these ingredients were hard to come by and expensive when sold on market shelves. Enter human ingenuity. Nature uses many of her popular flavors in multiple plants. Humans, who seem to be willing to try to eat just about anything, just kept tasting and experimenting until they figured out where those flavors were hiding.

Spice or Herb?

The words "spice" and "herb" are used interchangeably by most cooks to mean some source of seasoning added to recipes to enhance flavor. Technically, there is a difference. When we say herb, we mean the herbaceous, leafy part of the plant, used fresh or dry. Spices come from other parts of the plant and are typically dried. Spices can be bark (cinnamon), stigmas (saffron), root (ginger), or seed pods (cardamom). Sometimes, we can get both from the same plant. For example, dill gives us an herb when we use the leaf and a spice when we dry the seed.

The Search Begins

Vanilla

Consider, for example, vanilla. We get vanilla from the seed pod of the vanilla orchid from Central America and tropical areas around the Indian Ocean and the South Pacific. Europeans didn't experience this special spice until after Cortes brought it back from the New World.

But medieval Europeans were already familiar with the flavor. They found it in the low-growing ground cover, sweet woodruff (*Galium odoratum*). This light green, bushy perennial is found in the forests of temperate areas around the world. It doesn't look like vanilla. If you brush the foliage of the living plant, it certainly doesn't smell like vanilla. However, something wonderful happens when the fresh plant is added to wine or dried and added to tea: delicate notes of vanilla come through.

Pepper

Another popular spice, black pepper, has been known for centuries. Native to India, where people cultivated the trailing vine for its seeds, pepper was once worth its weight in gold. The properly dried seed was used as legal tender. Pliny the Elder complained in his writings about the huge amount of money that flowed from the Roman Empire to India because wealthy Romans just couldn't get enough of the spice.

Those explorers who found the New World as they searched for a new spice trade route also found red peppers. However, the fruit of capsicums (red and bell peppers) aren't *Piper nigrum* (black pepper). People eagerly sought out substitutes, like the seeds of the *Lepidium campestre*, or **field pepperweed**, where they could find them. Pepperweed is in the mustard family. The dried seeds make a fine pepper substitute.

Here's an interesting side note: you don't have to dry or grind plant parts to lend a hint of pepper to uncooked dishes. **Mustard flowers** have a peppery taste, as do **nasturtium** (*Tropaeolum majus*) and some **daylily** blossoms. Toss them on a salad just before serving for a beautiful, spicy dish.

Capers

Around the Mediterranean Sea, capers add flavor to fish dishes, spice up salads, and give pasta a real punch. Sadly, unless you live in an area with weather and land conditions similar to Turkey or Salina, you probably can't grow capers. You might be able to grow nasturtiums. Gardeners love nasturtiums for the cascade of rounded leaves and brightly colored, yellow, orange and scarlet flowers that deck the plant all summer long. The leaves and flowers add a peppery flavor to salads. Is it any wonder that the unripe seed pods are also peppery?

A poor man's caper can be made by pickling nasturtium seed pods. Start with 1 cup of firm, unripe seeds. Wash them in warm water, and then pat dry. Put the seed pods in ½-pint jar. (Be sure to use a jar that withstands boiling liquid.) Some cooks top the contents with a bay leaf for added flavor.

Boil 1 cup of white vinegar with 1 teaspoon of salt and 5–8 black peppercorns for about 10 minutes. Pour the liquid over the seed pods. Cap the jar and let it cool. Then store in a refrigerator for 3 months. At that point, your poor man's capers are ready to use.

Ginger

So many of our desirable spices come from tropical areas. Those of us living 15 degrees or more north or south of the equator are left envious of our tropical neighbors who can literally walk out the door and find or grow those aromatic plants we covet.

Consider the **ginger lily**, the source of that warm, pungent root that gives pumpkin pie and gingerbread houses their distinctive taste. In temperate zones, ginger has to be nursed along in a green house or a special, sunny part of the house.

Or, you could do as Native Americans did: search the woods for the root of *Asarum canadense* and *A. caudatum*—two types of **wild ginger**. The first is found most often on the east coast, the latter on the west. Neither is closely related to the ginger you get in the store, but both smell of ginger and will lend your dish a mild ginger flavor.

Anise

Gardeners are far more fortunate when it comes to anise (*Pimpinella anisum*). If you like the unique taste of the original jelly beans or chewy, black straps of licorice candy, you know anise, technically a member of the legume family. (Before we go any further, I should point out that, while anise and licorice are used interchangeably, they are two different plants—licorice is *Glycyrrhiza glabra*.) Like certain other spices, *Pimpinella* could once be used to pay off taxes. Charlemagne, in the ninth century, required the herb be grown in his royal gardens.

Of course, a major factor in the popularity of anise was its medicinal qualities. It was used to combat flatulence and to quiet indigestion. Romans thought it calmed epilepsy. Others used the seed to ward off lice. It alleviated coughs and was used as a sedative. Anise was also popular in the kitchen in cakes, candies, and syrups. No wonder people sought out plants that would provide similar taste sensations!

And, how fortunate that there are so many such plants available. In fact, you can grow an entire garden of licorice-flavored plants. **Fennel** (*Foeniculum vulgare*) is the first that comes to mind. Both the plant and seeds provide a delicate licorice flavor to recipes. **Tarragon** (*Artemisia dracunculus*) is another garden substitute for licorice or anise. The best substitute is French tarragon; Russian tarragon (*A. dracunculoides*) can be very unreliable in the amount of anise flavor available in the leaves. Both **cicely** (*Myrrhis odorata*) and **anise hyssop** (*Agastache foeniculum*) are anise substitutes, as is **chervil** (*Anthriscus cerefolium*). You can use anise and any of these licorice-flavored substitutes very safely, but note that true licorice can cause problems when used in large amounts for long periods of time. The FDA warns, "Don't eat large amounts of black licorice at one time. If you have been eating a lot of black licorice and have an irregular heart rhythm or muscle weakness, stop eating it immediately and contact your healthcare provider. Black licorice can interact with some medications, herbs and dietary supplements."

Substitutes: Geraniums and Basils

Finally, let's talk about **scented geraniums** (*Pelargonium* spp.) and **basils** (*Ocimum* spp.)—the gardener's substitute for just about everything under the sun! Europeans found scented geraniums in southern Africa. With over two hundred varieties available, they hit the mother lode. Scented geraniums can smell like rose, pineapple, coconut, lavender, myrrh, or peach. There are citrus-scented geraniums and mint-scented geraniums. Some smell like berries (raspberry or strawberry); some smell like eucalyptus or camphor. Victorian gardeners went crazy for scented geraniums, and for good reason: an ounce of pure rose oil can cost well over $200 per ounce today, while an ounce of attar of rose, the essential oil from a scented geranium, can be had for under $15. Scented geraniums still come and go in popularity in the garden for their relative ease of growth and maintenance. In temperate zones, these geraniums are annuals. However, gardeners can and do overwinter the plants in their homes for years of enjoyment.

Basils (*Ocimum basilicum*) are another group of plants that give a poor gardener a break. Even the novice gardener has grown sweet or Italian basil. Basil's range extends well beyond a flavoring for pizza. Can't afford or find star anise? Try Thai basil to lend your dish a clove-like flavor. Don't have a lemon tree outside your door? Grow a lemon basil plant to give a citrusy hint to your recipe.

Saffron

Over the centuries, the cost of spices rose and fell. Black pepper, once as good as gold, is now pennies per pound, but saffron (*Crocus sativus*) is still the most expensive spice in the world. Enter **safflower** (*Carthamus tinctorius*). To get one pound of saffron, you need to remove the stigmas from 75,000 saffron crocus blossoms. Safflower can be grown in any summer garden and produces many more flowers, which are the source of "bastard saffron." Good cooks will insist that there is no substitute for the flavor of saffron, and they are right.

In fact, none of these garden substitutes will exactly replace their exotic spicy cousins. That's not to say these humble alternatives aren't worth a try—especially if you are reconnecting with the rugged ingenuity of our ancestors, who were willing to taste a lot of wild plants to find that special one that could replicate the heavenly taste of those exotic, tropical spices.

Resource

"Black Licorice: Trick or Treat?" US Food and Drug Administration. Last modified October 6, 2015. http://www.fda
.gov/ForConsumers/ConsumerUpdates/ucm277152.htm.

JD Hortwort *resides in North Carolina. She is an avid student of herbology and gardening. JD has written a weekly garden column for over 20 years. She is a professional and award-winning writer, journalist, and magazine editor, as well as a frequent contributor to the Llewellyn annuals. JD has been active in the local Pagan community since 2002 and is a founding member of the House of Akasha in Greensboro, NC.*

Sage: A Story of Redemption

ᕻ by Anne Sala ᕻ

When I chose to write about sage, I didn't think I would enjoy the assignment. My first "bad herb experience" was with an obnoxiously over-flavored sage tea bread. I was seventeen and just starting to grow my own herbs. While I always kept a jar of dried sage in my cupboard, I did not grow it in my garden after that terrible tea bread. I feared the fresh stuff's resinous flavor would always be too difficult to control.

I am glad I challenged myself. Playing around with sage allowed me the freedom to figure out how I could add this versatile herb to my culinary repertoire. From now on, there will always be a sage plant growing at my home.

Salvia officinalis, or common sage, is an evergreen sub-shrub. Its leaves are soft and usually a dusty gray-green. In late summer, the plant puts forth spikes of purple or blue flowers. It is part of the Lamiaceae family, along with many other familiar, aromatic herbs, such as basil, mint, rosemary, oregano, thyme, and lavender. Common sage generally grows to be about a foot high, if planted in dry, chalky soil with good drainage and plenty of sun. While a perennial, the plant seems to lose its majesty after three years or so and is best replaced. When used as a companion plant, sage is beneficial to carrots, rosemary, and members of the genus *Brassica*, such as broccoli and cabbage. It has a detrimental effect on cucumbers and onions, though, and the sage plant itself will actually wilt and die if it grows too closely to rue (another lesson I saw play out in that first herb garden of mine).

Also like other members of its family, sage is native to the lands bordering the Mediterranean Sea, where it has been cultivated for thousands of years. The Greeks and Romans considered it a symbol of domestic virtue and dedicated it to Zeus and Jupiter. The Egyptians used it as a fertility drug, and others swore it could bolster a failing memory. Sage is a chief export from the region of the former Yugoslavia, and the dried sage that comes from the Croatian region of Dalmatia is considered to be some of the best in the world.

As a medicine, sage seems to do it all. The French call it *toute bonne*, or "all good," and its scientific name, *Salvia*, comes from the Latin word meaning "to save." Its essential oils contain thujone, borneol, and phenolic acids—all with antiseptic and antibacterial qualities. Healers have consistently turned to sage to cure sore throats, night sweats, upset stomachs, and rheumatic pain. Sage also has an antispasmodic effect, and its smoke—strangely enough—has been used to ease asthma symptoms.

Sage tea (which is surprisingly sweet and comforting), as well as sage in tincture form, is also used to relieve symptoms of menopause and to dry up mother's milk after a child is weaned. However, since sage has such an effect on the female reproductive system, it should not be used medicinally by pregnant women.

It is said that during the seventeenth century, Chinese traders were willing to exchange three cases of *Camellia sinensis* tea leaves for one case of dried sage leaves. During the bubonic plague, sage's fumigatory powers were sought as part of the popular four thieves vinegar, which, when sprinkled onto a person, would protect the wearer from the disease. Many different recipes exist, but they usually contain wormwood, cloves, sage, and garlic.

In the kitchen, ancient cooks discovered that combining sage with meat helped stave off spoilage. It also aids in the digestion of fatty foods (hence its presence in many kinds of sausage), like duck, pork, and chicken. Plus, sage helps reduce flatulence when combined with beans.

Sage leaves have a strange, fuzzy, waffle-weave texture. When used in cooking, they are usually chopped fine or strained out before serving to spare guests the unpleasant sensation of trying to chew one. This texture actually gets more unpleasant after drying the leaves, and their fibrous nature makes them hard to crumble. Instead, the leaves that are sold are usually ground up or "rubbed" into a powder. You can make rubbed sage at home, too.

After drying the sage leaves, place them in a colander. You can use either a fine mesh colander or a punched hole–style colander. Place the colander over a clean plate and rub the sage leaves against the bottom of the colander with your fingers. Everything that falls through the holes of the colander is the rubbed sage. Store it in an airtight container and use within a year.

Recipes

Poultry Seasoning

This recipe just tastes "right." Since I use the most poultry seasoning in holiday meals, like in stuffing for the turkey, or in comfort foods, like chicken and dumplings, I don't mind that this simple recipe tastes like the kind I used to buy in the store. That's the taste I remember from my childhood, and that's the taste I want my children to remember, too.

4½ teaspoons dried thyme

1 tablespoon dried marjoram

2¼ teaspoons dried rosemary, crumbled

2 tablespoons rubbed sage

1½ teaspoons grated nutmeg

1½ teaspoons ground black pepper

Depending on the size of your mortar and pestle or electric grinder, grind the thyme, marjoram, and rosemary separately or all together until they are a powder. Empty the powder into a glass jar. Add the sage, nutmeg, and pepper; then seal with a tight-fitting lid. Shake vigorously to mix. Makes about ¼ cup. Use within 1 year.

Sage-Scented Beef, Cabbage, and Potato

When winter snows are blowing, I like to imagine my medieval ancestors experiencing the same type of storm while making this exact dish. Inspired by a casserole featured in a cookbook by Lidia Bastianich, this hearty, one-pan meal comes from one of the northernmost portions of Italy, Valle D'Aosta, near the border with France and Switzerland. The flavorings are simple but essential. Garlic, wine, cheese, salt, and pepper can make almost anything tasty. Of course, the sage and rosemary are there for flavor, too, but I think their inclusion was originally for their ability to make fatty foods, like the tough cut of beef featured here, more digestible.

4 garlic cloves, peeled

8 fresh sage leaves

⅛ cup fresh rosemary leaves, stripped from the branch

2 tablespoons kosher salt

⅓ cup extra-virgin olive oil

4 tablespoons butter, softened

1¼ pounds red potatoes, sliced ½ inch thick

1 head green, napa, or savoy cabbage, about 1 pound, cored and sliced ½ inch thick across the grain

2 pound boneless beef chuck roast, sliced ½ inch thick

1 cup white wine

¾ pound fontina cheese, shredded

Preheat the oven to 425°F. Place the garlic cloves, sage, rosemary, and a pinch of salt in a heap on a cutting board. Mince all the ingredients until they begin to form a paste. Scrape the mixture in a bowl or measuring cup and combine with ⅛ cup olive oil. Alternatively, you can use a food processor.

Grease a large, high-side sauté pan or roasting pan with 1 teaspoon of butter and 1 tablespoon oil. Set aside.

Place the potatoes and beef in a large bowl and add 1 teaspoon salt, 2 tablespoons oil, and 1 heaping tablespoon of the garlic mixture. Toss to coat. Pick out half the potato slices from the bowl and arrange them in the pan. Cover with half the cabbage. Sprinkle with a teaspoon of salt.

Place all the beef slices in a single layer on top of the cabbage and dot with about 2 tablespoons of butter. Set the rest of potatoes on top, and then add the remaining cabbage. Sprinkle with another teaspoon of salt. Stir the wine into the last of the garlic mixture and pour over the top of the cabbage. Dot the top with the remaining butter.

Tent the pan with foil and bake until the meat begins to fall apart and the liquid is mostly evaporated (about 2½ hours). The mixture will have sunken down into the pan significantly. Remove the foil and spread the cheese over the top. Return the pan to the oven, uncovered, and bake until the fontina begins to bubble and brown (about 15 minutes). Allow the pan to rest for about 10 minutes before serving. Serves 4.

Sage and Cannellini Bean Bruschetta

Bruschetta is one of my favorite ways to endure the summer heat when it persists into the night. While most Americans think of bruschetta as an easy way to use up tomatoes from the garden, the key ingredients are actually the bread and olive oil. Additional toppings can be just about anything. A particular favorite of mine is beans marinated with an acid and herbs.

Sage has an affinity for both beans and lemons, so this recipe works very well. I was tempted to not make the bread and just eat the beans with a spoon.

1 day-old loaf of Italian bread, cut into ½-inch slices

1 13.4 ounce can low-sodium cannellini beans, drained and rinsed

6–10 fresh sage leaves, chopped

2 garlic cloves

1 teaspoon lemon zest

1 tablespoon fresh lemon juice

3 tablespoons extra-virgin olive oil

¼ teaspoon salt (or to taste)

⅛ teaspoon freshly ground black pepper (or to taste)

Preheat the oven to 400°F. Mince one garlic clove and place in a medium bowl with the lemon juice. Allow to mellow while preparing the bread.

Arrange the bread slices on a cookie sheet and toast in the oven until the bread begins to brown (about 5 minutes), but keep a close eye so they don't burn. Once the bread is toasted to your liking, remove the pan and allow to cool slightly. When the slices can be handled comfortably but are still warm, take the remaining garlic clove and rub over the surface of the bread. Arrange the slices on a plate and drizzle with 2 tablespoons of oil.

Add the beans to the bowl with the lemon juice and garlic. Use the back of a spoon to mash about ¼ of the beans into a paste. Mix in the rest of the ingredients. Taste and adjust the seasonings. Allow the flavors to blend at room temperature for about 30 minutes.

To serve, spoon a bit of the beans onto a slice of bread and eat accompanied by a glass of white wine. Serves 4.

Scallops with Sage Butter

Every fall, I bring my potted herbs inside in an attempt to lengthen their usefulness. Unfortunately, my home's dry winter air usually kills the plants before spring. When it looks like one of my herbs is about to take a turn for the worse, I often make a compound butter out of its remaining leaves. Using that butter to dress seared scallops is a fast and rewarding way to make a special meal.

This recipe takes the traditional, nutty-flavored brown butter sauce and adds the woodsiness of sage. When I serve scallops like this, it makes me feel like I am dining in Trieste, an Italian city on the eastern side of the Adriatic Sea, next to Slovenia. Sage grows wild there, and the dry environment makes the herb's scent particularly strong. Scallop recipes usually suggest removing the tough side muscle. I leave it on since it still tastes like scallop, and I don't want to waste a morsel.

For the butter:

   8–10 sage leaves

   1 stick (8 tablespoons) unsalted butter, room temperature

Place the butter on a cutting board. Tear the sage leaves into pieces, removing any tough stem pieces, and sprinkle on top of the butter. Using a sharp knife, chop the sage into the butter until the leaves are flecks about an ⅛ inch wide. Scrape the butter mixture onto a piece of wax paper, roll it into a cylinder, and chill. Use the butter within two weeks if kept in the refrigerator. If frozen, the butter should keep for 3 months.

For the scallops:

    1 pound dry-packed sea scallops

    Salt and freshly ground pepper

    1 tablespoon extra-virgin olive oil

    3 tablespoons sage butter

    3 fresh sage leaves, sliced into ribbons

    2 teaspoons fresh lemon juice or white wine

Remove excess water from the scallops with paper towels and sprinkle with salt and pepper. Heat the oil in a large skillet over medium-high heat. Add the scallops in a single layer and let cook without moving until they receive a crusty brown sear (about 3 minutes). Turn the scallops and add the butter. Allow the butter to foam and begin to brown. Monitor the heat and turn it down to prevent the butter from burning.

Once the butter has browned, bathe the scallops in it as they continue to cook. This should take an additional 3 minutes. Stir in the fresh sage leaves and lemon juice. Serve the scallops immediately with the butter sauce spooned over. Serves 4.

Cheesy Sage Muffins

I deliberately chose to make a baked good in order to assuage the damage done to me by that sage-infused tea bread. The sage flavor is prominent in this recipe but not overpowering. The sour cream and cheese add a tang and lighten the feel of the muffins. You can use any type of cheese you like. Cheddar is probably the best, but if you are going to make these with the ingredients you have on hand, even colby jack will taste fine. The muffins are best served warm and go well with soup or a roast with gravy.

1½ cups unbleached all-purpose flour

½ cup whole wheat flour

2 teaspoons baking powder

1 tablespoon fresh sage leaves, packed tight

½ cup shredded cheese

1½ teaspoons salt

1 cup sour cream

½ cup water

3 tablespoons olive oil

Preheat the oven to 350°F. Grease a muffin tin with butter. Stack and roll the sage leaves. Slice the leaves into fine shreds and then chop. Measure the sour cream into a small bowl and stir in the water and oil. Set aside.

In a large bowl, mix together the flours, baking powder, sage, cheese, and salt. Add the sour cream mixture to the dry ingredients and mix gently with a spoon or spatula until the flour is just moistened. Using 2 spoons, fill the muffin tin and bake. The muffins are done when the tops begin to brown and a toothpick inserted into a muffin comes out clean (about 25 to 30 minutes).

Cool the muffins for a few minutes in the tin before running a knife around the edges to loosen. Serve immediately or cool completely on a wire rack before storing in an airtight container. Makes 12 muffins.

Anne Sala *is a freelance journalist from Minnesota. Every year, her collection of potted herbs expands, and she's happy to report her rekindled love with sage has already influenced her plans for what she will plant—and cook—next summer.*

Nightshades

❧ by Magenta Griffith ❧

It is curious that one family of plants, the nightshades, contains both some of the world's most poisonous plants and some of the world's most popular foods. Potatoes, tomatoes, and peppers are all related to belladonna (deadly nightshade), jimsonweed (*Datura stramonium*), and mandrake. The Solanaceae family contains about 2,700 species, which also include such diverse plants as eggplant, chili peppers, and tobacco. They originated in a wide variety of places and in climates that vary dramatically: from rain forests that receive more than nine feet of rainfall annually to deserts with virtually no rainfall and to high mountains with regular snowfall and

subfreezing temperatures. They may contain deadly poison, useful drugs, or intense flavor. Potatoes are the fourth largest food crop in the world, with tomatoes and peppers not far behind. Even some poisonous varieties have medicinal purposes; for example, belladonna is the source of atropine, which is used to dilate the pupils of the eyes for examination and to treat motion sickness. The term "nightshade" may have been coined because some of these plants prefer to grow in shady areas and some flower at night.

Potatoes

Potatoes were first found in the Andes in South America, where they were domesticated approximately 7,000–10,000 years ago. There are over a thousand of varieties of potatoes, and they are grown in all parts of the world. Potatoes are an easy crop to grow and adapt readily to many climates as long as the weather is cool and wet enough. Potatoes do not keep very well in storage and are vulnerable to molds. All parts of the plant except the tubers contain the toxic alkaloid solanine and are therefore unsafe to eat. Solanine is also found in other plants in the family; it's what makes nightshade deadly, for example. Potato plants produce small green fruits that resemble green cherry tomatoes, and it may be that those poisonous fruits are what led people to think tomatoes were poisonous.

In 1845, a plant disease known as late blight, caused by a fungus-like microorganism, spread rapidly through the poorer communities of western Ireland, resulting in the crop failures that led to famine and mass migration, mostly to the United States, Canada, Australia, and Great Britain. (The influx of the Irish may be one reason there is so much Celtic Paganism in the United States today. The jack-o'-lantern is an

Irish import, for example.) Potatoes are used in many ways. They are boiled, baked, mashed, fried, deep fried, or grated and made into hash browns and pancakes. Potatoes are the traditional base for making vodka in Russia.

Tomatoes

Tomatoes were thought to be poisonous by Europeans because their bright, shiny fruit resembled nightshade berries. Tomatoes are also a New World plant, native to Peru, Bolivia, and Ecuador; the name comes from the Aztec word for them, *tomatl*. By 500 BC, tomatoes were cultivated as far north as southern Mexico. The stems and leaves are poisonous, but the fruit is not. When people first ate tomatoes, many were still using pewter plates, which were high in lead content. Because tomatoes are so high in acidity, they would leach lead from the plate, resulting in deaths from lead poisoning. No one made this connection between plate and poison at the time; the tomato was picked as the culprit. In some parts of Italy, the fruit was used solely as a table decoration; not until the late seventeenth or early eighteenth century was the tomato eaten. The tomato was also considered inedible—though not necessarily poisonous—for many years in Britain and the United States.

It became part of the cuisine by the late eighteenth century; by then, ceramics had replaced pewter as tableware. Some people claimed the fruit had aphrodisiac powers; in French tomatoes are called *pommes d'amour*, or "love apples." Tomatoes are often used raw but can be baked or broiled. The most common way to cook them is to reduce them into a sauce. Now, they are one of the most common garden plants in the United States. The species in the botanical name for tomatoes, *Solanum lycopersicum*, means "edible wolf peach."

Peppers

Peppers are another nightshade. Green, yellow, orange, and red peppers, as well as all varieties of chili peppers, belong to *Capsicum annuum*. (The black pepper that we grind and sprinkle on food comes from a different plant that is not a nightshade—*Piper nigrum*.) Another New World plant, the pepper has been grown for more than nine thousand years in Central and South America. While "pepper" was the English name, the name for this food in Spanish was *pimiento*, which referred to all peppers, not just the ones stuffed in olives. Peppers range from very mild and sweet to incredibly hot. Mild peppers don't contain the chemical capsaicin, which causes the burning sensation of chili peppers. The spice paprika comes from a mild- to medium-heat pepper (also *Capsicum annuum*). The amount of capsaicin in hot peppers is quite diverse and is measured in Scoville heat units. A yellow banana pepper is 100 or so on the scale, a jalepeño around 1000, and cayenne pepper around 30,000. The hottest pepper known, the Carolina Reaper, is around 1,600,000 or more.

Eggplant

When Europeans first encountered another member of the nightshade family, the eggplant, or aubergine, they gave it an intimidating reputation. They called it *mala insana*—"mad apple." Originally, many types of eggplants were white or yellow and smaller than the purple ones we find in stores today, hence the name. One of the few edible nightshades known to Europeans before the fifteenth century, eggplant is not of New World origin like potatoes, tomatoes, and peppers. Historians believe the eggplant may have its origins in India;

early accounts from a fifth-century Chinese record on agriculture suggest its cultivation in China as well. For centuries after its introduction into Europe, eggplant was used more as a decorative garden plant than as a food. Not until new varieties were developed in the eighteenth century were eggplants grown primarily to be eaten. Immature eggplants contain toxins, as do the stems and leaves. They are also sometimes bitter, which is why some recipes suggest they be sliced, salted, left to stand for a half hour to an hour, and then rinsed to remove the salt before using. Like tomatoes, they are technically a fruit—a berry. When cutting an eggplant, use a stainless steel knife; a carbon steel knife will react with it and turn black. Eggplant is sometimes used as a meat substitute, as in eggplant parmesan.

Tobacco

Tobacco is also a nightshade. While smoked and used for snuff as powdered leaves, it is poisonous. Nicotine, tobacco's principle active chemical, has been used as an insecticide. Other nightshades, even ones we eat, contain small amounts of nicotine: twenty pounds of eggplant contain about as much as a cigarette. A number of ornamental plants and flowers also belong to the nightshade family, including petunias.

Nightshade Recipes

The edible nightshades have increased the supply of food for humankind and added so much to the variety of cuisines. Can you imagine a world without pizza, salsa, or chili? Without, potato chips, french fries, or mashed potatoes on Thanksgiving? If we didn't have the nightshades, these dishes and many others would not exist.

Nightshade Salad

For the salad:

  1½ pounds red potatoes

  1 green pepper, chopped

  2 tablespoons fresh basil, chopped

  1 small red onion, chopped

For the dressing:

  ¼ cup vinegar

  2 tablespoons brown mustard

  2 tablespoons fresh lemon juice

  ½ cup extra-virgin olive oil

  Salt and black pepper to taste

Place the potatoes in a large pot and fill with about 1 inch of water. Bring to a boil, and cook until potatoes are tender. Drain, cool, and cut potatoes into quarters. Transfer to a large bowl and toss with green pepper, fresh basil, red onion, and salt and pepper. Set aside.

In a medium bowl, whisk together the vinegar, mustard, lemon juice, and olive oil. Pour over the salad, and stir to coat. Season with salt and pepper to taste. Serves 4.

Ratatouille

  1 eggplant, about 1–1¼ pounds

  2–3 tomatoes

  1 pound of zucchini, yellow summer squash, or a combination of both

  3 small onions (or 1 large)

2 green peppers or 1 green and 1 red, yellow, or orange

½ cup olive oil

2 garlic cloves, minced

1 teaspoon thyme

1 teaspoon marjoram

Salt and pepper to taste

Peel eggplant; cut into bite-sized pieces (1-inch cubes). Cut tomatoes, zucchini, and onion in similarly sized pieces. Remove seeds and membrane from green pepper and cut into 1-inch squares.

Brown onions and peppers in 2 tablespoons of oil. Remove them to a separate dish, then brown the eggplant and zucchini, adding oil 1 tablespoon at a time as needed. Then briefly cook the tomatoes with the garlic. Once all have been browned, combine them together into 1 pan; add herbs and salt and pepper; and continue to cook slowly, covered, for about 10 minutes or until all are tender. Serves 4.

Gazpacho

6 cups tomato juice (1 46-ounce can)

3 tablespoons lemon or lime juice

1–3 tablespoons olive oil

1 teaspoon soy sauce (optional—some brands of canned tomato juice are very salty)

2–3 cloves garlic, finely minced or pressed through a garlic press

1 cucumber, finely chopped or shredded

1 cup carrots, shredded

1 cup celery, finely chopped

1 green pepper, finely chopped or shredded

¼ cup green onion or chives, chopped

2 large tomatoes, chopped

Combine liquids; mix until blended. Add vegetables. Chill overnight or for at least a few hours. Serves 4. Feel free to experiment with how coarsely or finely you chop or shred vegetables. A food processor will make this easier but will turn it into a puree, rather than a liquid salad.

Magenta Griffith *has been a Witch since the 1970s and a high priestess for more than twenty-five years. She is a founding member of Prodea, which has been celebrating rituals since 1980, and is a founding member of the Northern Dawn Council of Covenant of the Goddess. Magenta, along with her coven brother Steven Posch, is the author of* The Prodea Cookbook: Good Food and Traditions from Paganistan's Oldest Coven. *She presents classes and workshops at a variety of events around the Midwest. She shares her home with a small black cat and a large collection of books.*

Herbs for Health and Beauty

Herbs for Teen Hormones

❧ by Dallas Jennifer Cobb ❧

Puberty is one of the most intense and (often) overwhelming times in life, filled with changing bodies, complex emotions, growth spurts, and a roller coaster of hormonal fluctuations. Many parents of usually calm children are perplexed and wonder where their little darlings went when they find themselves living with a teenage shape-shifter. Sweet and happy one day, surly and withdrawn the next. Previously pleasant and even-keeled kids can become hormonally raging, moody teenagers.

Recently, my thirteen-year-old daughter came home from school. "How was your day?" I asked. She looked at me and burst into tears.

"What's wrong?"

"I don't know," she said. "I just need to have some quiet time." Twenty minutes later she emerged from her room, saying, "I feel better now. I don't know why, but I just needed to cry."

While riding this hormonal roller coaster with my daughter, I have discovered that there are beneficial herbs for a teenager's hormones, natural substances that help calm and stabilize the tumultuous insides of our changelings. There are herbs that help with mercurial emotions, acne, anxiety and feeling overwhelmed, menstrual cramps and bloating, and even with attitude.

Help Needed

When my own daughter began puberty, I needed help. I went to other parents of teens and asked them, "What did you do to survive puberty?" While my daughter was technically still a kid, definite peaks and valleys of hormonal activity were evident, so I figured the behavior was linked to puberty. At times it was as if she were on an emotional roller coaster, and all she could do was scream or cry.

While other parents offered many pieces of advice (including the suggestion that I run away from home or purposefully overconsume alcohol), it was the herbal help that made the most sense. Herbs offered a gentle, effective, and natural way to support my daughter's body as it made its natural changes and provided some relief from the wacky side effects. I was surprised to learn that many of the so-called negative effects of puberty can be alleviated by paying attention to the health and proper function of the liver.

The liver is a huge, solid organ responsible for filtering our blood, removing toxins, and converting waste products that result from metabolic functions into urea. Urea is eliminated in the urine. Because it processes the toxins that result from the metabolizing of hormones, the liver works hard to keep hormones in optimum balance. During the changes, such as hormonal surges, brought about by puberty, the liver can be stressed.

The liver also creates bile, which helps to digest fats and carbohydrates. Synthesizing glutathione, an antioxidant, the liver also has a role in balancing blood sugar and creating red blood cells. When teens further stress the liver by consuming unhealthy foods and drinks containing refined sugars, fats, and caffeine, the result can be a liver that is overwhelmed and underfunctioning. With surges of hormones or unprocessed toxins in the bloodstream, teens can experience mood swings, energy fluctuations, acne, and a confused mental state.

With girls, these hormonal surges often appear as tearful, uncontrolled behavior; catty meanness; and occasional lethargy and mild depression. (Hello, estrogen.) In boys, the surges of testosterone common during puberty can produce impulsive, reckless behavior; defiance; and aggression. In both males and females, oily hair and skin, heavy sweat, smelly feet, and acne are common side effects.

In boys, the hormones associated with puberty are androgens, specifically testosterone, the primary sex hormone. For girls, the primary hormones that drive growth and development are estrogens. In addition to causing the growth and changes associated with puberty, estradiol also promotes the development of breasts and the uterus. Boys are also affected by estradiol, though it affects them later in age and at a more gradual level. Girls experience early growth spurts because of the quick rise in estradiol levels at an earlier age than boys.

While societally we have come to accept these changes in behavior as normal during puberty, they are most likely a result of a congested liver, one unable to efficiently process the surges of testosterone and estrogen coursing through the growing body. On the other hand, when the liver is functioning well, it processes hormones easily and keeps them in optimum balance. The hormonal surges of puberty are minimized as the liver works to maintain an internal state of equilibrium.

Using herbs can help the liver regain equilibrium and reduce the cycle of stress within the changing pubescent body. This will reduce the wild fluctuation of mood, emotion, energy, and attitude and improve the overall quality of health. Add in a few moderate changes to the diet, and many of these side effects can be sidestepped entirely. When the liver is supported to function optimally, it processes hormones and by-products easily, and many of the symptoms of hormonal fluctuation are greatly reduced.

Herbs for Teenage Hormones

There is a wide variety of herbs that have been useful in regulating teenage hormones and in treating the by-products of hormonal change. For whatever ails your teen, the herbs mentioned here (listed alphabetically) have a wide variety of helpful effects.

As with any use of herbs, the information here is for your enjoyment. If you want to use herbs to remedy your or someone else's ailments, consult your physician as well as a chartered herbalist, who can best prescribe a suitable remedy, recommend correct dosage, and teach you how to prepare it.

Angelica (*Angelica archangelica*) can be made into a tea and sipped before bed to help a teen wind down. It relieves insomnia and headaches, reduces anxiety, calms the nerves, and aids digestion. When your child suddenly starts to want to stay up later and later at night and becomes an ogre who sleeps until noon, try using angelica to sooth and calm, prepare for an early bedtime, and ensure proper sleep patterns. Coincidentally, angelica is rumored to have the power to cool sexual desires, so while the tea calms your teen before bed, it may also reduce that wild teenage libido. Another variation of angelica known as *dong quai* (*Angelica sinensis*) has been used to support establishing a regular menstrual cycle.

Chamomile (*Chamaemelum nobile*) is a versatile herb for teenage hormones. It has antispasmodic and anti-inflamatory qualities, relieves pain, and cleanses the liver. Chamomile calms nerves, reduces anxiety, eases menstrual cramps and upset stomachs, and relieves crankiness and restlessness. Chamomile calms itchy skin and can be made into a soothing balm for the treatment of acne. With a sweet, mild taste, chamomile tea can be sipped before bed to promote sound sleep and a positive outlook. It is sweet tasting and extra palatable with a little honey added. Mixed with lemon balm, it makes a tasty tea.

Chaste tree berry (*Vitex agnus-castus*) extract is used widely to regulate hormonal activity. While it should only be taken in small quantities, it is effective in supporting the establishment of a regular menstrual cycle. It can be beneficial to reducing acne breakouts associated with menstruation, and relieving premenstrual syndrome. Not just for females, chaste tree berry can help counter nighttime ejaculation in young men. Usually taken as a tincture, it takes about three months of continuous use to be fully effective.

Dandelion (*Taraxacum officinale*) is effective for stabilizing the changing body during puberty. It's a good source of vitamins, iron, potassium, and zinc. Dandelion stimulates the production of bile and regulates how bile flows from the gall bladder to the liver. Consuming dandelion tincture can improve overall liver function and health and stimulates kidney function. The kidneys work with the liver to help clear excess hormones from the system. Dandelion can relieve PMS symptoms because of the role it takes in detoxifying the liver, treating the root cause of fluid retention and associated weight gain. When taken as an infusion, dandelion root is bitter tasting but palatable if you add salt to it. Sweet additions don't mask the bitter taste.

Lemon balm (*Melissa officinalis*) is part of the mint family and is widely used to calm the nervous system, improve mood, reduce tension, and improve overall cognitive functioning. For teens, a cup of lemon balm tea in the morning can help them focus at school by reducing restlessness and promoting concentration.

Valerian root (*Valeriana officinalis*) has a natural tranquilizing effect and can be used more safely than common pharmaceuticals. Use the root to make a strong-tasting tea for teens who are beside themselves. Valerian induces calmness, promotes sleep, and calms the central nervous system. If your teen suddenly breaks into tears and doesn't know why, consider offering valerian.

Other Helpers

The other helpful practice I undertook was cleaning up my daughter's diet and removing substances that stressed the liver: refined sugars, empty carbohydrates, heavy fats and oils, and stimulants like chocolate and caffeine.

Too often teens overconsume sodas, juice, sports drinks, pizza, fast food, and snacks. These offer little nutritive value and cause havoc within the body, further stressing the liver. Other substances that stress the liver include alcohol, acetaminophen, and over-the-counter painkillers.

While we can't protect our kids from everything, as parents we can start some practices that support the health of the liver so that it can better cope with the environmental and lifestyle stresses that come along. If you, like me, have been mystified by puberty and how to help your kids through it, this list should offer a few ideas that you can customize for your family. These simple tricks may help out the kids you care about the most and help your changelings return to their sweet, centered selves. Because, after all, the health of our livers directly affects our overall health, and a poorly functioning liver will create a poorly functioning teen.

So when your daughter complains of cramps and you offer over-the-counter painkillers, you may actually be making the overall situation worse. And when your son sneaks a couple of beers with the boys to let off stress, he may actually be contributing to the greater stress on the liver. At this hormonally tumultuous time in your children's lives, herbs may be the answer to restoring balance.

Dallas Jennifer Cobb *practices gratitude magic, giving thanks for personal happiness, health, and prosperity; meaningful, flexible, and rewarding work; and a deliciously joyful life. She is accomplishing her deepest desires. She lives in paradise with her daughter, in a waterfront village in rural Ontario, where she regularly swims and runs, chanting, "Thank you, thank you, thank you." Contact her at jennifer.cobb@live.com or visit www.magicalliving.ca.*

Herbs for All Seasons: Essentials for Your Collection

by Sally Cragin

Sally Cragin

If you've worked with herbs for a few years, you probably have some "go-to" plants that are always in your medicine chest or herb cabinet. My husband enjoys cooking with curry, turmeric, and Indian herbs all year round—these items we seem to buy by the quart. For me, the mints (spearmint and peppermint) are essential for tea blends. However, the year is long, and during the warmer months, when the sun lingers in the sky, I find calming herbs, like chamomile, more appealing than I do in the winter months. During the long, cold winters, I look for herbs that are mood-elevating. (I'm in New England, where we have a very, shall

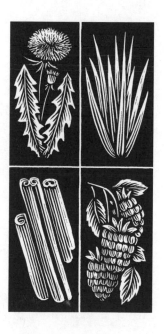

we say, "traditional" weather pattern that inevitably involves multiple yards of snow.)

Whether you grow your own herbs, purchase them at a farmer's market, or buy them in a store or online, be mindful that you store them in darkness and free from air or moisture. I like to buy herbs in small quantities during the growing seasons, as I know they're fresh.

Spring Herbs

Spring is a great time to clean out your house as well as look at your herb cabinet. If you haven't written dates on your jars or bags, consider tossing the lot and starting fresh. At various points, I was enthralled by some herb I hadn't heard of, and after a few experiments, I realized it wasn't going to be in my "hit parade" of herbs. Still, it took several more years to add it to our compost. Even though dried herbs have a long shelf life, you may as well get the best results by having top-quality products. (When you have to buy them, that is—foraging is usually free!)

Dandelions and **ferns** are quick out of the ground once the snow and cold have receded. Try to make sure you are gathering plants far from roadsides (to avoid exhaust fumes, lead in the soil, etc.). Tender dandelion leaves that grow from the center of the plant before it puts its flower forward are lovely when added to a salad or stew. The root can be dug up, dried, and used in teas. Ferns have a long colonial history, and before the Puritans arrived, local tribes boiled the stems and fronds and used the juice to dress their hair. Some people swear by fiddleheads, the fuzzy little spiral that unfurls into a frond, which can be boiled and eaten.

Of course, springtime is also when small, biting insects wake up and say, "Suppertime!" A number of herbs can be helpful for soothing insect bites, including **sweet Melissa**, **jewelweed** (which grows wild in wetlands), and **goldenseal** (which natives in the northeast used). Growing in the western United States, **yarrow** has insect-repelling properties. Encourage its growth, and see if insects diminish in numbers.

For some of us, immune systems may be taxed most during the spring. You may have heard of **tulsi**, or tulasi, tea (also known as holy basil). This herb has been part of Ayurvedic medicine for centuries as an immune system enhancer. The taste is mild, so drinking the recommended dosages (one to four cups a day) is easily done. If you have digestive difficulties that come from stress, tulsi may help, and it can also support your eyesight.

Parsley is another favorite, and it's easily grown inside. Sprinkle chopped leaves on anything from a panini to soup, or just chew the leaves for digestion enhancement. My husband is a master of the "weed salad," which can easily grow in your garden! Essential ingredients include **purslane**, which is rich in magnesium. This attractive little plant has tiny oval leaves and is literally a ground cover—it grows out, not up.

Summer Herbs

For some parents, summer brings stress, as the usual routines with the children have been interrupted. The transition from predictable to free-form days can take a toll, and some folks may want to experiment with calming herbs, plants, and natural remedies. **Kava kava** is a plant from the South Pacific and comes as a tea or a capsule. If you find that other calming substances can't touch your stress level, you may want to sample this remedy. Another stress-relieving herb is **licorice root**. It's grown all over—from Europe, to the Far East, to the Unites States. Licorice tea can help with digestion, and Chinese medicine considers it to have detoxifying effects.

Summer is also when you can get an inadvertent sun burn and find yourself at the end of the day feeling like the back of your neck or your cheeks are on fire. Last year, I brought a snip of our **aloe vera** plant on our beach vacation and every night rubbed it on my children's skin. We had, of course, doused them in sun block, but the aloe juice definitely helped their skin heal; they were ready for more beach fun the next day. (In my youth, the only preventative for too much sun was wrapping yourself in a towel, à la Lawrence of Arabia, which still is a very successful strategy.) Aloe plants are easy to grow and nearly impossible to kill. They enjoy full sun, and you can go weeks between watering them. Snap off a leaf and wrap it in plastic. Snip off an inch at a time and cut open the leaf. The aloe "gel" is quite thick, so you will find that a six-inch spike might last almost a week at the beach.

Summer is also a great time to grow your own herbs, and many farmers' markets will offer a wide array, either as cut plants or potted. I love the all-in-one pots that might have parsley, basil, chervil, dill, and other herbs. For those with limited space, having all your herbs together makes for easy access when cooking or creating remedies.

My favorite easy summer dish is **basil**, **tomato** slices, and sliced mozzarella, drizzled with oil and vinegar. There are so many different heirloom varieties of tomatoes that you can make a glorious platter of tomato salad in just a few minutes by arranging slices, covering with small bits of basil, and then adding mozzarella and dressing. (A family variant is a slice of tomato, plenty of basil, mayo, and mozzarella for a BMT sandwich!) Basil also has numerous health benefits, including supporting the immune system.

Fall Herbs

Now is the time to harvest. **Raspberries**, **blueberries**, and other plants are ready to go to sleep for another year, but before the frost comes in, do visit your berry bushes with a set of shears. Raspberry leaf tea is the easiest concoction for people of all ages, and making your own is easy. We cut back our bushes, so that the strongest branches will flourish next year, and let the leaves dry on the stalk in a bucket under our porch, where it's dark and dry. After several weeks, we take one stalk at a time and crumble the leaves into a large salad bowl. My children enjoy mashing the dried leaves with their hands, and when the leaves are smaller than a dime, it's time to pack them into sealed plastic bags. I make the tea a quart at a time (one handful plus four cups of water), let it steep, and drink it lukewarm or cold.

Some people find spring a more emotionally taxing time, but for those in the northerly latitudes, autumn's abrupt shortening of days (particularly after the clocks "fall back") can bring out emotional lows that make life difficult. **St. John's wort** has antidepressant effects, and for those who have mild depression, this herb may offer some relief. However, St. John's wort can also interact with other pharmacological substances, so consult your physician before adding this herb (which you can usually find in tablet form) to your diet.

Autumn is the time of year when the body craves warming drinks and teas. Fresh green salads may not be as appealing as a stew that includes some of the spectacularly colored vegetables such as squash, sweet potatoes, pumpkins, and carrots. All of those foods are loaded with beta-carotene, and other root veggies such as onions and turnips may help your body adjust to seasonal change. Nuts are also loaded with protein and help warm your insides. You may find you're craving **pepper**, especially the fresh-ground variety, which now can be found in a dizzying array of colors and flavors. Make a cheese log out of cheddar and chives, and then roll it in red peppercorns for a spicy treat.

Winter Herbs

The smells of winter so often include **cinnamon**—one of the most delightful, all-purpose spices. Many folks view cinnamon sticks as purely decorative, but I occasionally find myself chewing on one and enjoying the feeling of spice in my mouth. And if you sprinkle cinnamon on slices of apple, you're enhancing an already healthy snack with a spice that can regulate blood sugar. A pinch of cinnamon in coffee or tea will perk up your taste buds.

Astragalus is a mainstay plant for Traditional Chinese Medicine. It's used as an immune system enhancer and may help fortify your body against illness when used over time. It comes as a tincture, or you can purchase dried slices to add to soup (remove before serving). And if you have caught a dreaded cold, a number of herbs, spices, and plants are just waiting to be incorporated into teas. Pour hot water over a slice of **ginger** and add honey and lemon for a drink to open sinuses. **Sage** tea is also a great gargle if you have a sore throat.

However, winter is when we sometimes need a boost of energy, and how much coffee can you drink without getting jangly nerves? I decaffeinated myself back in 2012, and aside from a morning cup of black tea and perhaps some chocolate later in the day, I look for energy enhancement with **yerba mate** tea (which is a gentle energy boost), and products containing *Rhodiola rosea*. **Maca** (a Peruvian root) is another herb I'm experimenting with. It's known as a good vegetarian source of B12.

Don't underestimate the healing and soothing powers of aromatherapy with your herbs, either. Sleeping with a **lavender** pillow or taking some **valerian** tea as you get ready for bed will be relaxing.

All-Year Herbs

Of course, many herbs, spices, and plants are ones you'd reach for during any time of year: ginger can be added to lemonade (hot and cold), and thyme can be used for steam therapy as well as to make a salad more tasty. Spearmint tea will help you digest your meal, no matter what the season, and cardamom is delicious in iced tea as well as warm chai drinks.

Finally, consider that our knowledge about herb lore is only increasing, and this is primarily due to a centuries-long practice of record keeping across all cultures of people who are interested in herbalogy. You might consider keeping a log of herbal experiments; these need not be longer than a page and taped inside a kitchen cabinet. When you find an herb with multiple purposes, add it to your own herbalogy and enjoy experimenting!

Resources

Griffiths, Kathy. "Purslane." Dr. Christopher's Herbal Legacy. Accessed September 19, 2015.http://www .herballegacy.com/Griffiths_Medicinal.html.

"Herbal Medicine." University of Maryland Medical Center. Accessed September 5, 2015. https://umm.edu/health /medical/altmed/treatment/herbal-medicine.

Nordquist, Joseph. "The Health Benefits of Basil." Medical News Today. Accessed September 5, 2015. http://www .medicalnewstoday.com/articles/266425.php.

"Secret Natural Ingredient: Cinnamon Cures." Health.com. Accessed on September 19, 2015. http://www.health .com/health/gallery/0,,20307383_4,00.html.

Sally Cragin *is the author of* The Astrological Elements *and* Astrology on the Cusp, *which have been translated and sold overseas in a half-dozen countries. She serves on the Fitchburg School Committee (Massachusetts), teaches in the adult education program at Fitchburg State University, and is available to speak about readings, astrological or tarot. Visit "Sally Cragin astrology" on Facebook, or e-mail her at sally@moonsigns.net.*

Naturally Beautiful:
DIY Beauty Products

⪼ by Deborah Castellano ⪻

If you are concerned about not knowing what some of the ingredients are in your beauty products or if you have sensitivities or allergies, making some of your own beauty products can be fun to do with your family and friends! Homemade beauty products also make great gifts and can be less expensive than buying products at retail price. Once you have a little practice with the recipes, you'll be able to adjust them to suit any special needs you may have.

The first thing you need to do is find resources for containers, labels, and supplies for your beauty products. Some of my recipes can be made with items you can simply buy locally, but some things you may want to buy online. For example, if you don't want to use a little jar for your lip balm and would prefer a tube, you will need to buy lip balm tubes. I can personally recommend Specialty Bottle (www.specialtybottle.com), SKS Bottle & Packaging, Inc. (www.sks-bottle.com), the Lye Guy (www.thelyeguy.com), Nature's Garden Candles (www.naturesgardencandles.com), and Elements Bath and Body (elementsbathandbody.com). Make sure to cover your workspace with towels that can get dirty, and be sure to supervise all child helpers.

Exfoliating Lip Scrub

1 tablespoon honey, warmed

1 teaspoon sugar

Toothbrush

Small jar

Mix the honey and the sugar together; pour in small jar. Use the toothbrush over your lips with the honey and sugar mixture. Rinse from lips and from toothbrush.

Facial Toner for Sensitive Skin

¼ cup witch hazel

2 tablespoons rose water

6 drops rose essential oil

Small spritz bottle

Mix ingredients together in spritz bottle. Screw on cap and shake. Use after washing your face but before moisturizing.

Rejuvenating Body Scrub

½ cup coarse sea salt

¼ cup olive oil

4 drops orange essential oil

4 drops sage essential oil

Small jar

Mix ingredients together in the jar; seal tightly when not in use.

Fizzy Beauty Bath Tea

1 teaspoon quick oats

1 teaspoon dried milk

1 teaspoon dried rose petals

1 teaspoon powered honey

1 teaspoon flax seeds

4 tablespoons epsom salt

4 tablespoons baking soda

2 tablespoons citric acid

Small mason jar

Small muslin bags

Mix ingredients together in the jar and let sit out uncovered overnight. Mix again and then cover. To use, spoon into a muslin bag for a (mess-free!) bath.

Stress-Reducing Bath Oil

1 cup grapeseed oil

8 drops lavender essential oil

6 drops chamomile essential oil

4 drops sandalwood essential oil

Small mason jar

Mix ingredients together in the jar; seal tightly when not in use.

Fall Spice Solid Lotion Bars

4 ounces shea butter

4 ounces beeswax

¾ tablespoon vitamin E oil

4 drops clove essential oil

4 drops cinnamon essential oil

4 drops ginger essential oil

Silicone molds or ice trays

Small jars in which to keep the bars

Mix ingredients together over a double boiler on medium heat until smooth. Shut off heat and let the mixture cool for ten minutes. Pour into molds. Let the molds set overnight and then pop the bars out of the molds and into the mason jars.

Aloe Vera Shaving Gel

¼ cup aloe vera gel

2 tablespoons olive oil

1 teaspoon vitamin E oil

6 drops lavender essential oil

Small mason jar

Mix ingredients together in the jar; seal tightly when not in use.

Moisturizing Beard Oil

1 tablespoon jojoba oil

1 tablespoon coconut oil

1 tablespoon argan oil

1 tablespoon sweet almond oil

Brightening Strawberry Face Mask

    10 fresh strawberries

    ¼ cup bee pollen

    3 tablespoons honey

    1 tablespoon coconut oil

    5 drops rose essential oil

Mix ingredients in a blender until smooth. Apply to your face and leave on for 15 minutes. Rinse it off with warm water.

Shine-Boosting Shampoo

    ½ cup liquid castile soap

    ¼ cup coconut milk

    ¼ cup honey

    2 tablespoons coconut oil

    1 tablespoon vitamin E oil

    10 drops tea tree oil

    10 drops clary sage essential oil

    10 drops peppermint essential oil

    10 drops rosemary essential oil

    Bottle with pump

Mix all of the ingredients together in a mixing bowl until well blended and pour into the bottle.

Strengthening Conditioner

    1 cup coconut oil

    1 teaspoon vitamin E oil

    1 teaspoon almond oil

5 drops sandalwood essential oil

Bottle with pump

Mix ingredients together in a mixing bowl until well blended. Use a funnel to pour the mixture into the bottle.

Basic Four-Oil Cold Process Soap Recipe

My friend Bridgette Taylor, soap maker of the online store Essentiae (www.etsy.com/shop/essentiae), worked with me to create this recipe.

Ingredients:

14.4 ounces olive oil (any grade except pomace)

8 ounces coconut oil

6.4 ounces palm oil

3.2 ounces castor oil

12.16 ounces distilled water

4.36 ounces pure lye (sodium hydroxide) without additives

Tools:

Digital scale (measures pounds and ounces)

Large mixing bowl (for the oils)

Small mixing bowl (for the lye)

Small pouring pitcher (for the water)

2 stirring spoons

Spatula

Immersion hand blender

Mold(s) large enough to hold 48 ounces of soap total

Digital thermometer

Cooking spray

Plastic wrap

White vinegar, on hand in case of emergency

Well-fitting disposable gloves

Safety goggles

pH testing strips (or pH testing drops)

Butcher paper/parchment paper

Weigh your water and lye in separate containers. Add the lye to the water slowly, never the other way around. Stir well until the lye completely dissolves; it will become very hot. (Try not to directly breathe in the fumes.) Let the mixture cool to around 90°F. Melt the oils in the microwave until all the solid butters are liquefied. Let the oil mixture cool to a temperature under 100°F.

Prepare the molds. Spray the inside with cooking spray.

Add the lye water to your oils, stirring slowly. Use the hand blender to fully integrate the batter. After about 5 minutes (when the mixture starts to thicken), pour it into your molds. Use a spatula to get all the soap out.

Cover the molds with a layer of plastic wrap, and let your soap cure at room temperature for 24 hours. If your house tends to be cold and drafty, lay a thin towel over the molds to insulate them. After 24 hours, carefully remove the soap from the molds. Let the soap air dry for at least half a day so it's hard enough to be cut into sections.

Lay your soap out on butcher paper, and give it at least a month to harden and cure properly. The longer you let it cure, the harder and longer-lasting your soap will be. Turn the soap over at least once while it's curing.

Important Notes on Soap Making

- Never use aluminum or mixed metals with lye. Use stainless steel or plastic only.

- Use the pH strips to test the cured soap. Wet the soap a bit and rub a strip directly onto the soap. The pH should not be higher than 10. If it is, you've used too much lye.

- Make sure the room you make soap in has decent ventilation. Use a small fan to direct the fumes away from you.

- If you accidentally spill lye or soap batter on yourself, pour white vinegar on the skin then use water. The vinegar will neutralize the lye; water may spread the lye and cause more injury.

- You cannot substitute oil types or amounts without recalculating the correct amount of lye to use. To change ingredients, use a soap calculator such as www. soapcalc .net/calc/SoapCalcWP.asp.

Deborah Castellano *writes for many of Llewellyn's annuals and writes a blog with PaganSquare about unsolicited opinions on glamour, the Muse, and the occult. Her shop, The Mermaid and The Crow, specializes in handmade goods. She resides in New Jersey with her husband, Jow, and two cats. She has a terrible reality television habit she can't shake and likes St. Germain liqueur, record players, and typewriters. Visit her at www.deborahmcastellano.com.*

Heart of Gold: Turmeric, Saffron, the Capsicums, and Others

❧ by Susan Pesznecker ❧

There's a simple axiom in botany that says that in most cases the more brilliant a plant's colors, the richer it is in antioxidants. Antioxidants are substances that block chemical deterioration, which is associated with cellular damage, aging, and illness. Eating antioxidant-rich foods is believed to promote good health and possibly even a longer life.

The same rule applies to herbs: those with a deep gold, orange-gold, or red-gold color tend to be rich in antioxidants and in other constituents as well. A chemical constituent is a substance that creates a certain reaction. These are a few constituents commonly found in herbs:

Bitters: These have a bitter taste. The bitterness stimulates salivation and improves both appetite and digestion.

Carotenoids: These compounds create the yellow, orange, and red colors typical of many plants. They are moderate antioxidants and protect from photodamage.

Coumarins: These compounds help thin the blood and prevent clotting.

Curcumin: This brilliant yellow substance is responsible for turmeric's golden color. It may have an effect on digestive disorders, digestive cancers, and some psychiatric conditions.

Flavonoids: These act as pigments, imparting deep color. They are strong antioxidants and potent anti-inflammatory agents. They tend to protect the liver and strengthen circulation.

Mucilage: This gluey, sticky substance can coat intestinal surfaces, preventing irritation and thus relieving digestive disturbances and related diarrhea.

Proanthocyanidins: These impart red, blue, and purple colors to plants. Among the most powerful of antioxidants, they also support circulation and may protect the eyes.

Resins: These viscous substances are secreted by some trees and plants. They have a protective antibacterial nature.

Saponins: These compounds lather when rubbed with water, and they are among the most primitive of "soaps." Steroidal saponins may perform estrogen-like actions.

Steroids: These play an important role in cell building and are involved in building and maintaining hormone actions in the body.

Tannins: These are astringent in nature and thus are useful in staunching blood flow, drying up secretions, and checking infection. They may also be used to treat diarrhea.

Volatile oils: These are extracted from plants and used to make essential oils. Most are antiseptic and anti-inflammatory.

Adding these gold and red beauties to your herbal armamentarium will expand your herbal workings with wonderful results. As you read, please note that none of the information that follows is intended to serve as medical diagnosis or treatment; you should always check with your health care provider before using herbs medicinally. The kitchen suggestions, on the other hand, can be followed with confidence: I'm a darn good cook!

Calendula (*Calendula officinalis,* also known as pot marigold)
Calendula's bright gold-orange petals are collected in early to midsummer and sometimes again in early fall. A water-based infusion is useful for treating menstrual pain and upset stomach. The infused oil is a deep gold to orange color and can be used to make creams and balms that are both antiseptic and moisturizing. The plain essential (volatile) oil is used in vaginal suppositories to treat yeast infections.

Calendula's active constituents include bitters, flavonoids, mucilage, steroidal compounds (sterols), and volatile oils.

Cayenne (*Capsicum annuum*)
The dark red powder that we use in our kitchens comes from the cayenne plant. It creates a sensation of heat when taken internally and is regarded in Chinese medicine as having a "very hot" nature. Cayenne is a potent stimulant, acting as a general tonic to the entire body, stimulating blood flow and raising energy.

To use, dry the entire pepper and then chop coarsely or grind to a powder. A simple, hot, water-based infusion is excellent for treating colds, the flu, and respiratory conditions, as it stimulates cough and mucus flow; the same infusion can be gargled to relieve sore throats. Cayenne also excites and stimulates digestive functions. The infused oil, interestingly, does not burn or irritate the skin; it may be used as a massage rub for muscle aches, arthritis, and rheumatism. Cayenne's active constituents include capsaicin, carotenoids, flavonoids, volatile oils, saponins, and steroids.

In the kitchen, a pinch of cayenne powder can be added to anything from scrambled eggs to soup, stews, or chili to give them a little kick. I like to add a bit to mulled ciders and wine for extra warmth. Adding a pinch to hot chocolate creates a fiery mixture akin to drinking cacao of the ancient Maya.

Cinnamon (*Cinnamomum* spp.)

Cinnamon is another herb that is considered to be both warming and stimulating. The inner bark from the cinnamon tree is gathered in rolls, forming what we know as cinnamon sticks. These are typically used whole when herbcrafting and may be used whole or powdered in the kitchen. Cinnamon decoctions and tinctures stimulate digestion and kidney function, and they may also assist with menstrual difficulties. When used as a compress, a cinnamon infusion eases joint and muscle pain. The infused oil likewise makes a good massage oil for rheumatic pain, while a few drops of the oil in a steam inhalation are excellent for easing the congestion of colds and flu. Cinnamon's active constituents include volatile oils, tannins, coumarins, and mucilage.

Perfume your home by simmering hot water, cinnamon sticks, whole cloves, and orange peel on the stove. Not only will your home smell wonderful, but this infusion inspires the senses and is said to create a feeling of warmth and relaxation. Research suggests that pumpkin pie spice—the main ingredient of which is cinnamon—is said to awaken lust.

Mix three teaspoons powdered cinnamon, two teaspoons ginger, and a pinch of cayenne with enough honey to make a thick paste known as an "electuary" (a medicinal substance mixed with or conveyed in honey). Consume half teaspoons of the paste two or three times daily to ease the congestion associated with colds and the flu and to ease stomach upset. Store in the refrigerator. What your grandmother called a hot toddy is a warming drink that improves circulation and opens the airways. Place a spoonful of honey, a cinnamon stick, and the juice from half a lemon in a warm mug; fill with boiling water and, if you wish, a shot of alcohol—whiskey works well. Breathe the steam and sip the drink while it's as hot as possible. (A safety note: cinnamon is a uterine stimulant and should not be used medicinally by pregnant women or those trying to conceive.)

Paprika (*Capsicum* spp.)

Paprika, also known as Hungarian pepper, is one of the mildest members of the chili pepper family. It is available in many varieties, each with a different flavor profile and color. Paprika is used in the kitchen for its flavors and for the deep orange-red color it imparts to soups and sauces. It is also used as an elegant garnish. Heating the ground spice gently in a carrier oil releases an even deeper, richer flavor.

Besides its uses in cooking, paprika contains many of the medicinal qualities of the other capsaicins, albeit of lesser intensity. It is a moderately strong antioxidant and a warming spice, and it enhances circulation.

Saffron (*Crocus sativus*)

The herb we know as saffron consists of the stigmas—the tiny thread-like structures—found in the center of the saffron crocus. Saffron is one of the world's costliest and most valued spices by volume and weight; a single saffron crocus makes from one to four flowers annually, each bearing a few stigmas. It's a precious crop indeed. Saffron's active constituents include carotenoids, volatile oils, glycosides, and B vitamins.

Saffron threads are dark orange and impart a brilliant gold color when added to liquids or foods. They also have a unique flavor, making them prized in regional dishes such as Spain's *paella*, a mixture of seafood, chicken, rice, and saffron.

Recent studies suggest saffron's use in treating depressive disorders, including premenstrual syndrome and postpartum depression. However, due to saffron's exquisitely high price, it is not often used as a medicinal herb.

St. John's Wort (*Hypericum perforatum*)

St. John's wort is widely known for its psychoactive properties. The aerial parts (stems, leaves, and flowers) are dried and infused to make a tea that lifts the mood and has been found to be useful in treating depression. An alcohol tincture is even more effective for this. The flowering tops on their own create a brilliant red infused oil; this may be used on its own to treat joint and muscle pain and burns (after the skin has closed). The infused oil may also be used to make a cream, useful for treating all sorts of minor scrapes and lacerations. St. John's wort's active constituents include flavonoids and proanthocyanidins.

Turmeric (*Curcuma longa*)

Turmeric is widely used in kitchens for the deep golden color and special flavor it adds to soups, stews, tagines, and curries. It is also one of the most potent of antioxidant herbs, and it's long been used for treating digestive problems, liver disease, clotting disorders, high cholesterol, and inflammatory disorders. When applied to the skin and exposed to sunlight, it has strong anti-bacterial properties and is also used widely to treat psoriasis and other skin disorders. The decoction is used as a foot soak to treat athlete's foot. Turmeric's active constituents include volatile oils, curcumin, resins, and bitters.

My grandmother would pop us into a turmeric and cayenne bath at the first sign of a cold. She'd add two to four tablespoons of powdered turmeric and a teaspoon or so of cayenne to a hot bath; soaking in it induced an all-over warmth and sweat. When the water began to cool, we'd shower off, dress in clean flannel pajamas, and climb straight into a warm bed. It was a comforting process but is best-suited for adults and older children: you must be sure not to splash any of the bathwater into your eyes.

A Glossary of Herbal Preparations

These are approximate recipes; double the quantity of herb if using fresh, and chop first.

Water-based infusion: Add 15 grams of dried herb (small or aerial parts) to 250 milliliters of near-boiling water. Steep for 5 to 10 minutes. Strain and use.

Oil-based infusion (infused oil): In a saucepan, cover chopped fresh herbs with a carrier oil (olive, sunflower, etc.). Use a very low heat setting to warm the oil slightly. Maintain this warmth for several days (be sure to turn the stove off at night!). The goal is to evaporate water from the herbs slowly while infusing the herb's constituents into the oil. Cool, strain, and use. (For dried herbs, proceed the same way, but heating for a few hours to a day is sufficient.

Water-based decoction: Add 20 grams of dried herb to 500 milliliters of near-boiling water. Simmer (do not boil) until reduced to 150 to 200 milliliters. Strain and use.

Alcohol tincture: Use 100 grams of dried herb to 350 milliliters alcohol (vodka or Everclear) and 150 milliliters water. Store in a cool place for two weeks, shaking occasionally. Strain, press, and use.

Cream: Mix a small amount of warm infused oil with enough lanolin or grated beeswax to create the consistency you want. The mixture will thicken as it cools.

Resources

Chevallier, Andrew. *Encyclopedia of Herbal Medicine*. London: Dorling Kindersley, 2000.

Ody, Penelope. *The Complete Medicinal Herbal*. London: Dorling Kindersley, 1993.

Susan Pesznecker *is a writer, college English teacher, nurse, practicing herbalist, and hearth Pagan/Druid living in northwestern Oregon. Sue holds a master's degree in professional writing and loves to read, watch the stars, camp with her wonderpoodle, and work in her own biodynamic garden. She is cofounder of the Druid Grove of Two Coasts and the online Ars Viarum Magicarum, a magical conservatory and community (www.magicalconservatory.com). Sue has authored* Yule, The Magickal Retreat, *and* Crafting Magick with Pen and Ink *(all Llewellyn), and is a regular contributor to the Llewellyn annuals. Visit her at www.susanpesznecker.com and www.facebook.com/SusanMoonwriterPesznecker..*

Plant Therapy

❦ by Lupa ❦

It's the seven o'clock hour on a morning in July. The sun has just cleared the trees to the east, and the soft rays burn off the last of the dawn chill. My hands and knees are rooted in the soil of my plot at the local community garden, where I grow produce for my partner and me. Today is a day for weeding, and as I yank up popweed and thistles, I imagine that I'm methodically removing stressful thoughts from my mind as well. The physical activity gets my blood flowing and clears out the anxieties that plagued me the previous night, and the rising sun boosts my mood.

In midwinter I'm carefully watering my houseplants: swiss cheese vine, spider plants, a variety of rescued succulents left on the side of the road months ago. This is the hardest time of year for me—endless weeks of rain and cold and never feeling quite comfortable. But there's my little corner by the window where my indoor garden thrives. In absence of outdoor growth, tending to this tiny oasis has become one of the things that will help me get through to spring's longer days.

May gives its warmth and light to tulips and daffodils, early petunias, and the first roses of the year. I am fortunate enough to be invited to a tour of the therapeutic gardens at a local hospital. The garden director leads us through brick-lined pathways and broad-branched trees. At each stop we get a bit of history on how these gardens were planned and developed and learn of the research that supports their efficacy in helping patients recover more quickly. These cultivated places provide solace for the bereaved, physical therapy opportunities for the injured, and a moment of joy and gentle play for children fighting an array of illnesses. They are a much-needed change from closed-in hallways, beeping machinery, and the ever-constant pain of IV ports and blood draws.

Humans and Nature

It may seem odd to those of us who work with plants that the medical community—and science at large—is just now quantifying the benefits of gardening, hiking, and other exposure to the plant kingdom. Most of you reading this have had experiences similar to the ones I've described above. We know how relaxing it is to spend time with our hands in soil, coaxing little sprouts to grow. And we know this relaxation isn't just in our heads, either; we can bring others to our special green places to feel the same sense of safety and comfort.

So it is that when we engage in gardening and similar activities, we're being good to ourselves. We need exposure to nature, plants and otherwise, in order to be healthy. As a species, we evolved in wide, grassy savannahs and then later adapted to survive in almost every climate and habitat in the world. Until very recently, within the past several centuries or so, most humans lived in close relationship with the earth; even those who did not farm still hunted, visited the country-side, or traveled over land and water. It is ingrained into our very brains and bones, this connection to the world around us, and our delusion that we can somehow separate ourselves from nature is harming us as individuals and as a species.

Horticultural therapy is the deliberate application of this concept by trained professionals. These therapists help incorporate plants into their patients' lives, whether through gardening or other activities. Some therapists work with patients with physical ailments or those facing neurological issues that may affect their everyday functioning. Others focus primarily on the psychological benefits of plants on patients' mental health. Some may even delve into social work, teaching clients to garden both for food for themselves and their families and as a form of income.

But even the most specialized practitioners still take advantage of the effects that plants have on the whole person; a physical therapist knows that gardening is more mentally stimulating and fun than repetitive exercises in a gym, and a mental health counselor counts on the psychological boost that physical exercise offers. The time of seeing a human being as a collection of distinct parts is quickly giving way to a more systems-based view, in which one part is intricately connected to the rest and cannot be easily separated out. And when you improve one part of your health, every other part responds as well.

You don't need to be a trained horticultural therapist to understand and make use of this knowledge, of course. Let's look at some options for improving your life and health with the plants already in your life.

Through the Window, Out the Door

Let's start simple: take a look out the nearest window in your home or workplace. What do you see? If you're fortunate, your window looks out over trees or grass, maybe even a patch of woods or a park. I'm in a pretty urban part of Portland, but I can still see a big maple from my kitchen window and a pair of cherry trees from my tiny apartment porch. And I've worked in offices where the closest thing I had to a natural view consisted of a few tiny trees struggling in the dividers of the parking lot. But sometimes you just work with what you've got.

If it's possible, head outside and spend some time with the plants you see. Be aware of any restrictions on the land itself; your own yard (if you have one) is a pretty safe bet, but be mindful of the area and any limitations. If your window looks out on someone else's property you'll need permission before you go stomping all over their lawn to examine their rose bushes.

Make it a point to look out on this scene every day, paying special attention to whatever plants are present. Take note of any changes—are the leaves starting to grow back? Are there flowers? Are the leaves changing color as the weeks progress? Are there animals living in the plants? Does a particular plant look less healthy and thriving than it did a month ago? You might consider keeping a daily journal to note these changes and review them every so often. Over time you'll notice that the plants have a rhythm throughout the year, and with enough practice you can begin to anticipate the changes they're about to go through, even down to the week.

Finally, if you're feeling stressed, take a moment to watch the plants. Consider that no matter what the weather is like or what's going on around them, they still remain in place, breathing and photosynthesizing, putting forth seeds and pollen in the warm weather and conserving resources when it's cold. Focus on this constancy, and remember that your stress is temporary; the cycles of nature will go on, and so will you. If you can go outside, spend some time sharing breath with the plants, inhaling the oxygen they produce and giving them the carbon dioxide they need to live. There's so much more to life than whatever's making you stressed! Hold on to that thought, and then go back to what you were doing, relaxed and renewed and better able to focus.

Gardening (Indoor and Out)

If you have more time and resources to work with, gardening can be a great way to be more interactive with plants and their many benefits. By "gardening" I don't just mean having a large plot of land you tend to. A single house plant will suffice as well, if that's all you can manage; just make sure it gets the right amount of sunlight and other basic care. If you're new to gardening, plant nurseries, gardening books, and the Internet are all great resources for researching the needs of a particular species of plant.

In fact, the very act of caring for another living being can be really good for you! The physical activity involved in setting up your garden and caring for it daily helps keep you in good condition; just be realistic about your limitations if you're recovering from an illness or injury or are otherwise not in the best health. (You can always expand your efforts later as you get better, too.) The daily routine of watering and fertilizing the plants as needed, checking for parasites and diseases and treating as needed, and even harvesting produce can be meditative for some people. It's a chance to set aside the worries of everyday life and focus on the rewards (and challenges!) of a garden. And you have something lovely to look at, too, when the day is done, whether it be a potted plant on your windowsill or a garden that takes up most of your yard.

The stress-reducing exercise in the last section also works well with your garden. Additionally, daydreaming about future plans for your garden can help shake you out of a mental rut. If you've been feeling down, depressed, or like your life isn't going anywhere, take a look at where your garden is now, and then think about what you'd like it to look like three, six, or even twelve months from now. Let your imagination run with this—if you could grow any kind of plant in the space you have, what would you try? How might you arrange your garden if you started all over again? It's a good idea not to plant the same types of annuals in the same spot two years in a row, so how can you have your favorite plants while rotating the crops? For an indoor garden, which plants need to be repotted in larger containers, and what do you want to repot them in? Could you take a trip to a thrift store to see what sort of oddball household items might make fun and original planters? If you live in a small space, how could you make use of what room you have (including vertical space, like walls) to help your plants thrive? Use this planning period to break out of mental stagnation and give yourself something to look forward to, too!

Hiking and Other Outdoor Activities

We grew up in wilderness. Cultivated gardens and fields are fine in their own way, but nothing compares to wild places not dominated by humanity. If you're in a rural area, access to wilderness may be relatively easy for you; those of us in urban areas often have to do a bit more traveling. Depending on your physical health and ability, you may not be able to traverse the back country, but even being able to sit at a picnic table at a campsite or to drive or ride through a wilderness area can be beneficial.

When we are exposed to wild nature, it has an almost immediate effect on us. Our blood pressure drops, as do other stress responses in our bodies and brains. We stop having our attention violently pulled to and fro by the loud, demanding stimuli of advertisements and cars honking and people rushing by. Instead, we settle into what environmental psychologists Rachel and Stephen Kaplan term "soft fascination." Our attention is allowed to drift organically, wandering more gently, and only coming to hard focus in times of need (such as navigating a particularly challenging section of trail). It's not just that the wilderness is quieter; it's that its components knit together more harmoniously. It's what we evolved with and what we are still hardwired to thrive in.

Plants are an enormous part of the wilderness experience. We often think of them as a backdrop for more seemingly active parts of nature, like animals, or rarer ones, like hidden waterfalls. But plants are one of the crucial backbones of a wilderness place, and they have busy lives even if they are rooted in one place. You may not know many of the plants in the wild place you're visiting, but see how many individual species you can identify, even without their names. You'd be amazed at the diversity!

And wild plants still have the same effects as their more cultivated counterparts, too. Just spending time in the wilderness can be enough, whether you're sitting quietly or going for a fifteen-mile hike. But you can take the extra step to immerse yourself in the experience. Stop wherever you are in this wild place, and clear your mind. Let your thoughts drift away like clouds, and focus on what you notice with your senses. Then look at each of the plants around you, perhaps even touching the ones you know are safe. Recognize each one as an individual living being, every bit as wondrous as the wildlife you see, and know that you are surrounded by an amazing diversity of life that far outweighs the worries and problems you face. Be immersed in this wider world for a while and relax.

Lupa *is an author, artist, nature nerd, and wannabe polymath living in Portland, Oregon. She is the author of several books on totemism and nature spirituality, including* Nature Spirituality From the Ground Up: Connect With Totems in Your Ecosystem *(Llewellyn, 2016), and is the creator of the Tarot of Bones. Her primary website is http://www.thegreenwolf.com, and she can be contacted with questions or commentary at lupa.greenwolf@gmail .com.*

Rhodiola and the Adaptogens: Your Stress Relief

➤ by Diana Rajchel ➤

Medical professionals constantly ask, "Do you have any stress in your life?" For the average adult, this is enough to prompt hysterical laughter. Everyone has stress, and while a few lucky souls have managed to reduce their stress levels, the majority of us have been unable to reach that Zen state.

Stress isn't just in your head, nor is it a product of assuming the wrong attitude toward your environment. Just as you can strain your liver with excess alcohol and processed food, you can strain your brain and heart with excess adrenaline. Though we no longer have to outrun physical predators, we are still prey to deadlines, ego-driven coworkers, and psychological pressure from work, family, and the community. Our society gives us, at best, limited room to let our bodies process those adrenaline bursts.

We used to work off adrenaline by outrunning its trigger. Now you can't drop and do twenty push-ups while your boss yells at you unless you're in the military. Constant bursts of adrenaline without release impact the neurological system, inhibiting learning and memory access and the cardiovascular system and increasing the likelihood of heart disease and high cholesterol. They can mess up metabolism, prompting the body to store energy instead of burning it because emotional stress fools our bodies into a famine state. They also strain the immune system, making the body more vulnerable to infections.

Most people in the Western world have a lifestyle and life phases in which stress and consequent cortisol (the hormone released by the adrenal and pituitary glands) elevation is nearly constant. Making efforts to mitigate stress reduces the risk of some common diseases and disorders, especially heart attack and stroke. Exercise is the best solution, but injuries and other health conditions may make it difficult to get enough exercise to counteract the effects of stress. After exercise, we can reach for the next best thing: herbs. While no herbal formula can induce a complete lifestyle change, certain herbs may help by giving your adaptive system, the system that helps you deal with stress, a little extra support. These herbs are labeled adaptogens, based on the theory (not yet substantiated with empirical data) that they strengthen your cells against all forms of stress, and this reduces cortisol levels and counteracts tension.

As in the case of all substances, different bodies react differently to any chemical. It is always important to check a solid reference for possible undesired interactions between medications (prescription and over the counter) and herbs you may consume. The following herbs are among the best-known adaptogens. All have a relaxing effect upon consumption.

Adaptogenic Herbs

Ashwagandha (*Withania somnifera*)
An Ayurvedic herb, ashwagandha goes straight to the stress. Best known for its ability to reduce anxiety even when combined with alcohol, this root lowers cortisol levels significantly enough to help those suffering from insomnia. It also has a demonstrated ability to lower both blood sugar and cholesterol. The herb also has a high iron content, making it helpful to those suffering from anemia.

Astragalus (*Astragalus membranaceus*)
Astragalus is, above all, a potent anti-inflammatory. Elevated cortisol levels and high stress create constant inflammation. This herb not only counters that but also protects cardiac health and reduces the physical effects of aging. Practitioners of Traditional Chinese Medicine (TCM) use it to treat arthritis, lower blood pressure, relieve asthma symptoms, and reduce blood sugar.

Chrysanthemum (*Chrysanthemum morifolium*)
The yellow flower most associated with November birthdays actually has a proud medicinal history. Along with its use in reducing blood sugar, blood pressure, and cortisol, it actually makes a pleasant-tasting and soothing tea. Although

often used to increase alertness, its effect on cortisol levels makes it helpful to those trying to regulate sleep. While not as common in the continental United States, East Asian grocery stores here usually have some of this tea available.

Eleuthero (*Eleutherococcus senticosus*)

Best known as Siberian ginseng, the best data collected about eleuthero root was lost with the collapse of the Soviet Union. It is well recognized as an adaptogen, and while hailed as a resolution to the common cold (especially when taken with echinacea), there is still very little current data on this herb. Those who use the herb have reported that they often feel a boost of energy without the jitters or edginess that comes from caffeine.

Giant Angelica (*Angelica gigas*)

While all parts of this plant have use in herbal medicine, the root itself has a potent balancing effect on hormonal systems. It also gives a small boost to the immune system. However, only use giant angelica in a small dose, a maximum of around two tablespoons to one cup of water per day. It can cause high blood pressure when overused, reversing its cortisol-lowering effects.

Holy Basil (*Ocimum tenuiflorum*)

Also called *tulsi* in Hindi, this herb has a flavor similar to the culinary basil. Popular in Ayurvedic medicine for treating common colds and similar ailments, it improves blood circulation and settles stomach discomfort. It can also reduce blood sugar—a common problem for the chronically stressed-out—and is anecdotally reported as helpful to transgender people in need of balance when going off hormones for any reason. For those attempting to conceive, however, holy basil can interfere with fertility, so stop use if attempting to get pregnant.

Maca Root (*Lepidium meyenii*)

Maca draws attention from those seeking aphrodisiacs for women with reduced sexual desire. This tuber, a staple in the Peruvian diet, also treats general fatigue. It seems to regulate all hormonal systems, making it especially useful for women experiencing reproductive ailments. It's not good for those with thyroid conditions, but it makes a tasty tea for those seeking a small energy or libido boost. More interestingly, this leveled-out energy boost assists those with trouble sleeping as well.

Rhodiola (*Rhodiola rosea*)

Rhodiola is hailed by marketers as the greatest herb you've never heard of, and you may not hear of it much outside of here or GNC. Common names for the root include arctic root, king's crown, or rose root. Users believe it increases the body's ability to resist environmental stress and that it improves the benefits of exercise for the nonathletic. Drinking a tea made from rhodiola has a calming and centering effect.

Rosemary (*Rosemarinus officinalis*)

Rosemary is safest ingested in small doses, so it is popular as a meat rub seasoning. This antioxidant herb also can increase circulation and improve alertness, and in small doses it lowers cortisol levels in the blood stream, alleviating stress and helping clear out a noisy head. This is best used in a very small amount (perhaps a quarter teaspoon) with another herb. Overuse can lead to nausea and intestinal discomfort.

Schizandra Berry (*Schisandra chinesis*)
Called *wu wei zi* in TCM, this tart berry reduces cortisol levels, and, along with them, reduces anxiety. It was originally prescribed as a means of improving vitality. Unfortunately, very little data exists for its effect on pregnancy, so pregnant women should skip this one until more is known. These berries are not for snacking—regular users report that its nickname "five flavor plant" is literal and not all the flavors are good.

Shatavari (*Asparagus racemosus*)
Do not confuse this asparagus with the garden vegetable. This Ayurvedic remedy translates to "woman with 1,000 husbands" for addressing cortisol and fertility hormone imbalances in women, and it helps a great deal with gastric discomfort and ulcers. Though effective, it is now considered an endangered plant. Make use of maca, an already cultivated and managed plant, or ensure your shatavari is obtained from a sustainable source.

Not every herb works for every person: it may take trial and error to find what your body needs to sleep better, to feel more alert, and to think better. Yet when we find the herb that helps—by keeping us calm, by preventing that cold, or by giving us that little bit of extra strength—it's invaluable.

Selected Resources

"Angelica Gigas." Examine.com. Accessed November 2, 2015. http://examine.com/supplements/angelica-gigas/.

"Ashwagandha." Examine.com. Accessed November 2, 2015. http://examine.com/supplements/ashwagandha/.

"Asparagus racemosus." Examine.com. November 2, 2015. http://examine.com/supplements/asparagus-racemosus/.

"Eleutherococcus senticosus." Examine.com. Accessed November 2, 2015. http://examine.com/supplements/eleutherococcus-senticosus/.

"Holy Basil." WebMD. Accessed 11/2/2015. http://www.webmd.com/vitamins-and-supplements/holy-basiil-uses-and-risks.

"Maca." Examine.com. Accessed November 2, 2015. http://examine.com/supplements/maca/.

"Rhodiola Rosea." Examine.com. Accessed November 2, 2015, 2015. http://examine.com/supplements/rhodiola-rosea/.

"Rosemary." Medical Reference Guide. University of Maryland Medical Center. Accessed November 2, 2015. http://umm.edu/health/medical/altmed/herb/rosemary.

"Schisandra: Ultimate Super Berry." Medicine Hunter. Accessed November 2, 2015. http://www.medicinehunter.com/schisandra.

Weil, Andrew. "Astralagus." DrWeil.com. Accessed November 2, 2015. http://www.drweil.com/drw/u/REM00002/Astragalus-Dr-Weils-Herbal-Remedies.html.

Weil, Andrew. "Rhodiola Rosea." DrWeil.com Accessed November 2, 2015. http://www.drweil.com/drw/u/REM00033/Rhodiola-Dr-Weils-Herbal-Remedies.html.

Diana Rajchel *is a writer, tarot reader, creative coach, and community builder in San Francisco, California. Her book* Divorcing a Real Witch *is a Diagram Prize runner-up, and she is the author of* Mabon *and* Samhain *in the Llewellyn's Sabbat Essentials series.*

Herb Crafts

Herbs in Art

≫ by Suzanne Ress ≪

Since prehistory, human development has unfolded alongside and in symbiosis with plant development. Because plants and trees are immobile, we have never considered them to be threats, but, instead, we have embraced them with friendly curiosity.

Plants found to have beneficial properties (curative or aesthetic) and plants found to be essential for maintaining life (nutritional or useful in toolmaking and shelter building) have always been held in the highest regard. Many plants were considered so valuable by early humans that they were deemed sacred. Others became associated with particular gods or goddesses or with human qualities

or attributes, according to the plant's properties. These plants were often celebrated through artistic portrayal, in wall paintings, carvings, sculptures, and architectural motifs.

The Tree of Life

Of all plants, the Tree of Life was, across many if not all cultures, the most sacred and most represented in early artworks.

The idea of the Tree of Life is thought to have originated in ancient Chaldea (currently Iraq), nearly three thousand years ago. As it was depicted in ancient wall carvings, it was an invented tree species, sometimes resembling the lotus or pine. The image of the Tree of Life represented human life, death, and the afterlife, and it spread or was independently generated in cultures all over the world.

For northern Europeans, the Tree of Life was depicted as an oak or an ash tree. Ancient Middle Eastern cultures portrayed it as a date palm or cedar tree. Egyptians revered the sycamore, and Far Eastern cultures adopted the cassia and bo as their sacred trees. Aztecs and other ancient American cultures depicted wholly invented trees as their Tree of Life.

Perhaps using a tree to symbolize humanity was a way for our distant ancestors to pay homage to the life-sustaining plant world that surrounded them. Without plants, humans and other animate creatures cannot survive, so in a way the vegetative life all around us is our gift from the gods "personified."

Popular Plants in Art

For thousands of years, the following five plants have been used with great frequency in artwork of all kinds from a wide variety of cultures. All of these five plants can also be classified as herbal plants, for their healing and culinary properties.

The Lotus

The lotus has been considered sacred for over five thousand years in Far Eastern cultures. The lotus flower represents Buddha's birth, and for Hindus the lotus flower is Brahma's symbol of immortality. In Chinese and Japanese cultures the eight-petalled lotus plant symbolizes past, present, and future, because it sports bud, blossom, and seed head all at the same time. In artworks from these cultures, both ancient and modern, the lotus flower is a common subject for both its symbolism and its beauty.

The lotus plant also appears frequently in ancient Greek, Persian, Egyptian, and Maya artworks, where it was used as a decorative form in architecture, murals, engraving, sculpture, painting, and more.

As an herb, the lotus plant's seeds are used to soothe an upset stomach, its root aids digestion, and its leaves help regulate the menstrual cycle. Lotus stems can be eaten and are high in vitamin C and potassium.

The Lily

In Western art, the lily makes frequent appearances. In the Middle Ages and Renaissance the white lily symbolized purity and the virgin. It appears in paintings of the Immaculate Conception as a symbol of that act. Because of its long, flowing, graceful lines, the lily was a favorite motif in stained glass, ironwork, fabric design, and carved wood furniture of the art nouveau movement in Europe.

The lily is native to the Middle East and was revered as an emblem of motherhood in ancient Sumerian, Babylonian, Egyptian, Semitic, and Assyrian mythologies. The image of the lily appeared in ancient Greek art as the flower of Hera, goddess of the moon, birth, and woman.

The lily plant's root is used in China as an herbal remedy for coughs and sore throats. It is also calming and promotes sleep.

The Pomegranate

The pomegranate fruit, with its tough, leathery skin holding so many juicy, bright red seeds tightly inside it, has inspired artists from all over the world and was used in antique paintings to represent fertility and immortality. In Christian art the pomegranate came to symbolize the church, with all its members unified inside, or, alternatively, Christ's death and resurrection. This symbolic meaning is borrowed directly from earlier Roman mythology, where the pomegranate was the fruit ruling Proserpina's confinement in and return from the underworld in the spring.

In recent years it has been discovered that pomegranate juice is a powerful antioxidant, especially useful for athletes or other people under constant physical stress. The juice can also lower blood pressure. The fruit's juicy seeds are a curative for diarrhea, and the oil from its seeds promotes healthy, blemish-free skin.

The Rose

In every culture it has touched, the rose has represented beauty, youth, and love. The rose plant was first cultivated over five thousand years ago in gardens of western Asia and northeastern Africa. Roses have always been a favored subject of artists and poets, with the white rose representing innocence and charm and the red rose passion and desire.

For the Romans, the rose was the flower of Venus, goddess of love, and in artwork could also symbolize victory, pride, and triumph. In paintings from the European Renaissance period, a garland of roses represents the rosary of the Virgin Mary, and wreaths of roses worn by saints or angels mean they are experiencing heavenly joy.

Roses are a common flower in medieval heraldry, where a single small rose was the mark of the seventh son. The ten-petalled rose of the House of Tudor became the floral emblem of England after the War of the Roses in the fifteenth century (fought between the House of Lancaster and the House of York, both of which used a rose in their heraldic emblems).

The rose's petals, fruit, and leaves can all be employed as herbal cures. A rose tea, tonic, or infusion is soothing to the stomach and throat, can alleviate headache, and helps induce sleep. Rose hips are high in vitamin C, and are often eaten to prevent the common cold, flu, and mouth sores.

Other Common Herbs in Art

These are some of the herbal plants used most frequently in art the world over and throughout millennia, but if you take a good look at any art history book it is amazing how many different herbal plants are portrayed.

Bay Laurel (*Laurus nobilis*)
Since Roman antiquity, this popular kitchen herb has represented triumph, victory, eternity, nobility, and honor.

Bramble (*Rubus fruticosus*)
In medieval European art, these useful herbal plants represent error, sin, and the fall of mankind because of their thorny, fast-growing vines.

Daisy (*Bellis perennis*)
By the end of the 1400s, artists started using the daisy in paintings and on prayer book borders as a symbol of innocence. It is still thought of as representing innocence, freshness, and youth.

Hyssop (*Hyssopus officinalis*)
This herb portrayed penitence and humility because it has the reputation of growing in solitary, rocky places. It was also frequently used to mean baptism, as in the Psalm 51:7 of the Bible: "Purge me with hyssop, and I shall be clean."

Milk Thistle (*Silybum marianum*)
Because of its thorniness and a negative reference to it in the Old Testament, it came to symbolize earthly sorrow and sin. It was adopted by the Scots as their national flower emblem because it is said their English enemies were waylaid from the attack by having to cross fields of thorny thistles.

Poppy (*Papaver somniferum*)
It has long had a bad symbolic reputation in art, notwithstanding the beauty of its delicately distinctive flowers. It signifies extravagance, ignorance, indifference, sleep, and death!

Wild Clover (*Trifolium pratense*)
Also called shamrock, it figures especially, but not exclusively, in Irish art and originally represented the Trinity of Father, Son, and Holy Ghost. It is now meant to portray perpetuity.

History of Illustration

All of those plants, and many more besides, were often added to medieval and Renaissance European oil paintings for their symbolic meanings. They were hand painted on illuminated borders around religious scenes in books of hours and portrayed on carved and painted furniture, wall decorations, architectural fixtures, jewelry, metalwork, and heraldry.

Botanical illustration put the central focus of the artwork on the herbal plants themselves. Botanical illustration is believed to have had its start in the sixth century with the Codex Dioscorides, also known as the Codex Vindobonensis. This codex was a handmade copy of Greek artist Crateuas's illustrations, made by an unknown Byzantine artist in about 100 BCE, with text copied from what is believed to be the first herbal, *De Materia Medica*, which was written by Dioscorides in about 80 CE. Although the original *De Materia Medica* seems not to have survived, we know from the codex and later copies that it contained descriptions of six hundred plants useful as herbs and told when and where they could be found.

One of the most influential of the late medieval herbals was the *Pseudo-Apuleius Herbarius*, which linked antique and medieval botanical medicine. The author is unknown, but it was made in Greece around 300 CE. For many generations this was the base from which all other herbal illustrations were copied.

Medieval herbals were all painstakingly hand copied, usually by monks closed into their dimly lit monasteries. The illustrations made by these monks were not copied from life, but from the copy of the herbal they had on hand, which was itself a copy of a copy of a copy of a botanical illustration that was not very realistic to begin with. Thus, the illustrations in these medieval herbals, meant to aid in identifying plants for medical use, were often quite fanciful and bore no resemblance to the actual plant!

By the Renaissance period in Europe, accurate botanical illustration from life became an art form. Leonardo da Vinci and Albrecht Durer were just two of the artists of the time who drew and painted realistic renditions of herbs and flowers from nature.

With the widespread use of the printing press in the 1500s drawings and descriptions of herbal plants for home medical use could be circulated and seen by a great number of people, which increased general knowledge and interest in the subject. The early 1600s saw an explosion of popular illustrated herbals.

During the first half of the 1700s, Swedish naturalist Carl Linnaeus, in collaboration with artist Georg Ehret, published his illustrated system of botanical classification. This work became a basic of scientific study and had a great influence on popular culture.

During the 1700s and 1800s illustrated books about botany and horticulture were very popular. Many of the (often anonymous) illustrators of these books were women who, due to sudden unexpected changes in their economic status, found a way to earn a living through their artistic talent.

Art nouveau, with its elements of stylized plants and flowers, flourished in Europe from about 1885 until 1908, touching all aspects of art and design, including print making, painting, jewelry, ironwork, furniture, architecture, mosaic, and stained glass work. This style is characterized by graceful vine-like lines, inspired by plants to suggest growth and sinuousness. Favorite herbal plants depicted were honesty (*Lunaria annua*), lily, iris, geranium, horse chestnut, cattail, pomegranate, lady's mantle, grape and grape leaves, ivy, and magnolia.

Modern botanical illustration often takes its lead from botanical illustration styles of the past to create gorgeous, full-color, and extremely accurate works of art, usually in watercolor or colored pencil. Some of the works of modern botanical illustrators are breathtaking; it is as if you are seeing the actual plant in just the right light at a perfect moment.

It is worthwhile to take some time to observe herbal plants in art, for the artist's depiction of the plant elevates it to an immortal state, like that of a god, and reveals something about ourselves as well.

Suzanne Ress *earned an MA from Johns Hopkins University and has been writing for many years. Her first novel,* The Trial of Goody Gilbert, *was published in 2012, and she has since completed two more, as yet unpublished, novels, and begun work on a fourth. She is an organic farmer and beekeeper and lives in the foothills of the Italian Alps with her husband and many domestic and wild animals.*

Japanese Paper Streamers: The Mythical Origins of the Sakaki and Tamagushi

꜠ by Linda Raedisch ꜠

A host of lively spirits gathers around an uprooted evergreen tree to hang ribbons and what appear to be huge, curved icicles from the boughs. It could almost be Christmas, but instead of blown glass balls, a metal mirror winks among the leaves, and the tree in question is not a spruce or a fir but a *sakaki*, a glossy-leaved evergreen of the tea family.

No, I was not present to witness the above scene, which is part of an episode from the *Kōjiki*, a chronicle of ancient Japanese myth; the story was old already when it was written down in 712 CE. In the chapter titled, "The Door of the Heavenly Rock Dwelling," the purpose of decorating the sakaki (*Cleyera japonica*) is to lure the sun goddess out of the dark cave in which she has sealed herself. The episode, like our own Yule with its solar imagery and evergreen boughs, might be an echo of a prehistoric winter solstice rite.

The *Kōjiki* does not make for smooth reading. It is written in the language of myth: the "five hundred branches" of the sakaki are hung with "five hundred" jewels, each one eight ancient Japanese "feet" in length, and there's plenty of "heavenly" this and "heavenly" that. The trimmed-down version goes like this: the sun goddess, the radiantly beautiful Amaterasu, has had it up to here with her brother Susanō's crude antics. When Susanō tosses a flayed pony in through the roof of her weaving hall, this is the last straw. Amaterasu retreats inside a cave, thereby casting the world into darkness.

The sulking Amaterasu won't come out for anything until another goddess, Uzume, creates a ruckus outside. The Rubenesque Uzume (who, if you ask me, is the real heroine of the story) has taken matters in hand by dancing on top of a bucket just outside the cave. When Uzume swivels her hips and flashes her bottom, the other gods respond with uproarious laughter.

Amaterasu comes out of her sulk just long enough to wonder what is going on. She peeks outside the cave, and when she does so, the light of her own radiant person strikes the mirror which the assembled gods have placed in the sakaki tree. The sun goddess steps all the way out of her cave to see who this "other" dazzling deity might be. Of course, she soon realizes the ruse but too late to return to her hiding place, for the gods have strung a *shimenawa*, a fat rope of rice straw, across the entrance. I imagine Amaterasu must have had a good laugh herself in the end.

The detailed description that the *Kōjiki* gives of the dressed-up sakaki tree supports the idea that the "Door" incident is a reflection of an early solstice ritual. The tree itself was uprooted from the slopes of Heavenly Mount Kagu, and the five hundred "curved jewels" would have been oversized versions of the jade comma-shaped jewels still familiar to archaeologists who have unearthed them from ancient graves in Korea, where princes and princesses used to wear them suspended from their tall gold openwork crowns. In Asia as elsewhere, the winking of jewels and other glittering objects was supposed to invite the interest of kindly spirits while keeping the troublesome ones at bay.

In addition to the mirror and the jewels, the tree was hung with "pacificatory offerings"—that is, strips of cloth in white and blue. The white cloth would have been made from the inner bark of the *kozo* (a kind of mulberry), or perhaps of undyed, sun-bleached hemp, while the blue offerings would have been hemp cloth dyed with indigo, all highly revered materials which would later be used in the making of paper. The goddess Uzume's performance might have been an ingenious piece of improv, but the presentation of the tree with its carefully selected objects and ornaments created from sacred plants suggests a carefully prescribed ceremony to cajole the sun back to her proper place in the sky.

Compared to other sacred texts, the *Kōjiki* sometimes reads like an herbal. For instance, we are told that Uzume's dance costume included a club moss sash, that she wore a crown fashioned from a spindle tree, and that she carried a bouquet of bamboo-like *sasa* leaves. All this herbiness is not surprising considering the abundance of plants, trees, shrubs and flowers in Japan. It was this profusion of greenery which, over the millennia, made the islands so appealing to successive waves of migration.

There is actually not a lot said about the creamy-blossomed sakaki in the *Kōjiki* and other chronicles. In fact, the tree is mentioned in such a way that implies the reader should already be familiar with it. Why was the sakaki chosen for adornment rather than the cedar or the pine, which still graces the doorways of Japanese homes at the Lunar New Year? Perhaps because, unlike the needles of cedar and pine, the broader leaves of sakaki reflect the light of the sun, rather like our own glossy hollies.

Shinto

"The Door of the Heavenly Rock Dwelling" and the other tales in the *Kōjiki* were collected during Japan's Heian period. I won't bore you with dates; the Heian is easily distinguished from later eras by the striking appearance of its court ladies, who wore their hair loose and long—so long that it trailed over the floor. They padded their torsos with excessive layers of silk under which they wore red trousers so voluminous it must have made walking difficult. They also stained their teeth black, shaved off their eyebrows and painted them on again higher up the forehead. This was a period of high fashion, a headlong rush in pursuit of the latest thing, and the latest thing almost always came from China or Korea: silk, paper, incense, printed characters, and religion in the form of Buddhism.

It was also at this time that the native Japanese religion of Shinto became crystallized. In response to all the new ideas flowing into the islands, there was also a reaching back for that which was "purely Japanese." Before about 700 BCE, Shinto had not had a name, nor had it been considered a proper religion. It was simply a way of living that acknowledged the influence of one's ancestors as well as the spirits which everyone knew to dwell in each tree, flower, rock, river, and mountain. Shinto means, roughly, "way of the gods," as opposed to the imported "way of the Buddha."

The gods, deities, or spirits in question are known in Japanese as *kami*: the sun goddess' full name is Amaterasu-no-mi-kami. How many kami are there? Well, the official Shinto count is "eight-hundred ten-thousand many," which basically means "a lot." The ancient Japanese liked to play fast and loose with their numbers. By telling us that the sakaki from Heavenly Mount Kagu had five hundred branches, the author of the *Kōjiki* simply wants us to know that it was a healthy specimen. If said author could visit one of our Christmas tree lots, he would not ask for a full, well-rounded tree; he would say, "Show me something with five hundred branches."

The *Kōjiki* is now an accepted part of the Shinto canon. Pure white paper, which also came into its own during the Heian period, is now an integral part of Shinto ritual, replacing the earlier cloth offerings. Those flowing red trousers? They're still worn by *miko*, Shinto shrine maidens, while on duty within the shrine precincts. And what of sakaki? *Cleyera japonica* is also native to southern China, Taiwan, and the Buddha's own Nepal, but it is only within the context of Shinto that it is considered sacred. The sakaki probably acquired its status in Japan long before Heian days, and it too has long outlived them.

The presence of at least a slender branch of sakaki is a must wherever weddings, ground-breakings, roof-raisings, and a host of other important rites are performed. It often appears in the form of a *tamagushi*, a snippet of sakaki to which a *shide* has been attached. What is a shide? English language authors sometimes refer to them casually as "paper streamers," but the word refers to a very specific, though variable, form. Shide are those zigzag, lightning bolt–shaped strips of white paper that you can also see dangling from the rice straw shimenawa to mark off a sacred site or tied to a branch of pine as a New Year's decoration.

Below, you'll find instructions on how to fold a shide and attach it to your sakaki branch to make a tamagushi.[1] Is there more than one way to fold a shide? Yes. Is there a proper way to fold a shide? Yes. Is this it? No; the "proper" way requires pure white Japanese *washi* paper to be either torn or cut with a knife reserved for that purpose alone and is probably best done by a Shinto priest. I know what you're thinking: if this is not going to be a proper tamagushi, then why bother? For one, by folding your own shide, you'll never again take for granted those ubiquitous "paper streamers." If you've already done some origami, you've probably heard that it owes its existence to the Buddhist monk who carried the first sheets of paper into Japan. The truth is that *origami*, "folded paper," along with its sister art, *kirigami*, "cut paper," evolved from the sacred forms of Shinto. (Origamists are fond of pointing out the similarity between the words *gami*, "paper," and

---

1. Unless you happen to live in a region to which *Cleyera japonica* is native, you will probably be unable to get your hands on a sakaki branch. Even in Japan, oak, box, and cedar are sometimes used. You might also consider another member of the tea family such as camellia or stewartia, an evergreen such as one of the smoother-leaved hollies, or even—why not?—a snippet of your Christmas tree.

kami.) But perhaps the best reason for creating a tamagushi is the fact that it is an exceedingly pretty ritual object, whether or not you intend to offer it to the gods.

Tamagushi

To make a tamagushi, you will need a 5 × 8-inch piece of white paper, scissors, a ruler, a pencil, string, and a sakaki branch.

Fold your piece of paper in half like a book. Using a pencil, lightly mark 4 vertical lines, separating the paper into 5 strips that are 1 inch wide. Alternate sides and cut 3 inches of each line, keeping the strips connected.

Hold the paper in your hand as shown in the first figure of the diagram. Starting on the left, fold the first strip toward you and upward so that the crease is at the end of the cut. Fold the second strip away from you and downward, creasing at the end of the cut, so that your paper looks like the second

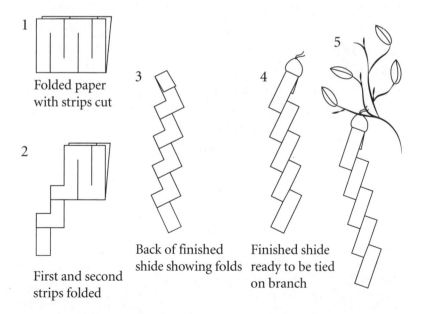

1

Folded paper
with strips cut

2

First and second
strips folded

3

Back of finished
shide showing folds

4

Finished shide
ready to be tied
on branch

5

figure. Fold the third strip toward you and upward, and the fourth strip away from you and downward. Fold the very top of the last strip toward you to make a hook, and your paper should now look like the third figure of the diagram, the back of the shide. Erase all pencil marks, and slip a loop of string under the hook. Tie the finished shide near the top of your sakaki branch.

Resources

Ashkenazi, Michael. *Handbook of Japanese Mythology.* New York: Oxford University Press, 2003.

Ekiguchi, Kunio and Ruth S. McCreery. *Japanese Crafts and Customs: A Seasonal Approach.* New York: Kodansha International, 1987.

Hughes, Sukey. *Washi: The World of Japanese Paper.* New York: Kodansha International, 1978.

The Kōjiki. Translated by Basil Hall Chamberlain. Accessed September 8, 2015. http://sacredtexts.com/shi/kj/kj023.htm.

Nobutaka, Inoue. "Sakaki." June 2, 2005. Encyclopedia of Shinto. Accessed August 30, 2015. http://eos.kokugakuin.ac.jp/modules/xwords/entry.php?entryID=312.

Linda Raedisch is *a reader, papercrafter, tea drinker, house-cleaner, and intercontinental traveler as well as the author of* The Old Magic of Christmas: Yuletide Traditions for the Darkest Days of the Year *(Llewellyn, 2013). She is most often found at the crossroads of the magical and the mundane.*

Raffia Projects

❧ by Autumn Damiana ❧

If you like crafting, you have probably come across a popular product called raffia. It is a natural, eco-friendly, fibrous, stringy, grasslike material that is typically used to tie bows or gift tags around packages, candles, canned goods, soap, wine, and just about anything else that you want to give a homespun, shabby chic, or vintage appeal. Raffia is also commonly used to make Hawaiian grass skirts, to tie plants to stakes, or as a filler material in packaging. More classic, historical uses for raffia show just how much further this medium can be taken. Hats, baskets, wreaths, mats, purses, and many other, more complex designs have been made from raffia.

These traditional crafts are as beautiful as they are functional but unfortunately require great skill to create. And yet, raffia shouldn't be dismissed as a simple ornament that is added to other knickknacks as an afterthought, either! The craft projects in this article will hopefully get you excited about raffia as more than just string for tying bows.

So what is raffia? Surprisingly, it's not a type of grass at all. Raffia is a dried fiber that comes from a genus of palm trees (*Raphia*) that includes about twenty different species. The long, ribbon-like strands that are sold commercially are stripped from the fronds of the *Raphia farinifera* or *Raphia vinifera*, which are native to Madagascar and parts of Africa. Raffia palms have the longest fronds of any palm tree, which is why raffia can be comprised of strands measuring sixty feet or more. While these palms are now grown in tropical areas all over the world, the largest raffia plantations are still located in Madagascar and its surrounding islands in the Indian Ocean.

Raffia also plays an important role in the economies of Central and West Africa and the Philippines. People in the Democratic Republic of the Congo use raffia fronds to make a type of cloth out of them the same way villagers in the area have been doing for centuries. By stripping the palm frond into sections still attached to the stem, a loom is created onto which other raffia strands are woven. The resulting raffia cloth is then dyed, decorated, and sold or traded, often to make ceremonial costumes. In Nigeria and Cameroon, raffia is a valuable resource used to make everyday necessities, like mats, hammocks, rope, and fishing nets; bags, hats, shoes, and other accessories are also crafted for export. Families in Tanzania have recently become involved in sustainable raffia production, where raffia palms are now being cultivated on homesteads rather than being over-harvested from surrounding forests. And in the Philippines, where basket-making is a major enterprise, raffia fibers are prized as a cheap, durable, and easily dyed material used for weaving.

Here are a few tips on what to look for when purchasing raffia. For one, the raffia that is found in craft stores is typically sold in a bundle by weight. This is the most inexpensive raffia available, as the bundle will have strands of varying lengths and thicknesses, but all of the following craft projects can be made with this grade of raffia. Also, a bundle of raffia can be separated into more manageable "hanks," and individual pieces of raffia can be sorted based on length, thickness, or uniformity. Long strands of higher-grade raffia in more even thicknesses are available (usually online), although they are more expensive. In addition, buyers should beware, because most of the "raffia" that is sold in spools is not raffia at all but is either paper or a shinier synthetic material made to look like raffia. Natural raffia is light beige, and dyed raffia always has a matte appearance. Try these three fun projects that you can make using raffia.

Raffia Cinnamon Broom

A small, hand-held broom makes a perfect Halloween decoration, especially when made with black or orange raffia. Be careful, though, because the dye on natural raffia will come off when wet! A broom also makes an excellent good-luck gift for a new marriage and is said to ward off evil and misfortune when hung in the home.

Materials:

14–20 (or more) pieces of raffia

Hot glue and glue gun or double-sided tape

One long cinnamon stick, at least 5 or 6 inches (These are typically sold around the holidays, sometimes with scent added.)

Scissors

Ribbon, embroidery floss, jewelry charms, sequins, feathers, dried flowers or herbs, etc. (optional)

Select a strong, thin piece of raffia to be your anchoring strand—one that won't come apart or shred easily.

Attach the other pieces of raffia to this strand using lark's head knots, making the ends hang down more or less even with each other. Pull the knots snug, but not too tight, and don't worry about placing them too close together. For now, just attach as many as you want along the anchoring strand facing the same direction. I recommend 12 at the very least. They can be of different widths or lengths, as long as the shortest strands after being knotted are at least 3 or 4 inches long—you can trim them to be even later. These will be the broom "straws" on your cinnamon stick handle.

When you are done adding the knotted pieces, slide them along the anchoring strand until they are grouped closely next to each other, and then pull each knot tight.

Next, attach the straws on the strand to the end of the cinnamon stick using hot glue or double-sided tape. If you are using tape or have a lot of straws knotted along a lengthy anchoring strand, I suggest spiraling the anchoring strand up the cinnamon stick. When these have been secured, you can either trim the ends of the anchoring strand if they are fastened in place or tie the two ends together.

With a thick piece of raffia or a ribbon, tie a band around the outside of all the straws and the stick. This finishing touch keeps all the straws from sticking out sideways and helps hold them in place. I like to use embroidery floss, winding it around and around the broom and then threading on a jewelry charm where I tie it off.

Now, if you like, you can use the scissors to trim the bottom of the broom so that all the raffia straws are even. Decorate the broom with ribbon or embroidery floss, glue on sequins or feathers, add dried flowers or herbs, etc.

Miniature Raffia Herb Wreath

These make wonderful herbal napkin rings, fragrant window or kitchen decorations, or Christmas tree ornaments when a ribbon or a hook is added. If the knotted ends of the raffia strand are long enough, you can always hang your wreath from those as well.

Materials:

A lengthy, sturdy, preferably unsplit piece of raffia 2 feet or longer

Large crochet hook

Sprig of herb with a woody stem, such as rosemary

Piece of ribbon and/or ornament hook (optional)

First, take the long piece of raffia and using the crochet hook, make a single chain stitch with large loops. The loops should be big enough to stick your pinky finger through. This may take some practice, even if you are adept at crochet, because raffia is stiff and does not behave like yarn. The raffia chain should be 1 or 2 inches longer than your herb sprig.

When you are satisfied with the chain, tighten each end so that it will not come undone. Next, using the stem end like a needle, weave your herb sprig through the raffia chain, passing it over and under the loops. The leaves of the herb sprig will pull off if your chain is too tight or you try to drag the herb through the loops, so go slowly and have patience with this step.

When you have woven the sprig all the way through, carefully bend the chain into a circle and tie the raffia ends together. This will create a small herb wreath that has a raffia crisscross pattern around it. The advantage of the raffia chain outer layer is that it will help hold the herb spring and its leaves together even when the herb dries out; plus, it just looks nice!

Seasonal Raffia Dolly

Corn husk dolls have roots in many different cultural traditions, and these raffia dollies are a simple twist on that old favorite. Unlike corn husks, which have to soak in water to become pliable and can be difficult to shape, raffia is a flexible, ready-made resource that lends itself well to this craft and is in season any time of year. If you've ever made a corn husk doll, you can apply your experience to these directions, and if you haven't, I suggest that you research it online because the basic construction is the same.

Materials:

Large bundle of raffia

String, yarn, twine, etc. (optional)

Hot glue and glue gun (optional)

Grab a 1-inch-thick hank of raffia that has strands of roughly equal length (thickness of the strands does not matter). Fold the hank in half. Grasp the hank about 1 to 2 inches below the folded end. Tie a piece of raffia or string, yarn, or twine around the hank where you are holding it. This will make the doll head.

Grab another slightly smaller hank of raffia. Holding this hank horizontally, place it inside the folded vertical hank, resting just under the head. The two hanks should be perpendicular to each other, so they look like a cross.

Now, if you tie off the vertical hank just below the horizontal hank that you just placed, this will make the waistline of the doll. The cross hank of raffia that is sandwiched in place will become the doll's arms.

That's it for the basic construction! From here you can do a number of things to your doll, like tie the ends of the arms at the wrists and trim the ends. You can leave the raffia strands loose below the waistline to look like a skirt, or you can separate the skirt into two hanks, tying them off at the ankles to make pants. There is also the option to braid the raffia arms or legs of the doll to make more substantial limbs.

Lastly, add decorations. The size of the raffia hanks that you use to construct your doll will determine the overall size of your finished project. A small doll may use an acorn cap as a hat. A larger doll can have moss or yarn glued to the head as hair. Bay leaves or dried rose petals strung on thread make wonderful aprons or overskirts. And of course you can make fabric clothes with buttons or other embellishments. The best thing about this project is that there are so many ways to customize the doll using colors, flowers, herbs, and other seasonal accents, like a sprig of holly for winter or a flower for spring.

More Ideas

- With a tapestry needle, sew raffia into embroidery patterns on cloth for texture.
- Wrap and glue raffia around bowls, jars, bottles, or candle holders to give visual appeal. You can also glue on herbs, flowers, pinecones, berries, spices, etc.
- Using a flower loom (such as the ones offered by Boye or Provo Craft), make decorative raffia flowers (see tutorials online).
- Tie pieces of raffia together to make a long strand and use it to weave a God's eye on crossed sticks glued together.
- Braid, weave, or knot raffia into friendship bracelets, adding beads if you like.

The beauty of this resource is that not only is it sustainable, biodegradable, and eco-friendly, but it is also inexpensive—you are free to experiment with it to your heart's desire. Raffia is a remarkable resource that lends itself well to a variety of craft projects, and it can be used for so much more that most people give it credit for!

Autumn Damiana *is an author, artist, crafter, and amateur photographer. She is a Solitary Eclectic Cottage Witch who has been following her Pagan path for almost two decades and is a regular contributor to Llewellyn's annuals. Along with writing and making art, Autumn is currently finishing up her degree in early childhood education. She lives with her husband and doggy familiar in the beautiful San Francisco Bay Area. Visit her online at autumndamiana.com.*

Pomanders:
Scents and Sensibility

≫ by Natalie Zaman ≪

To every season, there is a scent: those first earthy traces, long trapped under the frost, that hang in the air of spring mornings; the heady perfume of flowers made more potent by the heat of the summer sun; the smoky bite of bonfires stoked with dry leaves and seasoned wood that drift on autumnal breezes.

And winter? December sparkles with the fragrance of pine and balsam, but there are warm scents that tell winter tales too: the spicy tang of citrus and clove, the seasonal incense that's neatly packaged in a pomander.

"Pomander" can refer to both a scent and the container that holds it. The word itself is derived from

pomme d'ambre—apple of amber—and like most ancient monikers, it's a name that's layered with meaning. *Ambre* can refer to ambergris, often the base used to create pomander perfumes. It can also be a nod to the color of amber: gold. *Pomme* is French for "apple," its Latin root *pomum*, revealing a connection to the Roman goddess of the orchards, Pomona. In her School of the Seasons, Waverly Fitzgerald offers further connections: Pomanders were a representation of the "golden ball of dominion," the pommel of a sword used for swearing oaths, while three golden balls were St. Nicholas's symbol—pomanders are linked to Christmas and New Year celebrations.

There are also mythological connections. In his race against Atalanta, Melanion used golden apples to distract the goddess to win the race—and her. The golden apples in the garden of Hesperides granted immortal life; one of Heracles's labors was to procure one of these precious jewels. And when Paris awarded the golden apple meant "for the fairest," to Aphrodite, he unwittingly started the Trojan War.

In the Middle Ages and Renaissance when classical themes and folklore were woven into courtly society, pomanders were fashionable pieces of jewelry a wearer could touch to his or her nose when confronted with bad odors (a regular occurrence when folks bathed but once a month at best). It was also believed that the perfume in pomanders prevented infection. These apple- or ball-shaped pendants were fashioned from precious metals, ivory, and even wood, intricately carved and jeweled with perforations incorporated into their designs, the better to disperse the scent within. Elaborate specimens were hinged and sectioned so that one bauble could house several scents at once.

Elizabeth I owned several pomanders and wore them dangling from a belt around her waist, but not everyone could afford this luxury. Less expensive to acquire and so more widely accessible were pomanders made from actual fruit and spices. Now more ornament than personal, portable aromatherapy, pomanders are easy to make with ingredients and materials you may already have in your kitchen, pantry, and craft stash.

Nostradamus's Pomander Perfume

On her blog, *The Anne Boleyn Files*, Claire Ridgway shares Nostradamus's own recipe for pomander balls, which included "labdanum gum as obtained from goats beards and sheeps bellies in the fortunate lands of Arabia." The recipe also called for storax and benzoin, but you can create similar pomander balls with a less exotic base: beeswax holds scented herbs and oils and maintains shape while glitter and fabric trims hint at the jewels of centuries past.

1 dozen dried rose buds

1 tablespoon of powdered orris root

Gold glitter

Rose oil

Musk oil

Amber oil

4 × 4-inch sheet of red or pink beeswax

Straight pin

Gold beads that can be threaded onto the straight pin

Gold fabric trims

Wire cutting tool

Tapestry needle

Stretchy gold cord

Grind the rose buds and orris root with a mortar and pestle. Transfer them to a bowl, add the glitter and a few drops of each oil, then stir the mixture until all the ingredients are thoroughly combined.

Cut beeswax sheet into dime-sized squares, tear them into small pieces, and add them to the mixture. Stir the ingredients so that the wax is evenly distributed with the flower mixture.

Knead and squeeze the ingredients together to form a solid mass. The heat from your hands should be sufficient to soften the beeswax. If not, you can set the bowl in a sunny spot or in a pan of hot water to soften the wax. (Never put beeswax in a microwave—it is highly flammable, and your mixture may heat unevenly and cause burns.)

Keep turning and kneading the flowers, glitter, and beeswax until all is distributed as evenly as possible, then roll it in your hands until it forms a sphere a little larger than a golf ball. Add more of any of the materials if necessary. You can adjust the scent by adding more or less of any of the oils.

Slide a few beads onto the straight pin and set it aside; this will be used to finish the pomander. To form the "container," wrap the sphere with the metallic trim 3 or 4 times—don't cover it; patches of the glitter and flowers should peak through. Hold the threads in place by pressing the straight pin into the end of the trim when you're done wrapping; try to begin and end in the same place. Use a wire cutter to shorten the pin if necessary. Cut a length of gold cord, thread it underneath the fabric trim, and tie a loop for hanging. The beaded straight pin should be on the bottom of the pomander.

Alternatively, you can form smaller versions of the pomander balls. Instead of wrapping them with fabric trim, use a tapestry needle to thread them on gold stretchy cord like beads to fashion aromatic bracelets.

The Cardinal's Faire Orange

Most folks who lived during the Middle Ages and Renaissance didn't have the funds to buy jeweled pomanders, but one man certainly did. Henry VIII's ill-fated advisor Cardinal Thomas Wolsey was known for his extravagance—at one point his enemies estimated that he was richer than the king—but when it came to pomanders, simplicity was more efficacious. In the city registers, George Cavendish, one of the cardinal's servants wrote, "Cardinal Wolsey's pomander was an orange, with the substance taken out and filled up with sponge and aromatic vinegar." Wolsey is often credited with inventing the "poor man's pomander," although that's not completely certain. But the "Cardinal's faire orange" is the predecessor of the pomander most folks know today. They are simple to make, smell sweet and spicy, and, thanks to the cloves, have the added benefit of keeping moths at bay.

1 orange with a medium-weight skin

Permanent marker

Straight pin

1 1.25-ounce jar (or more) of whole cloves

Ground cinnamon

Tapestry needle

A length of ribbon 24–36 inches long

Using the permanent marker, draw dots on the orange's skin;

each dot marks where you will place a clove. Make patterns: vertical or horizontal rows, lattices, a swirling spiral from the top or bottom of the fruit, or a central image. Drive the straight pin into each dot before pushing the cloves into the orange according to your pattern. This will make it easier to insert the cloves (though some of us still end up with sore fingers).

Alternatively, you can cover the entire orange—just be sure to keep a small area at the top and bottom clear so you can insert the ribbon, which will serve as a hanger. When all the cloves are in, place your orange in the bowl of cinnamon and roll it around. This will soak up and dry any juice and help preserve the fruit. Tap off the excess powder.

Thread the ribbon through the tapestry needle, then carefully pass it through the orange, in through the bottom and out through the top. Pull the ribbon through so you have some length, then pass the needle back through the top and out at the bottom so that you have a loop at the top of the fruit and two loose ribbon ends at the bottom.

Slide off the tapestry needle, then pull the loop so that the ribbons on the bottom are even. Knot off the loop (make sure it's large enough for hanging), then slide the orange up the ribbons so that it lies tight against the knot. Secure the pomander on the ribbon by tying a tightly knotted bow at the bottom.

Cloven Apples

Oranges aren't the only fruit that can be used to make a pomander. Apples—from which the pomander gets its name—are also sweet-smelling gifts with a New Year's tradition. In Scotland, "Hogmanay" refers to New Year's celebrations as well as apples preserved with cloves and rosemary that are given as gifts at this time of year. In 1932, Laura Ingalls Wilder wrote about a similar apple that her mother received at Christmas in *Little House in the Big Woods*: "Aunt Eliza had brought Ma a large red apple stuck full of cloves. How good it smelled! And it would not spoil, for so many cloves would keep it sound and sweet." Create a version of this New Year's gift with four simple ingredients:

1 apple

1 1.25-ounce jar (or more) of whole cloves

Twine

Several sprigs of rosemary

Screwdriver or awl

Cover the entire apple in cloves, keeping a small area at the top and bottom clear. Cut two lengths of twine and braid it, using the sprigs of rosemary as the third strand. Pierce the apple with the awl or screwdriver and thread the rosemary-twine braid through it. Tie the ends so that the apple hangs on it like a pendent. Keep the apple in your kitchen or give it as a gift with wishes for warm winter blessings.

The Calennig

This Welsh pomander and talisman for a plentiful harvest can look like one of Delia Deetz's sculptures from *Beetlejuice*. The literal translation of *calennig* is "New Year's Gift," but more specifically it's an apple propped up on a tripod of twigs with a fourth inserted into the side for a handle. The apple is studded with cloves and "planted" with evergreens (usually boxwood and holly) which may in turn be adorned with raisins and hazelnuts—all symbolic of wealth and plenty. Essentially, it is a fruitful year symbolically created in a single piece of fruit.

Like the word pomander, "calennig" has two meanings: the object and the celebration, which may come from Ka-lends, a Roman new year festival. At Calennig (which used to last through Twelfth Night in some parts of Wales), children would carry the calennig from door to door in the early hours of New Year's day singing songs for coins (usually given to silence the singers). A calennig will make a unique center-piece for your holiday revels—and is easy to craft from items you can harvest wild and buy at the supermarket.[1]

1 apple

4 sturdy twigs cut to the same length, about 6–9 inches long

Whole cloves

3 holly sprigs or boxwood sprigs

Gold glitter (optional)

Insert 3 of the twigs into the fruit so that it can stand on them like legs. Insert the last twig into the side of the fruit. Your apple should not rest on this last twig; it will serve as the calennig's handle.

Insert the evergreens and then the cloves into the fruit. There is no specific pattern for placing greens or cloves, but you can incorporate patterns or symbolism into your calennig. For example, place the evergreens so that they look like they are growing out of the fruit. Form symbols or initials with the cloves. If you wish, sprinkle your calennig with gold glitter

---

1. See a calennig being made in this video: https://www.youtube.com /watch?v=qyPu6Wx3IOw. But be warned—the presentation is done com-pletely in Welsh!

to make it more festive—for your table or to enhance your performance if you will be singing door to door.

Blwyddwyn Newydd Dda!

Happy New Year!

Resources

Fitzgerald, Waverly. "Celebrating Midwinter." The School of the Seasons. Last modified 2003. http://www.school oftheseasons.com/pdfdocs/midwtrcrafts.pdf.

Hessayon, Dr. D.G. *The Bedside Book of the Garden: A Garden Miscellany*. New York: Expert Books, 2008.

Mair, Fiona. "Make a Tudor pomander." Time Traveller Kids. Last modified September 15, 2013. http://time travellerkids.co.uk/news/make-a-tudor-pomander/.

"New Year's Gift." National Museum Wales. http://www .museumwales.ac.uk/faq/calennig/.

Ridgway, Claire. "Pomanders." The Anne Boleyn Files. http://www.theanneboleynfiles.com/resources/tudor -life/pomanders/.

Weston, John. "Old Welsh Christmas customs." Data Wales. Last modified 1995. http://www.data-wales.co.uk/xmas .htm.

Wilder, Laura Ingalls. *Little House in the Big Woods*. New York: Harper Collins, 1981.

Willis, Gwenllian. "Sut i wneud calennig." YouTube video, 3:02. December 17, 2012. https://www.youtube.com /watch?v=qyPu6Wx3IOw.

"Wills and inventories from the registers of the Commissary of Bury St. Edmonds and the archdeacon of Sudbury." *Works of the Camden Society*, no. 49 (1850): 259.

Natalie Zaman *is a regular contributor to various Llewellyn annual publications. She is the coauthor of the Graven Images Oracle deck (Galde Press) and writes the recurring feature* Wandering Witch *for* Witches & Pagans Magazine. *Her work has also appeared in* FATE, Sage Woman, *and* newWitch *magazines. When she's not on the road, she's chasing free-range hens in her self-sufficient and Pagan-friendly back garden. Find Natalie online at www.nataliezaman.blogspot.com or at www.broomstix.blogspot .com, a collection of crafts, stories, ritual and art she curates for Pagan families.*

A Garden to Dye For

⤜ by Monica Crosson ⤚

When I turned forty, a friend of mine introduced me to the art of spinning natural fiber. It was from her that I purchased my first spinning wheel, a small Ashford Traveller. It's an inconspicuous model that stores easily in a corner of my craft room until the first bite of winter takes hold and it is brought downstairs to its place of honor next to the woodstove. There, I spend the dark, chilly evenings rhythmically pressing the foot pedal and working the roving to spin it into yarn that can be transformed into the only items I can crochet—hats and scarves.

It was later, after joining a local spinning and knitting group, that I learned about dyeing roving to create an endless palette of colors. I started by using acid dyes that, with a little vinegar and a pot of hot water, turned my plain yarn into one-of-a-kind works of art. "This year, kids," I would tease as I crocheted. "You're going to have the coolest hats and scarves in town."

This was always followed by sarcastic comments like, "Yay! We can't wait to look like the Weasleys!"

It was on a particularly dreary March afternoon, when spring still felt like a dream, that I gathered with my spinning and knitting group tightly around a small woodstove at a member's tiny home. The musky scent of lanolin filled the small room, which was made alive by the striking golden hue of the yarn one of our more avid craftswomen was working with.

"I love that color," I remarked.

"Oh," she said. "That's from black-eyed Susan."

"Really?" I was intrigued. I didn't know we had people in our group who worked with natural dyes.

"You should visit my garden this summer." She smiled. "That is, if you're interested in a dye garden."

"I look forward to it!" I don't think she knew it at the time, but she had created a monster.

I wasn't very patient as the browns and ocher of winter's decay bursted into the riotous shades of green and dappled yellows of spring. When I wasn't reminding her of my upcoming garden tour at our monthly spinning and knitting gathering, I was e-mailing her so she wouldn't forget. As the greens deepened and the richer jeweled flowers of summer began to blossom, I started calling. "Are you ready for me, yet?" I would ask.

"Let's wait another week," she would say. "I want you to really be able to appreciate the garden."

Finally, one honey-colored afternoon in July, I was able to see a real dyer's garden.

To be honest, I had built up the place so highly in my imagination that I remember being slightly disappointed when the small home and garden I came upon wasn't the thatched fairy-tale dwelling surrounded by the quintessential English cottage garden complete with gnomes. It was a plain, ordinary, ranch-style home, and the gardens . . . Well, they were lovely but maybe a little weedier than I expected.

But after a few minutes of hands-on education on dye plants, I was completely hooked. I found that I already had a lot of the plants she used. Others I didn't need to grow: the dye material could be harvested soundly from wild plants growing in nearby fields. There were only a few of the more colorful dye plants that I would grow from seed or get small starts through mailorder. A new garden venture—I was absolutely giddy!

A Colorful History

What is the appeal of dye plants? Is it the color and beauty of the plants themselves? How about the alchemic magic of extracting red from the yellow blossoms of St. John's wort or blue from the green leaves of indigo? Maybe it's the connection to our past and sustaining old traditions. For me, it's a little of all of that, and though I am just a "dabbler" in the fiber arts, I enjoy the satisfaction of self-sufficiency, knowing I created something truly from the ground up.

Ever since our most ancient ancestors started to create, they endeavored to add color to their world. They used pigments extracted from minerals to keep their stories alive through cave paintings and decorated ceremonial objects. The earliest written record of the use of natural dyes goes all the way back to China in 2600 BCE. Red fabrics found in King Tutankhamun's tomb showed traces of alizarin, a pigment extracted from madder. The Romans described a people (the Picti) who painted themselves with the blue pigment extracted from woad. Later, purple was extracted from the trumpet-like shell of *Hexaplex trunculus*. It took over 8,000 of these creatures to produce just one gram of dye, making it so expensive only royal families could afford to wear it.

It wasn't until the 1800s that the first chemical dye was created by a mixture of prussiate of potash and salt. And in 1856, while trying to find a cure for malaria, William Henry Perkin discovered the first synthetic dye stuff, which he called "mauve." It was the beginning of a new era.

Getting Started

Before you get out there and place those first beautiful plants into their new homes, let me answer a few basic questions about dye plants.

First of all, Where does the color come from? All plants produce chemical compounds called pigments. Pigments only constitute a small percentage of the overall dry weight of a plant, and dye plants' pigments can be extracted and used to dye natural fiber.

What is the color range I can expect from my dye garden? Many plants give shades of yellow, tan, brass, or gold. A dull olive green, orange, and browns are fairly common as well. Reds can be obtained by several plants (though they tend to be on the rusty to orange side of red), and very few plants will give you blue dyes. Some of the more brilliant natural colors (turquoise, purple, pink, and bright green) come from insects or shellfish. Minerals will produce rich reds, yellows, and ocher.

Will my dye plants give me consistent results? It's best to have a serendipitous approach when it comes to using natural dye. It is very difficult to get an exact match every time you make up your dyebath no matter how careful you are with measurements. Shades can vary slightly, so I recommend that you dye enough yarn per dyebath to finish whatever project you are planning.

Is the plant's color an indication of what color my yarn will be? Not always. As mentioned earlier, the sunny yellow flowers of St. John's wort will give you a rusty shade of red, and you will get blue from the green leaves of indigo. Most dye plants, including their green leaves, will give you shades of gold, brown, and tan.

Mordants

Most yarn works best when it is pretreated with a bit of a metallic compound. A mordant is an element which aids the chemical reaction that takes place between the dye and the fiber so that the dye is absorbed. It helps with fading and creating brighter colors. Sometimes (depending on the mordant/fiber combination) you can create a very different dye. Take hollyhock (*Alcea rosea*) blossoms for instance: if you mordant wool with alum you will get a burnt purple color, but if you mordant with tin, it will become a shade of olive green.

Aluminum: The compound used for mordanting is alum (potassium aluminum sulfate). Using alum tends to brighten your dye bath. Using too much can give your yarn a sticky feel.

Tin: The compound used for mordanting is stannous chloride. It too brightens colors, especially red, oranges, and yellows. Adding too much tends to make some fibers brittle.

Iron: Ferrous sulfate is generally used as the mordant for fiber. Iron darkens colors and brings out the greens. Using too much can make your fiber brittle.

Copper: Use cupric sulfate for mordanting. It will deepen colors and create brilliant blues. This mordant is a lot less harsh than iron.

Chrome: The compound to use is potassium dichromate, which is almost exclusively used on wool and mohair. It brightens colors and softens the fiber. Because of some of the health dangers from prolonged exposure to chrome, some dyers prefer not to use it at all.

Breaking Ground

The great thing about dyer's plants is that they do not require a special garden. You can dedicate a few rows of your vegetable garden to them or just include them in your established flower beds. The most important thing to remember is that most dye plants (like most flowering plants) need a spot where they will get at least six hours of direct sunlight. Since you will be harvesting from these flowering beauties often, you will also have to consider your layout. Keeping them within a reach of no more than four to five feet is ideal.

If you plan on creating a separate bed for your dyer's garden, prepare your soil like you would for your vegetable or flower garden. Remove the sod and any debris or roots. Dig in deep to loosen the soil and remember to work in a lot of compost. This will improve drainage and help retain water and nutrients. Top it off with a layer of mulch.

A Rainbow of Dye Plants

Here is a list of some of the most common dye plants. Most of these you probably already have. You may find plants such as madder, woad, or indigo in a well-stocked nursery, or you can order seeds and starts online.

Dye Plant	Type	Height	Space per plant	Yield (for 4 oz. wool)	Color	Harvest
Dahlia (*Dahlia* hybrids)	tender perennial	1–5 ft.	1–4 ft.²	4–8 flowers	all flower colors (discard white): yellow, gold, orange	1st year
Goldenrod (*Soldago* spp.)	perennial	up to 5 ft.	4 ft.²	tops of 4 plants	bright gold to dark brown	2nd year
Hollyhock (*Alcea rosea*)	usually biennial	4–8 ft.	3–4 ft.²	8–12 flowers	darker flowers: purple, lilac, olive green, brown; lighter flowers: yellow, gold, brown	1st year (annual strains)
Indigo (*Indigofera suffruticosa*)	tender shrub	3–6 ft.	1 ft.²	leaves of 2–4 plants	from leaves only and brightest when in bloom; dusky to dark blue	1st year

Dye Plant	Type	Height	Space per plant	Yield (for 4 oz. wool)	Color	Harvest
Madder (*Rubia tinctorum*)	perennial	2 ft.	4 ft.^{2}	roots of 2 plants	orange red, coral, deep rusty red	3rd year
Marigold (*Tagetes erecta, T. patula,* & hybrids)	annual	1–2 ft.	1 ft.^{2}	flowers and leaves from 4–6 plants	leaves: soft yellows; flowers: yellow, gold, orange	1st year
Marjoram (*Origanum majorana*)	perennial	1 ft.	2 per 1 ft.^{2}	tops of 24 plants	gold, green, orange, dark brown*	1st year
Purple basil (*Ocimum basilicum* var. *purpurescens*)	tender perennial	2 ft.	1 ft.^{2}	tops of 18 plants	greens, mauve, brown, gold†	1st year
St. John's wort (*Hypercium perforatum*)	perennial	2–3 ft.	2 ft.^{2}	flowers from 24 plants	rusty reds, golds, olive green‡	2nd year
Sunflower (*Helianthus annuus*)	annual	4–10 ft.	2–4 ft.^{2}	flowers of 12 plants	greenish gold, tan*	1st year

☙ Herb Crafts ☙

Woad (*Isatis tinctoria*)	biennial	2–3 ft.	1 ft.²	leaves of 24 plants	dusky blue; reuse leaves for pinkish beige	1st year
Yellow bedstraw (*Galium verum*)§	perennial	2–3 ft.	4 ft.²	roots from 4 plants; tops from 6–8 plants	flowers: golden yellow; roots: coral, rusty reds	2nd year
Yellow cosmos (*Cosmos sulphureus*)	annual	1–3 ft.	2 per 2 ft.²	flowers from 12 plants	golden yellow, bright orange, rusty brown	1st year
Zinnia (*Zinnia elegans*)	annual	1–3 ft.	1 ft.²	flowers from 16–24 plants	soft yellow, golds, browns**	1st year

* Colors depend on mordant used.

† Purple basil is part of a group of flowers called anthocyanins, whose colors can be unpredictable and shift drastically in response to the pH of the mordant in the bath.

‡ St. John's wort releases its color over time, and the color can change dramatically with continued soaking.

§ Yellow bedstraw can be invasive. It is best to plant it in a contained area.

** All flowers produce these colors, but darker flowers yield more dye than lighter ones.

Plants to Avoid

There are some dye plants you might not want to add to your garden: most are invasive and some are illegal. Included in this list are ragweed, redroot pigweed, dock, bindweed and cocklebur. If you want to use them in a dyebath, these plants can be easily obtained in vacant lots, roadsides, or fields. In several northern and western states (including Washington, where I live) purple loosestrife, a European import that clogs wetlands, is considered an invasive plant and is illegal to grow in gardens, but it is legal to grow in the southern United States. If you are not familiar with a plant, please check with your local University Extension Office's Master Gardeners to find out more.

Remember, even if you're just a dabbler, like me, creating a dye garden can be very rewarding. Besides the dyebaths that can make your fiber arts truly one of a kind, you will have a garden that is brushed with beauty, splashed with pleasant scents, and tinted with a long and colorful history.

Resources

Bliss, Anne. *North American Dye Plants*. Loveland, CO: Interweave Press, 1993.

Buchanan, Rita. *A Dyer's Garden: From Plant to Pot; Growing Dyes for Natural Fibers*. Loveland, CO: Interweave Press, 1995.

Monica Crosson *is a Master Gardener who lives in the beautiful Pacific Northwest, happily digging in the dirt and tending her raspberries with her husband, three kids, three goats, one dog, three cats, many chickens, and Rosetta the donkey. She has been a practicing Witch for over twenty years and is a member of Blue Moon Coven. Monica writes fiction for young adults and is the author of* Summer Sage. *Visit her website at www.monicacrosson.com.*

Herb History,
Myth, and Lore

Rabbits in Little Velvet Jackets: Natural History in Beatrix Potter's Fairy Tales

❧ by Thea Fiore-Bloom ❧

Beatrix Potter (1866–1943) created an enchanted story garden, peopled with blue-velvet-clad rabbits and talking hedgehogs. She set her fantasy stories against backdrops of real plants, like foxglove and bracken fern. Herbs too poke their green, leafy heads between the pages of almost every one of the farmer and author's artful adventures for children.

Fiction with Fragrance

Herbs do more than merely decorate Potter's pages; they enhance the tales by infusing them with the illusion of fragrance. "A good deal of what I would call the sensory appeal of Potter's books has to do with her incorporation of herbs into

her work. I don't know exactly how to explain it, but Beatrix Potter's stories have a fragrance," said Marta McDowell, horticulturist and author of *Beatrix Potter's Gardening Life*, in my interview with her.

Potter was a gifted botanical illustrator and consummate storyteller. She conveyed the physical likeness of aromatic plants in a manner that somehow encourages her audiences to forget they are reading a book. As McDowell puts it, "Beatrix Potter's herbs are drawn so you can almost smell them. Potter's garden stories tend to be at the height of the season. So the lavender is blooming and the sage is out, and you can just imagine being out there in the middle of it, smelling it all."

The imagined smell, touch, and even taste of herbs in the tales contribute to the enchantment we feel as we wander about Beatrix Potter's watercolored gardens, glades and warrens. Potter suspended the disbelief of her story's readers, young and old alike. She accomplished this through the accurate depiction of more than just herbs.

The Science in Her Fiction

Potter's knowledge of natural history and her keen science-based drawing, allowed her to place her talking fantasy animals amongst illustrations of plants, mushrooms, and insects that would impress any botanist, mycologist, or entomologist. "She insisted on all the science and naturalism in her own stories to be exactly true," said McDowell. For example, in *The Tale of Miss Tittlemouse*, a toad named Mr. Jackson encounters a butterfly tasting sugar cubes (atop a lovely china cup). This butterfly is no generic winged thing; it's an accurately etched *Vanessa atalanta*, commonly known as the Red Admiral.

McDowell said, "If you read Beatrix Potter's stories, its not outrageous to think, 'Oh, there actually *are* rabbits that wear little velvet jackets'; because everything else is so real, it increases the reality of the things that are fantasy."

Ever look closely at Beatrix Potter's mushrooms? They are not only beautiful, but they are scientifically correct as well. Potter completed hundreds of professional-level fungi paintings. She experimented with spore germination and even wrote an academic paper on her pioneering findings. (That paper was presented at the Linnean Society in April of 1897).

When Potter's toads have a tea party, as in *The Toads' Tea Party* (1902), they are not seen sitting at a table in the form of a cartoonish mushroom. Potter's toads have their tansy cake on a meticulously rendered toadstool of a table, with each scallop-shaped toad chair a part of a cluster bracket fungus, *Polyporus squamosus*. This mushroom group was sometimes called "dryad's saddle," referring to the dryads of Greek mythology and folklore (wood nymphs who favored oak trees) who conceivably were envisaged saddling and perhaps riding such comfortable mushrooms.

Pet Rabbits and Potting Sheds

Beatrix Potter's drawings of rabbits and mice are so real and engaging because they are the culmination of countless hours spent drawing from life. The animals she employed most often as models were from her own exotic menagerie of pets: rabbits (Peter Piper being one), mice (Xarifa being her favorite), guinea pigs, ferrets, hedgehogs, and even salamanders.

Potter and her brother loved the life sciences from early childhood on. They had a miniature museum with a laboratory in their nursery/study. It was replete with microscopes, dissection tools, fossils, books, and insects both alive and dead.

Potter's drive for accuracy and excellence didn't stop with the outdoor settings in her books. Her meticulousness extended into the domestic interiors of her stories as well. Potter collected vintage mahogany furniture and often used it for sketching the period backdrops for her cottage-centered fantasies.

Like many inspired novelists, poets and artists of our own day, Potter drew inspiration from detailed studies of locations she found fascinating. Many of Potter's discoveries took place in the grand historic manor houses where her family summered in Great Britain. For example Mr. McGregor's potting shed in *The Tale of Peter Rabbit* was a replica (down to the geraniums, clay pots, and gardening tools) of a potting shed Beatrix had once happily stumbled upon at Bedwell Lodge in Hertfordshire in 1891. McDowell said, "You know the places she went to create these stories were *real* worlds [real homes, real gardens, and real hillsides]. And sort of the only thing that is added are the details of her imagination, but they are all layered on top of actual things."

Even the textiles Potter used to add texture to her interior scenes and the clothing she dressed her characters in were the results of her inspired research. Potter painstakingly copied the luscious, embroidered silk waistcoat that the mice work on in *The Tailor of Glouster* (1903) from a period waistcoat she repeatedly sketched in detail during visits to the Victoria and Albert Museum in London. The city, with its science and art museums, engaged Potter's quick mind, but it was the countryside that held her heart.

The Restorative Power of Gardens

The gardens and hills of the Lake District were not only a place of great creative inspiration, but also a source of solace for the artist. The English earth supported Potter all her life, but perhaps she called on the land's restorative properties most strongly after the heartrending early death of her fiancé, publisher, and muse, Norman Warne.

"There are definite chemical, psychological benefits to working in the soil and being out in the garden and seeing things grow," said McDowell. "Beatrix Potter immediately starts to garden after she acquires her first piece of property, and that was in the very [first] months after Norman died. It is reasonable to assume that the land helped Potter a great deal in her own life." Potter helped the land a great deal in return. Over the course of her lifetime she purchased and saved more than four thousand acres of Lake District farm country, later to bequeath it to the public through the National Trust.

Additional Resources on Beatrix Potter

Plan a visit to Beatrix Potter's Garden and Home Museum (www.nationaltrust.org.uk/hill-top), or join the Beatrix Potter Society (beatrixpottersociety.org.uk). Keep up with the news for Hill Top and current exhibitions at the Beatrix Potter Gallery at the National Trust's blog (www.beatrixpotters-patch.blogspot.com).

The Armitt Museum (www.armitt.com) in the Lake District is known as an eccentric, small gem of a museum and houses a collection of Beatrix Potter's original material and ephemera alongside that of other artists and writers.

The Perth Museum (www.pkc.gov.uk) in Perthshire has a small but lovely collection of Potter's mushroom studies and also gives visitors access to her inspiring correspondence with her influential mentor in the natural sciences, Charlie McIntosh, who also happened to be her postman.

Suggested Reading

Buckley, Norman and June Buckley. *Walking With Beatrix Potter: Fifteen Walks in Beatrix Potter Country.* London: Frances Lincoln, 2007.

Lear, Linda. *Beatrix Potter: A Life in Nature.* London: St. Martin's Griffin, 2008.

Linder, Leslie, ed. *The Journal of Beatrix Potter (1881–1897).* Forward by Judy Taylor. London: Fredrick Warne, 1966.

McDowell, Marta. *Beatrix Potter's Gardening Life: The Plants and Places that Inspired the Classic Children's Tales.* Portland: Timber Press, 2013.

Taylor, Judy, ed. *Beatrix Potter's Letters.* London: Frederick Warne, 1989.

If you like English mysteries, you may like *The Cottage Tales of Beatrix Potter* or *The China Bayles Herbal Mysteries* by Susan Wittig Albert (http://www.cottagetales.com/index.shtml).

Thea Fiore-Bloom, *PhD, is a freelance writer, artist, workshop leader, and children's literacy volunteer with a doctorate in mythology. Fiore-Bloom's work is inspired by world heritage sights, the homes and biographies of artists and writers, and the objects and stories of the people she meets in her own backyard. She can be reached at theafiorebloom@gmail.com.*

The Painted Celt: Woad in Ancient and Modern Use

✺ by Tiffany Lazic ✺

The image of Mel Gibson's face streaked blue in the film *Braveheart* has become an iconic imprint on our imaginings of ancient Celtic warriors. Since that 1995 film, it is an image which has occurred again and again, in cinema notably with the Woads of *King Arthur* and the Macintosh clan of Disney/Pixar's *Brave*. The distinctive deep blue color is a favorite for tribal tattoos, often reflecting intricate Celtic knotwork patterns. It has become seemingly irrevocably associated with the Celts, particularly to excite feelings of courage and insight. There is something about that specific shade of woad blue that evokes both a proud surge in the heart and an inspired wave in the brow.

Historic Claim

Strong as this association may be, there are thin threads that link woad with those ancient warriors, other than one ever-so-brief sentence in Julius Caesar's *Comentarii de Bello Gallico* in which he wrote that the "Britons dye their bodies with woad, which produces a blue colour and gives them a wild appearance in battle." From that small observation the Picts got the name by which we know them. The Romans called them *Picti*, or "Painted Ones." But Caesar never made it as far north in Britain as the land of the Picts, and when it comes to information about the Celts from the Roman perspective, one must exercise some discernment: there was a certain amount of propaganda at play.

What we do know is that woad was highly valued for the dye that could be extracted for coloring wool. It was the only colorfast blue available to the ancient peoples of the West. There is archeological evidence that woad seeds were collected and stored in Neolithic times, and blue-dyed textiles have been found at sites attributed to the Hallstatt Celts (eighth to sixth centuries BCE), the very first Celts to make their European appearance.

Though woad plants themselves are quite hardy and can be found across Europe and Asia, they do not thrive more than two years in one spot. In ancient times, those devoted to woad production lived nomadic lives, taking down the sheds built for processing and rebuilding them in new locations. Later, the technique of field rotation was utilized to provide more stability of place, and certain locations, such as Toulouse, France, became quite wealthy as a result of the thriving trade. By 1392, the German town of Erfurt was so wealthy from woad it established its own university.

However, as with so many commercial ventures, the lucrative woad trade became threatened due to a couple of key complicating factors. By the 1500s the huge land requirements for growing woad were thought to have contributed to a massive food supply shortage in Britain, and Queen Elizabeth I issued a complete ban on growing woad. After two years the ban was amended to allow for restricted cultivation. Around the same time European woad merchants were becoming uneasy due to distant threats from India. The indigotin that is produced in woad (*Isatis tinctoria*) is identical to that produced by indigo (*Indigofera tinctoria*), but indigo is far easier to cultivate than the soil-draining woad. With Vasco da Gama's discovery of a direct sea route to the East, the slow introduction of indigo from Asia, which had begun solely geared toward artists as pigment for their paints, began to reach its arms ever further. An international union of woad growers called the Woadites was formed to put pressure on governments to restrict the import of indigo, even going so far as to spread claims that indigo caused fabric to rot and to call it "the Devil's dye." By the mid-1600s, popular attitude seemed to change to "if you can't beat them, join them." Cultivation of indigo in the New World was aimed at loosening the Indian monopoly and increasing availability in Europe, sounding the death knell for large-scale production of woad.

Dyers' Skill

Creating the distinctive blue dye from the leaves of the woad plant is a long and somewhat arduous process. Though the leaves naturally turn blue as they age, it is the young leaves in a plant's first year that must be used in order to obtain the beautiful blue dye for which it is known. A dyer covers roughly chopped leaves in a pot or jar with almost boiling water, letting it sit for about ten minutes. Once steeped, the leafy liquid must be cooled down very quickly. If using a metal pot, the whole concoction can be placed in another larger tub of cold water; however, this will not work if using a glass jar, as glass may break from the temperature shock. Once cooled, the mix must be strained to remove the leaves. Gloves are recommended lest the dyer become painted blue as well. Those who worked in woad production could often be identified by the blue stain on their hands and under their fingernails.

There are two very important steps to coaxing the beautiful woad blue: adding an alkali and aeration. In ancient times, urine would be used as the alkali, which would also produce a strong odor. Queen Elizabeth I put restrictions on how close woad production could be to her palaces. Less-noxious ingredients such as ammonia, potash, or soda ash are also effective in creating the necessary pH balance. Using a hand or electric mixer provides aeration which is indicated by the liquid turning green and producing a froth. Fabrics dyed in this liquid will appear greenish-yellow initially but will turn blue if left to dry in the air.

Woad balls were also highly valuable because they could be stored and more easily transported. The leaves would be ground, formed into palm-sized balls, and left to dry for three weeks to a month. The balls, once transported, could be broken up into a fine powder and allowed to ferment in water, a process known as couching, which took several days and allowed for further breaking down the plant material without reducing the level of indigotin. Once completed the resulting substance could be dried again, ground to a powder, and stored for later use. The amount of indigotin in the resulting dye made a range of blues—everything from quite light hues to the deep blue associated with the painted Celts.

Healing Properties

Reference to the healing properties of woad also stems back to the time of the Romans. Woad is an astringent healing herb that can staunch bleeding and reduce inflammation. Though much has been made of the terrifying woad-streaked Celtic visages, there is some credence to the thought that the use of woad by warriors was more practical than aesthetic—a battle preventative for potential wounds.

The seventeenth century herbalist Nicholas Culpeper references woad's effectiveness in dealing with matters of the spleen, stating that the application of a plaster of woad reduces pain and alleviates hardness. He also somewhat inexplicably and mysteriously states that woad is destructive to bees, which he attributes to its extreme effectiveness of dyeing and binding and suggests, with yet another reference to the association of woad with urine, that diseased bees can be cured by placing a bowl of urine near them with pieces of cork floating in it so that the bees will not drown.

Symbolism

Though the information regarding the use of woad as an herbal remedy is somewhat sparse, there are many references to its symbolic use. Perhaps regarding the Painted Celts, woad is said to aid in shape-shifting, allowing self-transmutation, and strengthening one's spiritual connection. Working with woad also has its challenges. It is not easy to cultivate. It is not easy to extract the dye. Even in the dye extraction, there is no guarantee of precise color tone. It emanates the message that things of beauty and rarity are always worth the struggle to attain them.

Benefits of Blue

Whether you are working with woad from a textiles perspective, exploring its healing properties, or tapping into its rich symbolism, this is a fascinating plant with a long tradition in the West, particularly Britain, France, and Germany. The next time you drape yourself in that exquisite rich, deep blue or whiff its earthy incense, allow yourself to be uplifted, feeling proud, capable, and confident. Allow yourself to be transformed into your strongest, most resilient self. Allow yourself to become painted in the incomparable beauty of woad blue.

Resource

Culpeper, Nicholas. *Culpeper's Complete Herbal: A Book of Natural Remedies for Ancient Ills*. Ware, UK: Wordsworth Editions, 1995.

Tiffany Lazic *is a registered psychotherapist and spiritual director with a private practice in individual, couples, and group therapy. As owner of the Hive and Grove Centre for Holistic Wellness, she created and teaches two self-development programs. An international presenter and keynote speaker, she has conducted workshops for many organizations in Canada, the United States, and the United Kingdom. She serves on the Board of Trustees for the Sisterhood of Avalon and is the founder of Kitchener's Red Tent Temple. She is the author of* The Great Work: Self-Knowledge and Healing Through the Wheel of the Year *(Llewellyn, 2015).*

Herb Names

⊰ by Suzanne Ress ⊱

Herbal plants have many wonderful qualities: their scents,
their healing properties, their culinary uses, their beauty, and even
their colorful names! Most common
herb names in English were given in
medieval times or earlier, and they
reflect an older way of speaking and
thinking.

Some common herb names in
English are variations of their original Greek names, given to them several thousand years ago. Other names
are translations or corruptions of the
herb's botanical Latin name, assigned
in the Middle Ages. Almost all common names for herbs are descriptive
of their medical use, appearance, or
other outstanding qualities.

feverfew
mugwort
foxglove
pennyroyal
henbane
broom

The Worts

Herbs with names like liverwort, mugwort, nipplewort, and lungwort sound old-fashioned and slightly amusing to us now, but in Old English the word *wort* simply means a medicinal herb. All herbs with wort names have some beneficial, often medical quality or qualities. **Liverwort** (*Hepatica triloba*) was used to treat liver congestion; **mugwort** (*Artemisia vulgaris*) was used in beer brewing; **nipplewort** (*Lapsana communis*) was used to treat breast ulcers; **lungwort** (*Pulmonaria officinalis*) made a soothing expectorant that restored elasticity to the lungs.

Other interesting wort names are lousewort, woundwort, milkwort, stitchwort, spearwort, butterwort, plaguewort, spiderwort, pearlwort, pennywort, ribwort, horsewort, stonewort, masterwort, starwort, and moonwort.

St. John's wort (*Hypericum perforatum*) is likely one of the most well-known worts of current times. Its other common names are Grace of God and Touch and Heal, and it is believed that it reaches the apex of its healing powers on the eve of St. John's Day, June 23. It was, and still is, used to relieve headache, back pain, varicose veins, ulcers, sunburn, and more.

Another wort is **motherwort** (*Leonurus cardiaca*), also commonly called lion's ear or lion's tail. It is a calming herb, used for nervous problems. **Ragwort** (*Packera aurea*), sometimes known as coughweed, was used to bring on suppressed menstruation. **Soapwort** (*Saponaria officinalis*), one of the principal medicinal herbs of the Middle Ages, was used to wash itchy, pimply, or otherwise problematic skin. Many worts are still considered valuable alternatives to modern synthetic pharmaceutical concoctions, when used as directed.

The Banes

A bane is an herb with poisonous qualities, and the name comes from the Old English word *bana*, which means death, destruction, murderer, or poisonous.

The root of **dogbane** (*Apocynum androsaemifolium*), also called bitterroot or milkweed, was used in combination with less potent herbs as a cathartic and emetic. Eating the leaves can be fatal to livestock and dogs.

Wolfsbane (*Aconitum napellus*), another name for monkshood, is poisonous in all of its parts to humans and animals. Even touching its pretty, indigo-colored flowers can cause serious harm. Its juice was once used on arrowheads and was strong enough to be fatal to the most ferocious wolf. Minute quantities were used to treat severe pain.

Henbane (*Hyoscycamus niger*), sometimes called black nightshade, is poisonous in all of its parts, but was once used sparingly in love potions and aphrodisiacs and as a sedative in cases of insanity. Contrary to what one may think, its name does not refer to poultry. *Hen* was the root of an Old English word that means death.

Sowbane (*Chenopodium rubrum*), also called hogsbane or red goosefoot, is fatal to swine. As far back as Neolithic times at least, it was eaten by humans as a nutritious cooked foodstuff. It comes from the same family as quinoa (*Chenopodium quinoa*), an important nutritious staple for indigenous peoples of Peru, Bolivia, and Chile.

Banewort, a name which would seem contradictory, is an old-fashioned name for deadly nightshade, also known as belladonna (*Atropa belladonna*). It is an extremely poisonous plant but was once used by shamanic-type priests for astral projection and hallucinatory visions. Its Latin name, *bella-donna* (beautiful woman), refers to its use in olden times in the form of eye drops to dilate the pupils of women who wished to look seductive. Before the Middle Ages it was sometimes used as an anesthetic for surgery, but its main historical employment was as a deadly poison.

The **nightshade** family is very interesting indeed! It includes such exotic sounding plants as black nightshade, enchanter's nightshade, malabar nightshade, and stinking nightshade, as well as the homely staples potato, tomato, eggplant, pepper, hot pepper, and tobacco. The Latin family name Solanaceae refers to these plants' ability to store up energy from the sun during the day for growth and flower blooming at night or in the shade.

Other Colorfully Named Herbs

Broom (*Cytisus scoparius*), also called Scots broom, is self-explanatory once you look at the shrubby plant's long, tough, straw-like stems. It was once also called the "genista plant," from which the large and powerful European royal family, the Plantagenets, derived their name. The family emblem was the broom plant.

Costmary, or **alecost** (*Tanacetum balsamita*), includes the word "cost," which comes from the Greek *kostos*, meaning "spicy." Mary refers to the Virgin Mary, a mother goddess. Costmary's alternate common name, alecost, makes reference to the herb's use in beer brewing. Its leaves were added to the brew to clear and preserve it, as well as to impart a sharp, bitter, balsamic flavor. Costmary's leaves can also be rubbed on insect bites and stings to relieve the pain.

Devil's bit (*Succisa pratensis*) is a pretty, purple wildflower with a root that looks like it has a bite taken out of it, and who but the devil could have bitten from below ground? It was believed that because the plant was so useful to human beings, the devil bit off its root in malice.

Eyebright (*Euphrasia officinalis*) was widely used in the form of a weak infusion of the fresh herb to treat eyestrain and inflammation. Its Latin name, *Euphrasia*, comes from Greek and means cheerfulness or gladness.

Feverfew (*Tanacetum parthenium*), strangely, is not known to have ever been employed as a fever reducer. However, first century Greek records reveal it was used as an anti-inflammatory. In the Middle Ages it was commonly prescribed as a remedy for migraine headaches and head colds. The dried leaves also make an effective insect repellent.

Foxglove (*Digitalis purpurea*) is also known as fairy fingers or fairy glove; its Latin name means reddish fingers. It is thought that the name foxglove is a corruption of "folks' glove," where "folk" refers to fairies.

Heartsease (*Viola tricolor*) is a common, old-fashioned name for wild pansy. A decoction made from its purple, white, and yellow flowers was used to ease the pain of a broken heart. It is still considered a valid heart tonic, which reduces the build up of plaque in the arteries.

Honesty (*Lunaria annua*), also sometimes called the money plant, was believed to draw good luck when hung inside the home. Its disk-shaped seed pods resemble silver coins but also, in their shiny translucence, look like candid full moons, the epitome of honesty. The name honesty became common in the sixteenth century.

Horehound (*Marrubium vulgare*) brings to mind an image of a wolf-like creature covered in hoary frost. In truth, it evolved from *hārhūne*, the Old English name for the downy plant. *Hār*, meaning "hoary," refers to the woolly underside of its silvery-green leaves. Its botanical name comes from Hebrew and means "bitter juice."

Knitbone, another name for comfrey (*Symphytum officinale*), was thus called because the mucilaginous secretions of its leaves are strong enough to be used as a bone-setting plaster.

Lady's bedstraw (*Gallium verum*), a sweet-smelling herb, was originally called Our Lady's bedstraw. It was thought to have been one of the three plants that made up the hay in the Christ child's manger where he was born. Its Latin name, *Gallium*, which comes from *gal* (milk), refers to its use as a substitute rennet for cheese making.

Lady's mantle (*Alchemilla vulgaris*) is the common name that came about in medieval times for this valued herb, and it referred to the cloak of the Virgin Mary (Our Lady), to which its leaves bear a resemblance. The herb was considered to be a woman's protector, used to regulate menstruation, ease menopause symptoms, reduce inflammation of the female organs, and ease painful swelling in postlactating breasts. Its Latin name, *Alchemilla*, comes from the Arabic word for "alchemy," meaning a magical transformation.

Meadowsweet (*Filipendula ulmaria*) is the common name for an herb sometimes also called bridewort, and is a corruption of the Old English *meadesweet*, meaning "mead sweetener," because the plant was used to flavor mead. Its botanical name, *Filipendula*, comes from *filum* (thread) and *pendulus* (hanging), which well describe the plant's fibrous hanging roots. This herb's white, lace-like flowers were strewn in sacred places for weddings and made into garlands for brides. The whole plant can be used as a remedy for stomachaches and diarrhea.

Self-heal (*Prunella vulgaris*) has a long-standing reputation as an aid to the body's natural healing power. A decoction of the dried herb was used to cure coughs, chest colds, and sore throats. A poultice of its leaves speeds the healing of wounds. It is also sometimes called all-heal or woundwort.

Southernwood (*Artemesia abrotanum*) is also known as old man or lad's love. This woody herbal plant is native to the southern countries of Eurasia and to northern Africa. It was widely used in aphrodisiacs, and worn in young mens' buttonholes to attract women with its fresh, camphor-like scent. The English common name, old man, was donned upon it to create a coupling with its relative, old woman (wormwood).

Speedwell (*Veronica officinalis*) was one of the principal herbs used medicinally in medieval times. Speedwell reputedly heals all ills, including respiratory problems, stomach ailments, headache, mouth and throat sores, gout, and chronic skin problems.

Passionflower (*Passiflora incarnata*) is an herbal plant named solely for its appearance by Jesuit friars when they first encountered it in its native South America in the 1500s. In the center of each dramatic-looking flower are five red anthers representing the five wounds Christ suffered on the cross. The raised triple styles are supposed to represent the three nails, and the corona at the center is imagined as Christ's crown of thorns. The flower's white calyx represents a halo. Contrary to its name and appearance, passionflower is a soothing herb, used widely in relaxation-inducing tisanes and teas.

Pennyroyal (*Mentha pulegium*) is an evocative name for this strong, minty herb, useful as an insect repellent. It was once widely employed as an abortifacient. Its common name is a corruption of the Latin word *pulegium* (which means flea-repelling) to the easier-to-pronounce "penny," plus *real*, which has transformed to "royal."

Viper's bugloss (*Echium vulgare*) is a pretty, blue-flowered herb often considered an invasive weed in hay fields that got its common name in the Middle Ages. According to the doctrine of signatures, its central stem resembles a snakeskin, and its flowers are shaped like snakes' heads. The flowering tops were chopped up to make a poultice for treating vipers' bites and boils. Bugloss comes from the Greek *buglossos*, which means "ox's tongue": the plant's leaves are rough and shaped like tongues.

Witch hazel (*Hamamelis virginiana*) is a small tree, unrelated to the hazelnut tree (*Corylus avellana*), whose bark and leaves make a soothing lotion for sunburned or itchy skin. Divining rods and wands were commonly made from it, too; hence, it became known as the witch's hazel.

Wormwood (*Artemesia absinthium*) is sometimes called old woman for its witchy associations. Wormwood is the primary herbal ingredient in absinthe liquor, and is rumoured to induce a state of near insanity when used to excess. The herb was once mainly employed as a vermifuge. Its flowering tops were ground to a powder and swallowed to expel intestinal worms in man and beast. Like the other *Artemesia* species, wormwood has woody stems.

After taking a closer look at some common and botanical herb names, it becomes ever more apparent how important these plants were to our ancestors and how lucky we are that these names survive to reveal a bit of each herb's history and use. There are so many enjoyable facets of herbs, not the least of which are their illustrative names!

Suzanne Ress *earned an MA from Johns Hopkins University and has been writing for many years. Her first novel,* The Trial of Goody Gilbert, *was published in 2012, and she has since completed two more, as yet unpublished, novels and begun work on a fourth. She is an organic farmer and beekeeper and lives in the foothills of the Italian Alps with her husband and many domestic and wild animals.*

The Ancient History of Herbs

~ by Elizabeth Barrette ~

The history of our relationship with herbs is long and colorful. Today people use herbs for many purposes, including culinary, medicinal, magical, spiritual, crafting, and so forth. Many modern varieties have been adapted and cultivated for human preferences, some over thousands of years. Others remain very similar to the wild plants that our ancestors first began gathering.

Types of Herbal Medicines

Most early medicines came from plants, with a few exceptions coming from mineral or animal sources. At first people gathered wild plants. Discarding the unused portion near camp encouraged the regrowth of

favored species. Over time, this casual use evolved into true domestication. People began farming fruits, vegetables, and grains. They planted gardens of herbs for diverse purposes.

The most basic division of herbal medicines lies between simples and formulas. A **simple** is one herb taken in large quantity. Chamomile, ginger, mint, and willow are popular for this method. Simples are easy to make and use, so they are an excellent addition to the herbal medicine chest. They were probably the first approach. **Formulas** consist of multiple herbs that may have similar properties or different ones. You might combine several painkillers together for a stronger effect but a lower chance of overdosing on any one herb. Alternatively, a blend for treating colds might use different herbs to relieve cough, fever, and stuffy nose. Formulas consist of several herbs or several *dozen*. Among the most complex were alcohol tinctures from the medieval and Renaissance periods, recipes for which survive today as bitters used for culinary flavoring or mixed drinks.

Liquid delivery includes such things as infusions, decoctions, and tinctures. In an **infusion,** hot water is poured over herbal ingredients. This works well for tender parts such as flowers and leaves, which give up their essence easily and could be ruined by higher temperatures. A **decoction** places the herbs into boiling water for a time. This works well for extracting the essence from roots, bark, nuts, and other hard materials. A **tincture** uses alcohol and water to draw out the active ingredients from herbs and preserve them for a long time in a compact format. This developed later in history, as it required more sophisticated methods of brewing and bottling.

Semisolid remedies come in forms from almost liquid to rather stiff. They include such things as lotions, creams, ointments, salves, and oxymels. A **lotion** is a slightly thickened liquid still runny enough for a squirt bottle. It's made from water, herbal infused oils, and sometimes essential oils. The water means that lotion doesn't keep as long as some other forms, but it spreads the farthest over skin. A **cream** has more oil than water, so it is thicker, usually kept in a wide-mouthed jar. An **ointment** is a soft, sticky substance that is too thick for a bottle but too loose for a tin. It is made from herbal infused oils or fats, wax, and sometimes essential oils and can spread a long way. It is usually dispensed from a tube, although it may come in a wide-mouthed jar. **Salves**, with their creamy or waxy texture are thick and stiff enough to stay in a tin. They are good for coating small areas of skin and are made from herbal infused oils or fats and wax. Historically, animal fats were often used for many of these, but because fats tend to go rancid fast, botanical oils are preferred today. **Oxymels**, an excellent choice for sore throats or cranky children (but never infants), infuse herbs into honey and vinegar, and are typically bottled.

Solid preparations hold their shape outside a container, although they may be fairly soft. These include things like balms, lotion bars, soap, and ice. A **balm** is made from wax, herbal infused oils, and essential oils and has the highest proportion of wax. Its stiff texture suits it for a push-up tube or a tin. **Lotion bars** and **deodorants** are basically balms with a slightly softer texture and additional ingredients. **Soap** is made from a fat and a base, plus essential oils and/or dried herbs. Real soap is usually hard or slightly squishy; liquid "soap" is more often a detergent. **Ice cubes**, an excellent means of storage if you have a freezer, may be made from herbal tea or pureed herbs. Regular use of ice is only a few centuries old.

Herbs in Prehistory

Herbs and other plants have been part of history since *before* recorded history. From archaeology, we know that people began to inter the dead with flowers many thousands of years ago. The earliest known example at this time comes from Shanidar, where forensic science detected pollen in larger amounts than normal from natural sources, implying that one or more of the bodies found there may have been put to rest with flowers around 60,000 years BCE.

A later and more concrete example comes from the vicinity of Mt. Carmel around 12,000 years BCE. Numerous bodies were buried over a bed of herbs. Scientists found impressions in the earth left by the plants, some so detailed as to indicate particular species still growing nearby, such as *Salvia judaica*, a type of wild sage. Furthermore, the clarity of the impressions indicated that the herbs had been picked while their stems were strong, at the height of their flowering season, rather than later when they would have been softer and left blurry marks, if any.

Wonders of the World

Among the Seven Wonders of the World was the Hanging Gardens of Babylon. It was most likely built around 600 BCE by King Nebuchadnezzar II, as a gift for his homesick wife, Amyitis. However, some accounts attribute it to the Assyrian Queen Semiramis, whose five-year reign began in 810 BCE, so the king may have inherited an earlier piece of hardscaping and simply expanded upon it.

Although we tend to think of "hanging" gardens to mean pots or flats suspended by lines, the most probable format for the Hanging Gardens of Babylon is that of terraces forming an artificial mountain. Modern misconceptions stem from imperfect translations: the Latin word *pensilis* and the Greek *kremastos* refer to "overhanging," as in terraces or balconies, not just things hanging from a chain.

Another possibility is arbors, pergolas, or similar structures used to support grapes, hops, and other climbing plants. Likewise, strawberries and smaller running plants can be grown in gutters or pots hung from a frame to facilitate harvest. Such structures often stand tall enough that people may walk underneath and harvest fruit from the vines overhead. Garden bowers of these types emerged in ancient Egypt where formal gardens aimed to extend the greenery beyond the few natural oasis areas and the banks of the Nile.

What kinds of plants grew in the Hanging Gardens of Babylon? Ancient writers described planters big enough to hold large trees. Wild almonds (*Prunus dulcis*) have been found in archaeological sites from as early as 3000 BCE. Grapes (*Vitis vinifera*) were cultivated wherever they would grow, and most of our modern cultivars descend from a species found in Iran from around 2000 BCE. They symbolize divine inspiration and abundance. Trade in olive oil (*Olea europaea*) began somewhere between 3000 and 2000 BCE. This healthy source of vegetable fat is a vital source of calories in harsh conditions. Quince (*Cydonia oblonga*), a bitter fruit popular in sweetened preserves, is native throughout the Middle East. European pears (*Pyrus communis*) did not emerge directly from the wild, but rather from cultivation and careful crossbreeding that dates from about 1000 BCE. Common figs (*Ficus carica*), ranging from the Middle East to western Asia, were among the first plants ever cultivated by humans. They provide a dense source of energy.

Roman Gardens

Gardens in Rome, like those of Egypt, tended toward formal styles. Although they began as a practical source of herbs, fruits, and vegetables, they soon grew more elaborate. The Romans loved geometry and incorporated raised beds, urns, columns, and paths in aesthetic patterns. Buildings often had planted courts adjoining them. Philosophers, physicians, and other professors often taught outdoors in garden spaces where they could point out plants to students.

Certain features distinguished Roman gardens. Porticos were walkways flanked by columns, sometimes also covered. Groves of trees featured plane and cypress. The leaves of the bay laurel had religious as well as culinary applications. Fountains and other waterworks abounded. Shrubs of many types were pruned into topiary. Myrtle, box, and yew also made hedges in larger gardens. Small gardens used woody herbs such as thyme for these purposes. Large villas belonging to wealthy Romans would divide ornamental plants, vegetables, and medicinal and culinary herbs into separate areas.

Herbs favored for culinary and medicinal uses included basil, hyssop, mint, and savory. Popular flowers included costmary, crocus, iris, lamb's ear, poppy, and rose. Orchards featured trees such as apple, apricot, fig, olive, pear, pomegranate, and quince. Grapes were grown wherever possible. By 100 CE greenhouses had emerged for growing warm-weather plants like grapes and melons in colder regions.

Another feature was the *lucus,* or sacred grove. This was a cultivated forest or wooded park that often contained an *aedes,* or small shrine housing divine images. Other landscaping features might facilitate making offerings and other actions important to the Roman faith. Therefore, holy herbs such as bay laurel, olive, rose, and sage often made up part of the plantings.

Monastery Gardens

During medieval and Renaissance times, the common people tended to use casual gardens. Nobles and monks, however, continued the tradition of formal gardens. Monasteries in particular became famous for their elaborate gardens filled with herbs. The *herbularius,* or medicinal garden, provided many of the healing supplies of the day. The *hortus,* or kitchen garden for vegetables and seasonings, supplemented the much more expensive spices imported from other lands.

Monastery gardens typically used geometric shapes, such as squares, rectangles, circles, and ovals. Naturally, crosses were popular, and so were elements borrowed from Celtic culture, including the Celtic ringed cross, trefoil knots, and all kinds of intricate knotwork. Both Norse and Celtic cultures contributed to the use of stone benches and tables, sometimes carved with flowers, runes, knotwork, or Latin sayings.

One interesting feature of monastery gardens was the placement of the most beautiful and aromatic herbs closest to the hospital. These herbs included roses and lilies, followed by horehound, lavender, lemon balm, mint, rosemary, sage, and others. This design kept the medicinal herbs close to where they would be used, and it offered bedridden patients an inspiring view and ambulatory ones a pleasant place to sit outdoors within immediate reach of staff.

Farther out grew rangier herbs such as angelica, anise, comfrey, fennel, leeks, mallow, mustard, and yarrow. Orchards included apple, pear, quince, and other fruit trees. These often featured beehives for honey and wax. Honey formed the base of oxymels; beeswax went into salves, ointments, and balms. Large monasteries may have featured forests with crops of acorns, hazelnuts, and other edibles. Juniper could be trimmed into topiary or hedges and also provided useful berries and aromatic wood.

Another purpose for herbs lay in making dye. Because many of these plants were poisonous, they usually had their own section of the garden. These included madder (pink to red), tormentil (red), marigold (yellow to orange), onion peels (orange), agrimony (yellow), St. John's wort (yellow to red), weld (yellow), foxglove (green), woad (green to blue), elderberry (blue to purple), deadly nightshade (purple), hops (brown), and meadowsweet (black). Strewing herbs such as mugwort, pennyroyal, rue, and woodruff were grown in large quantities to deter pests. Other toxic plants used for killing pests or parasites included hemlock, henbane, and wormwood.

Elizabeth Barrette *has been involved with the Pagan community for more than twenty-six years. She served as managing editor of Pan-Gaia for eight years and dean of studies at the Grey School of Wizardry for four years. Her book* Composing Magic: How to Create Magical Spells, Rituals, Blessings, Chants, and Prayers *explains how to combine writing and spirituality. She enjoys magical crafts, historic religions, and gardening for wildlife. Visit www.ysabetword smith.livejournal.com or www.penultimateproductions.weebly.com.*

Crop Lore: When the Plants Talked Back

❧ by Diana Rajchel ❧

In pre-Industrial Europe, many farmers and their workers often held an animistic view of the world well into Christian times. They often saw the various grains they raised as not just alive but as in some way sentient—and from that sentience sprang the idea of related spirits, some of which manifested in humanlike forms. Early folkloric accounts often read like an *X-Files* record of common crop pests, whether a haunting came in the form of an especially clever goat or as the ghost of a particularly persistent neighborhood busybody. The nineteenth-century folklorists labeled these accounts tales of "corn spirits" or of "the corn spirit," even

though these personas came attached to any type of crop. This happened because, in the United Kingdom, the term corn was used interchangeably for all grains—maize, the North American crop commonly thought of as corn, came to Europe long after these folk tales came to life.

Especially in Germany, farmers associated specific eerie happenings to the intervention of Germanic and Norse gods. As Christianity gradually replaced the culture of polytheism, these gods became spirits. Animism—in this case a belief in living, breathing fields with spirits appearing among them— did not disappear until well into the twentieth century.

Crop Creatures

While some of these spirits appeared benign—the Irish described the bending of corn as fairies marching across it, and the Russians told of *ljeschies*, faun-like creatures that took a kind view toward farming practices and whatever else kept humans out of their woods—others saw the creatures living within the crops as adversarial at best. The Germans had a series of demons responsible for various crop maladies. The *Erntebock* was an invisible creature that actually stole part of the harvest. In April, just as the grain began growing, they had to deal with the *Aprilochse*, a mysterious spirit that infested and ruined crops in different ways. Each grain demon filled a specific, delegated role in the ever-important process of antagonizing the farmer or gardener.

Certain animals, often livestock, also played the part of common crop spirits instead of crop pests. The *Farre* (little bull) infested corn and wheat fields, the *Gerstenwulf* took the form of a wolf that disrupted the barley, the *Graswolf* (also a wolf) disrupted pastures, the *Hafenboch* was a supernatural goat that ran amok in oat fields, the *Halmbock* was a goblin that hid in straws and stems, biting people as they gathered them, and the *Kartoffewult* was a goblin that hid among the potatoes. The descriptions of these creatures bear a strong resemblance to the gopher in *Caddyshack*. Some merely existed to annoy. Others appeared quite dangerous: when harvest workers fell ill in the fields, those around often described the incident as the *Kornwulf* taking them.

In ancient Greece, sows—simultaneously crop pests and sacred animals—often represented Demeter and had a role in the Eleusinean rites, as did rams. Both animals were used in ritual sacrifices at the beginning and end of harvest. At the beginning of plowing seasons, the ancient Greeks threw pigs into the cave of Demeter, and in medieval England, the tradition of the sacrificial ram continued, served as a meal to the harvest workers during the feast of St. John the Baptist. Over time the last sheaves came to be named after cows, rams, sows, and horses—suggesting a direct relationship between corn spirits and the animals sacrificed to ensure a good harvest. Different villages throughout Europe developed tales of mysterious sows found in the fields at harvest. Germany and Russia often expanded the lore to include tales of white dogs, wolves, and women in white appearing in the fields.

Women in White

In eastern Europe, the corn spirits took on tones of ghosts or fae. Polish lore tells of the *Dziwozony*, a race of tall, wild women that lived in the forests. Often compared to Amazons, these supposedly square-headed women stole human children and left changelings in their place as well as attacked men working in remote fields. The farmers seemed especially bedeviled at harvest. Bulgaria and Russia had similar tales of wild women, adding that they lived underground and spent their lives learning the secrets of herbal medicine.

While Slavic men feared ambush by the Dziwozony, women and men alike feared *Poldunica*, a name that translates roughly to "Lady Midday." This spirit appeared either as a woman in white, an elderly woman wandering the fields, or as a twelve-year-old girl carrying a whip. She floated high above the fields on violent gusts of wind. Anyone she touched died immediately. She ambushed women at harvest—especially those who had recently borne children. In what is now the Czech Republic, people described her as a woman with horses' hooves for hands, slanted eyes, and wild hair. Polish accounts also told of a woman in a white robe carrying a sickle; in the summer she lived in the woods and chased field workers that strayed into her territory. She interrogated any harvest worker she caught about the harvest and proper growth procedures. If her victims answered incorrectly, they became deathly ill.

In a similar vein, Serbs told of a woman in white, sometimes young and sometimes old, that accosted people found alone at harvest. She would insist they speak with her for an hour about practices in growing hemp and flax: anyone who answered incorrectly was punished with a wasting illness. The Serbs called her *Pripoblnica*; she also appeared to workers in the fields at noon, guarding the crops and punishing children who walked on the grain, like a bogeyman who was beneficial to parents.

Male Spirits

Meanwhile, male forest spirits appeared at night to reap the corn and bind the sheaves. The mistresses of the farms often brought these helpers food as thanks. The Russians called these beings *ljeschies*—faun-like spirits who lived in the woods but reportedly helped farmers in distress.

Russia, always a bit different from its Slavic siblings, had two major male crop spirits. *Polevik* appeared to overtired harvesters as tall as the corn, and then before their eyes shrank to the size of grain stubble. Some lore said that he ran away before the reapers as they cut with scythes and then jumped into the hands of the final reaper as he cut the last sheaf. To cut the last sheaf was considered good fortune in some communities, but in ones with Polevik, the reaper was viewed as having death living in his hands. This spirit appeared at any time between noon and sunset; workers avoided sleeping in the fields lest Polevik ride over them with his horse.

In addition to the prankish taskmaster, Russian harvesters also honored *Belun*. This helpful spirit appeared only during the day and as a mysterious stranger who helped guide people who lost their way in the tall fields.

Humans and the Harvest

The harvest was closely associated with all finality; those who depended on crops understood the grain as a being that sacrificed itself for greater survival. Parents often told their children that Death lived in the fields, to keep them from playing there during harvesttime. Encounters with many of the legendary entities led to serious illness. While common diseases of the time certainly played into this lore, the connection between spirits and crops also expressed the conflict that is the harvest season: all that work for all that growth and beauty that is all inevitably consumed in the end.

The universal idea of a corn spirit or a series of crop spirits speaks to the intimate connection between humanity and what it sows. As the hunter-gatherer lifestyle evolved into agrarian society, people began feeling the connection to the food that they raised from seed. The act of growing and harvesting from season to season inevitably lead to thoughts on mortality. While most modern gardeners look to the simple pleasures of cyclic work, our ancestral farmers had to face daily how little control human beings really have in this world. Living at the mercy of the elements fed our ancestors' collective imagination: those who grew the food for survival found both allies and enemies in its spirit. This animistic view also led to a degree of empathy with the crops.

The deepest reflection of the human condition is its meditation on what it means to be born only to die. This meditation happened annually for the food growers of the past, amidst the worries for health of family and livestock. This seems especially true in Germany, where the people built folklore around the corn spirit's ultimate resentment of the people who consumed it. The entity might take a harvest worker with it into death out of anger at its lot. We may think of these as silly superstitions now, legends used to make children behave, but beneath the surface is empathy, an awareness—of our utter dependence on nature and how the crops might have thoughts about their own dependence and ultimate death—that gives the tiniest ring of truth to each of these strange accounts.

Sources

Chambers' Encyclopedia: A Dictionary of Universal Knowledge. London: William & Robert Chambers, 1912.

Folkard, Richard. Plant Lore, Legends and Lyrics: Embracing the Myths, Traditions, Superstitions, and Folk-Lore of the Plant Kingdom. London: Sampson Low, Marston, Searle, and Rivington, 1884.

Gentleman's Magazine. "A Sheaf of Corn Lore." Gentleman's Magazine 301, no. 2 (1906): 607-622.

MacCulloch, John Arnott, and Jan Machal. The Mythology of All Races Vol. III: Celtic Slavic. Edited by Louis Herbert Gray. Boston: Marshall Jones Company, 1918.

Diana Rajchel *is a writer, tarot reader, creative coach, and community builder in San Francisco, California. Her book* Divorcing a Real Witch *is a Diagram Prize runner-up, and she is the author of* Mabon *and* Samhain *in the Llewellyn's Sabbat Essentials series.*

The Almond:
Ancient Harbinger of Spring

by Doreen Shababy

While some food writers call the almond the king of nuts because it is so nutritious, what's good for the king is good for the queen and everyone else in the castle too. From Spain, France, and Italy to Greece, Turkey, and North Africa, many Mediterranean cultures consider the almond queen of nuts.

In Human Culture

Almonds are considered "a symbol of sweetness and fragility." In *Nectar and Ambrosia*, Tamra Andrews notes, "The mythic figure of the tree as woman, or as mother, is common to many cultures." Several myths describe a princess turning into an almond tree, including Phyllis of Thrace, who died of a broken heart; Jasmina of Morocco, whose lover died in battle; and princess, Hatim who gave freely of her wealth to the impoverished, like a Moroccan Robin Hood—like an almond tree. People recognized that the almond, like a mother, was generous: it provided nuts and oil for food and body care, even shells for fuel.

However, like all nuts, the almond is also representative of the male principle. An old Phrygian myth from ancient Turkey tells of the virgin goddess Nana, who became pregnant after cosseting an almond in her bosom, subsequently giving birth to the vegetation god Attis. The biblical Aaron's rod, bursting into bloom on the holy tabernacle, is believed to be an almond branch; the blossoms became a model for the Menorah, as specified in the book of Exodus.

In the ancient Hebrew language, the almond was called *shaked*, meaning "to watch for," "to awaken," or "to make haste." This translation possibly refers to the early blooming habit of the almond—the flowers appear before the leaves unfurl. Cultivated many centuries ago, the oil was used in ancient Rome and the Levant, and almond remnants have been discovered in excavations beneath the ancient palace at Knossos, at an even deeper, Neolithic level.

The almond is associated with the Virgin Mary of Christian tradition, symbolizing divine grace. Indeed, many iconographic representations of the Mother Mary depict her image within a "vesica piscis" or "mandorla," an almond-shaped framework (formed by two overlapping circles) within the piece of art; this shape is also associated with the vagina. Paintings representing Mary and the infant Jesus often show almond branches in the iconography.

Almonds are so intrinsic to human culture that there are two structures in our brain called the amygdalae (which comes from the Latin and Greek words for almond) or "amygdala nuclei," which are about the size and shape of an almond. Generally reaching full potential in females before males, the amygdala is part of the limbic system and is associated with decision-making, emotional reactions, and memory. Does the scent of toasted almonds stir up any memories for you? The connection between memory and aroma—including phero-mone detection—are linked with this ancient part of the brain.

The Ancients Grew Almonds, and We Do Too

In *The Folklore of Trees and Shrubs*, author Laura Martin notes that "even in the wild, today's almond is considered a natural ancient hybrid of three wild species found in eastern and central Asia." While the tree most likely originated in Asia and parts of Russia, and while the Phoenicians are credited with spreading it to the western world, it wasn't until the late 1500s that almonds arrived in the Americas. We eat the almond much to our nutritional benefit today, and it's interesting and perhaps even sobering to consider what it means not only to cultivate the land but also to take plants forth and distribute them in other places and in new environments. Perhaps there is something innate about wanting to plant food, something vital and satisfying; some might call this desire the introduc-tion of invasive species. Although the ancient Romans set the standard for organized, well-managed gardens in their fashion, people still communed with wild plants as well as the plants they tended like their own children, like something they loved. And they still do.

The sweet almond tree, *Prunus dulcis* (or *P. amygdalus*), can grow twenty to thirty feet tall, maturing to a spreading dome shape. The *Western Garden Book* describes the almond fruit as "a leathery, flattened, undersized green peach," which doesn't sound very appetizing. The fruit we see on the tree is technically the hull (or mesocarp), which in turn splits open to reveal the shell (endocarp), which contains the actual kernel. Almonds need pollinators from other varieties for fertilization, although some are self-fertile. The fruit (the kernel is technically considered a "drupe") grows from the previous years' new growth and on the two- or three-year-old spurs. Almonds belong to a large group of fruit-bearing trees including the apricot, peach, and cherry, all part of the huge rose family, Rosaceae. California is the largest producer of almonds in the world, and nearly a million beehives are trucked there for February pollination.

Almonds on Our Skin

The tradition of using almond oil for personal body care is as ancient as its use for food. Almond oil is non-drying and widely used in fine cosmetics. It is commonly used for massage therapy and even to condition the wood of oboes and clarinets.

Almond Oil Hand Treatment

To make a traditional hand conditioner, take 1 ounce each cocoa butter, almond oil, and beeswax. Melt them all together, then store in a small wide-mouth jar. Slather this on your hands, knuckles and cuticles at bedtime, don a dainty pair of cotton gloves for sleeping, and wake up to smooth, supple skin. This treatment works for feet as well, wearing cotton socks.

While your sweetie might not like you wearing gloves or socks to bed, the results are worth it. You can also mix a dab of honey with almond oil and use as a fabulously moisturizing facial mask.

Almond Oil Hair Conditioner

Try this simple recipe for a penetrating scalp and hair conditioner, similar to the parsnip hair conditioner I wrote about in my book, *The Wild & Weedy Apothecary*. Gently heat up a small amount (about 3 or 4 ounces) of almond oil. Starting at the scalp, work in some of the warm oil, saturating the hair out to the ends. After all is coated, wrap your hair with plastic (only your hair!), then a towel, and then wait at least 15 minutes. Finish by cleansing with a good herbal shampoo.

Almond Meal Facial Cleanser

Almond meal made from the ground nuts is also used for skin care. The most common method is to use the meal for a facial cleanser that is safe for sensitive skin. You can make your own by grinding fresh almonds in a blender, or purchase some if you use a lot in baking. To use, put a pinch or two of the meal in the palm of your hand. Moisten it with water, honey, yogurt, or even rosewater (ooh la la!), and gently use it to massage the skin of your face and neck. Let it dry a bit, and then rinse with plain water followed by your favorite facial toner. Honey helps the skin retain moisture while the almonds smooth the skin and even skin tone. This is a fabulous treatment for the skin of middle-aged herbalists and others who like to spend a lot of time outdoors.

Almond Milk Lotion

You could also try your hand at making almond milk lotion, a product the Grande Dame of Herbalists, Jeanne Rose, calls "a fine moisturizing agent" which will help tighten pores and diminish dryness. Grind 1 handful of almonds, simmer in enough milk or water to cover them for 15 minutes. Strain, cool, and apply. It doesn't get much easier than this. Keep in fridge for 2 to 3 days. Makes 1–2 cups.

Almonds in the Kitchen

Homemade Almond Milk

Almond milk was frequently substituted for dairy milk during the Middle Ages, mostly because milking cows weren't readily available to the average person. My favorite recipe is fresh and light. Take 1½ cups almonds, rinse well in a colander, then place in a bowl large enough for you to cover the almonds with plenty of water to soak overnight. Drain the soaked almonds (you can leave the skins on or remove if you wish), place in the blender with 4 cups of cold water. Start out on slow speed (it will be very noisy!), then pulverize the almonds for about 30 seconds. Let rest a couple of minutes, then blast them again for another 30 seconds.

Set out a large bowl with a strainer over it and line it with cheesecloth or something similar, like a nut milk bag (yes, Virginia, there is such a thing). Pour the milky pulp into the lined strainer; most of the liquid will go through. Next, pull up the corners of the cloth together so nothing can escape, and squeeze the remaining liquid out of the pulp. Toss the pulp into the compost and refrigerate the milk for up to 3 days. Makes 4 cups.

Almond Paste

Here is a splendid recipe for homemade almond paste (marzipan), which is simple to prepare and delightfully free of chemicals and preservatives. You will need a food processor.

1½ cups almonds

1½ cups confectioner's sugar

1 egg white

1–2 teaspoons almond extract (to taste)

Blanch the almonds by soaking for 1 to 2 minutes in boiling water, and then slip off their skins. Grind the almonds in a food processor until smooth. Add remaining ingredients and process again until smooth. Divide into ½-cup portions, storing in air-tight containers. Refrigerate for 1 month or freeze up to 3 months. Makes about 2 cups.

Use this homemade almond paste to make dainty sweets: *pasti di mandorle* is used in Sicily to make small cakes often decorated with candied dried fruit; *amygdalota* might be found at a Greek wedding; in India, a sweet dessert called *badam halwa* is prepared using ground almonds and saffron.

Meal and Flour

Ground almonds, almond meal (with skins), and almond flour (without skins) are used in baked goods such as muffins and breads, especially in gluten-free and Paleo diets. I have adapted dozens of recipes, from banana bread to blueberry pancakes, using almond meal or flour, with good results. You can't completely switch almond flour for wheat (there are other considerations), but even when I wing it, I usually get lucky. The following recipe uses all-purpose flour, but you could replace the wheat with your favorite gluten-free blend if you desire.

Gingered Almond Tea Bread

  ½ cup butter

  ½ cup natural sugar

  2 eggs

  1½ cups all-purpose flour

  ½ cup almond meal

  2 teaspoons baking powder

  ½ teaspoon salt

  ¼ cup chopped candied ginger

Heat oven to 350°F. Grease and flour a standard-size bread loaf pan. Cream the butter and sugar together until light and fluffy, then gradually beat in the eggs until well blended. Mix the dry ingredients in a separate bowl, then fold into the butter blend; stir in ginger. Turn into the prepared loaf pan and bake for 45 to 50 minutes or until done. Cool 10 minutes in the pan before removing and cooling on wire rack.

Dreaming of Dessert

Dreamlore suggests that when young lads or maidens dream of almond blossoms, they will soon meet their beloved, and when a married person dreams about the blossoms, it indicates a sweet love life. I wonder what it means to dream of cakes and cookies, fruits and nuts . . . Probably time to start baking!

Resources

Andrews, Tamra. *Nectar and Ambrosia: An Encyclopedia of Food in World Mythology*. Santa Barbara, CA: ABC-CLIO, 2000.

Atlas, Nava. *Vegetariana*. Garden City, NY: The Dial Press, 1984.

Bianchini, Francesco and F. Corbetta. *The Complete Book of Fruits and Vegetables*. New York: Crown Publishers, Inc., 1975.

Buchman, Dian Dincin. *Herbal Guide to Natural Health and Beauty*. Garden City, NY: Doubleday & Company, Inc., 1973.

Cartland, Barbara. *The Romance of Food*. Agincourt, Ontario: Methuen Publications, 1984.

Grieve, Mrs. M. *A Modern Herbal*. New York: Dover Publications, 1971 (unabridged republication of 1931 work, Harcourt, Brace & Company).

Martin, Laura C. *The Folklore of Trees and Shrubs*. Chester, CT: The Globe Pequot Press, 1992.

Rose, Jeanne. *Jeanne Rose's Herbal Body Book*. New York: Grosset & Dunlap Publishers, 1976.

———. *Kitchen Cosmetics*. Los Angeles, CA: Panjandrum Books, 1978.

Sunset Books. *Western Garden Book*. Menlo Park, CA: Sunset Publishing Corp., 1988.

Weschcke, Carl. *Growing Nuts in the North*. St. Paul, MN: Webb Publishing Co., 1953.

Doreen Shababy *is the author of* The Wild & Weedy Apothecary. *She lives in northern Idaho and has surrounded herself with herbs and wild plants for decades, making and selling herbal remedies and concocting fabulousness in the kitchen. Doreen is fascinated with food history and has lately been involved with organic, gluten-free baking. She practices various and spontaneous forms of energy work, including Reiki and Source Connection, and she loves working with tarot and other oracle cards. Please visit her at www.doreenshababy.com and www.wildnweedy.com.*

Moon Signs, Phases, and Tables

The Quarters and Signs
of the Moon

Everyone has seen the moon wax and wane through a period of approximately 29½ days. This circuit from new moon to full moon and back again is called the lunation cycle. The cycle is divided into parts called quarters or phases. There are several methods by which this can be done, and the system used in the *Herbal Almanac* may not correspond to those used in other almanacs.

The Quarters

First Quarter

The first quarter begins at the new moon, when the sun and moon are in the same place, or conjunct. (This means the sun and moon are in the same degree of the same sign.) The moon is not visible at first, since it rises at the same time as the sun. The new moon is the time of new beginnings of projects that favor growth, externalization of activities, and the growth of ideas. The first quarter is the time of germination, emergence, beginnings, and outwardly directed activity.

Second Quarter

The second quarter begins halfway between the new moon and the full moon, when the sun and moon are at a right angle, or a 90° square, to each other. This half moon rises around noon and sets around midnight, so it can be seen in the western sky during the first half of the night. The second quarter is the time of growth and articulation of things that already exist.

Third Quarter

The third quarter begins at the full moon, when the sun and moon are opposite one another and the full light of the sun can shine on the full sphere of the moon. The round moon can be seen rising in the east at sunset, then rising a little later each evening. The full moon stands for illumination, fulfillment, culmination, completion, drawing inward, unrest, emotional expressions, and hasty actions leading to failure. The third quarter is a time of maturity, fruition, and the assumption of the full form of expression.

Fourth Quarter

The fourth quarter begins about halfway between the full moon and the new moon, when the sun and moon are again at a right angle, or a 90° square, to each other. This decreasing moon rises at midnight and can be seen in the east during the last half of the night, reaching the overhead position just about as the sun rises. The fourth quarter is a time of disintegration and drawing back for reorganization and reflection.

The Signs

Moon in Aries

Moon in Aries is good for starting things and initiating change, but actions may lack staying power. Activities requiring assertiveness and courage are favored. Things occur rapidly but also quickly pass.

Moon in Taurus

Things begun when the moon is in Taurus last the longest and tend to increase in value. This is a good time for any activity that requires patience, practicality, and perseverance. Things begun now also tend to become habitual and hard to alter.

Moon in Gemini

Moon in Gemini is a good time to exchange ideas, meet with people, or be in situations that require versatility and quick thinking. Things begun now are easily changed by outside influences.

Moon in Cancer

Moon in Cancer is a good time to grow things. It stimulates emotional rapport between people and is a good time to build personal friendships, though people may be more emotional and moody than usual.

Moon in Leo

Moon in Leo is a good time for public appearances, showmanship, being seen, entertaining, drama, recreation, and happy pursuits. People may be overly concerned with praise and subject to flattery.

Moon in Virgo

Moon in Virgo is good for any task that requires close attention to detail and careful analysis of information. There is a focus on health, hygiene, and daily schedules. Watch for a tendency to overdo and overwork.

Moon in Libra

Moon in Libra is a good time to form partnerships of any kind and to negotiate. It discourages spontaneous initiative, so working with a partner is essential. Artistic work and teamwork are highlighted.

Moon in Scorpio

Moon in Scorpio increases awareness of psychic power and favors any activity that requires intensity and focus. This is a good time to conduct research and to end connections thoroughly. There is a tendency to manipulate.

Moon in Sagittarius

Moon in Sagittarius is good for any activity that requires honesty, candor, imagination, and confidence in the flow of life. This is a good time to tackle things that need improvement, but watch out for a tendency to proselytize.

Moon in Capricorn

Moon in Capricorn increases awareness of the need for structure, discipline, and patience. This is a good time to set goals and plan for the future. Those in authority may be insensitive at this time.

Moon in Aquarius

Moon in Aquarius favors activities that are unique and individualistic and that concern society as a whole. This is a good time to pursue humanitarian efforts and to identify improvements that can be made. People may be more intellectual than emotional under this influence.

Moon in Pisces

Moon in Pisces is a good time for any kind of introspective, philanthropic, meditative, psychic, or artistic work. At this time personal boundaries may be blurred, and people may be prone to seeing what they want to see rather than what is really there.

January Moon Table

Date	Sign	Element	Nature	Phase
1 Sun	Aquarius	Air	Barren	1st
2 Mon 4:57 am	Pisces	Water	Fruitful	1st
3 Tue	Pisces	Water	Fruitful	1st
4 Wed 11:20 am	Aries	Fire	Barren	1st
5 Thu	Aries	Fire	Barren	2nd 2:47 pm
6 Fri 3:18 pm	Taurus	Earth	Semi-fruitful	2nd
7 Sat	Taurus	Earth	Semi-fruitful	2nd
8 Sun 5:06 pm	Gemini	Air	Barren	2nd
9 Mon	Gemini	Air	Barren	2nd
10 Tue 5:49 pm	Cancer	Water	Fruitful	2nd
11 Wed	Cancer	Water	Fruitful	2nd
12 Thu 7:08 pm	Leo	Fire	Barren	Full 6:34 am
13 Fri	Leo	Fire	Barren	3rd
14 Sat 10:52 pm	Virgo	Earth	Barren	3rd
15 Sun	Virgo	Earth	Barren	3rd
16 Mon	Virgo	Earth	Barren	3rd
17 Tue 6:16 am	Libra	Air	Semi-fruitful	3rd
18 Wed	Libra	Air	Semi-fruitful	3rd
19 Thu 5:09 pm	Scorpio	Water	Fruitful	4th 5:13 pm
20 Fri	Scorpio	Water	Fruitful	4th
21 Sat	Scorpio	Water	Fruitful	4th
22 Sun 5:45 am	Sagittarius	Fire	Barren	4th
23 Mon	Sagittarius	Fire	Barren	4th
24 Tue 5:43 pm	Capricorn	Earth	Semi-fruitful	4th
25 Wed	Capricorn	Earth	Semi-fruitful	4th
26 Thu	Capricorn	Earth	Semi-fruitful	4th
27 Fri 3:37 am	Aquarius	Air	Barren	New 7:07 pm
28 Sat	Aquarius	Air	Barren	1st
29 Sun 11:10 am	Pisces	Water	Fruitful	1st
30 Mon	Pisces	Water	Fruitful	1st
31 Tue 4:46 pm	Aries	Fire	Barren	1st

February Moon Table

Date	Sign	Element	Nature	Phase
1 Wed	Aries	Fire	Barren	1st
2 Thu 8:50 pm	Taurus	Earth	Semi-fruitful	1st
3 Fri	Taurus	Earth	Semi-fruitful	2nd 11:19 pm
4 Sat 11:44 pm	Gemini	Air	Barren	2nd
5 Sun	Gemini	Air	Barren	2nd
6 Mon	Gemini	Air	Barren	2nd
7 Tue 2:03 am	Cancer	Water	Fruitful	2nd
8 Wed	Cancer	Water	Fruitful	2nd
9 Thu 4:41 am	Leo	Fire	Barren	2nd
10 Fri	Leo	Fire	Barren	Full 7:33 pm
11 Sat 8:52 am	Virgo	Earth	Barren	3rd
12 Sun	Virgo	Earth	Barren	3rd
13 Mon 3:43 pm	Libra	Air	Semi-fruitful	3rd
14 Tue	Libra	Air	Semi-fruitful	3rd
15 Wed	Libra	Air	Semi-fruitful	3rd
16 Thu 1:41 am	Scorpio	Water	Fruitful	3rd
17 Fri	Scorpio	Water	Fruitful	3rd
18 Sat 1:52 pm	Sagittarius	Fire	Barren	4th 2:33 pm
19 Sun	Sagittarius	Fire	Barren	4th
20 Mon	Sagittarius	Fire	Barren	4th
21 Tue 2:08 am	Capricorn	Earth	Semi-fruitful	4th
22 Wed	Capricorn	Earth	Semi-fruitful	4th
23 Thu 12:17 pm	Aquarius	Air	Barren	4th
24 Fri	Aquarius	Air	Barren	4th
25 Sat 7:24 pm	Pisces	Water	Fruitful	4th
26 Sun	Pisces	Water	Fruitful	New 9:58 am
27 Mon 11:52 pm	Aries	Fire	Barren	1st
28 Tue	Aries	Fire	Barren	1st

Times are in Eastern Time.

March Moon Table

Date	Sign	Element	Nature	Phase
1 Wed	Aries	Fire	Barren	1st
2 Thu 2:43 am	Taurus	Earth	Semi-fruitful	1st
3 Fri	Taurus	Earth	Semi-fruitful	1st
4 Sat 5:05 am	Gemini	Air	Barren	1st
5 Sun	Gemini	Air	Barren	2nd 6:32 am
6 Mon 7:54 am	Cancer	Water	Fruitful	2nd
7 Tue	Cancer	Water	Fruitful	2nd
8 Wed 11:45 am	Leo	Fire	Barren	2nd
9 Thu	Leo	Fire	Barren	2nd
10 Fri 5:07 pm	Virgo	Earth	Barren	2nd
11 Sat	Virgo	Earth	Barren	2nd
12 Sun	Virgo	Earth	Barren	Full 10:54 am
13 Mon 1:28 am	Libra	Air	Semi-fruitful	3rd
14 Tue	Libra	Air	Semi-fruitful	3rd
15 Wed 11:11 am	Scorpio	Water	Fruitful	3rd
16 Thu	Scorpio	Water	Fruitful	3rd
17 Fri 11:00 pm	Sagittarius	Fire	Barren	3rd
18 Sat	Sagittarius	Fire	Barren	3rd
19 Sun	Sagittarius	Fire	Barren	3rd
20 Mon 11:31 am	Capricorn	Earth	Semi-fruitful	4th 11:58 am
21 Tue	Capricorn	Earth	Semi-fruitful	4th
22 Wed 10:28 pm	Aquarius	Air	Barren	4th
23 Thu	Aquarius	Air	Barren	4th
24 Fri	Aquarius	Air	Barren	4th
25 Sat 6:06 am	Pisces	Water	Fruitful	4th
26 Sun	Pisces	Water	Fruitful	4th
27 Mon 10:11 am	Aries	Fire	Barren	New 10:57 pm
28 Tue	Aries	Fire	Barren	1st
29 Wed 11:48 am	Taurus	Earth	Semi-fruitful	1st
30 Thu	Taurus	Earth	Semi-fruitful	1st
31 Fri 12:40 pm	Gemini	Air	Barren	1st

April Moon Table

Date	Sign	Element	Nature	Phase
1 Sat	Gemini	Air	Barren	1st
2 Sun 2:27 pm	Cancer	Water	Fruitful	1st
3 Mon	Cancer	Water	Fruitful	2nd 2:39 pm
4 Tue 6:13 pm	Leo	Fire	Barren	2nd
5 Wed	Leo	Fire	Barren	2nd
6 Thu	Leo	Fire	Barren	2nd
7 Fri 12:20 am	Virgo	Earth	Barren	2nd
8 Sat	Virgo	Earth	Barren	2nd
9 Sun 8:34 am	Libra	Air	Semi-fruitful	2nd
10 Mon	Libra	Air	Semi-fruitful	2nd
11 Tue 6:42 pm	Scorpio	Water	Fruitful	Full 2:08 am
12 Wed	Scorpio	Water	Fruitful	3rd
13 Thu	Scorpio	Water	Fruitful	3rd
14 Fri 6:27 am	Sagittarius	Fire	Barren	3rd
15 Sat	Sagittarius	Fire	Barren	3rd
16 Sun 7:05 pm	Capricorn	Earth	Semi-fruitful	3rd
17 Mon	Capricorn	Earth	Semi-fruitful	3rd
18 Tue	Capricorn	Earth	Semi-fruitful	3rd
19 Wed 6:52 am	Aquarius	Air	Barren	4th 5:57 am
20 Thu	Aquarius	Air	Barren	4th
21 Fri 3:43 pm	Pisces	Water	Fruitful	4th
22 Sat	Pisces	Water	Fruitful	4th
23 Sun 8:32 pm	Aries	Fire	Barren	4th
24 Mon	Aries	Fire	Barren	4th
25 Tue 9:56 pm	Taurus	Earth	Semi-fruitful	4th
26 Wed	Taurus	Earth	Semi-fruitful	New 8:16 am
27 Thu 9:39 pm	Gemini	Air	Barren	1st
28 Fri	Gemini	Air	Barren	1st
29 Sat 9:48 pm	Cancer	Water	Fruitful	1st
30 Sun	Cancer	Water	Fruitful	1st

Times are in Eastern Time.

May Moon Table

Date	Sign	Element	Nature	Phase
1 Mon	Cancer	Water	Fruitful	1st
2 Tue 12:12 am	Leo	Fire	Barren	2nd 10:47 pm
3 Wed	Leo	Fire	Barren	2nd
4 Thu 5:47 am	Virgo	Earth	Barren	2nd
5 Fri	Virgo	Earth	Barren	2nd
6 Sat 2:20 pm	Libra	Air	Semi-fruitful	2nd
7 Sun	Libra	Air	Semi-fruitful	2nd
8 Mon	Libra	Air	Semi-fruitful	2nd
9 Tue 1:01 am	Scorpio	Water	Fruitful	2nd
10 Wed	Scorpio	Water	Fruitful	Full 5:42 pm
11 Thu 12:59 pm	Sagittarius	Fire	Barren	3rd
12 Fri	Sagittarius	Fire	Barren	3rd
13 Sat	Sagittarius	Fire	Barren	3rd
14 Sun 1:37 am	Capricorn	Earth	Semi-fruitful	3rd
15 Mon	Capricorn	Earth	Semi-fruitful	3rd
16 Tue 1:50 pm	Aquarius	Air	Barren	3rd
17 Wed	Aquarius	Air	Barren	3rd
18 Thu 11:52 pm	Pisces	Water	Fruitful	4th 8:33 pm
19 Fri	Pisces	Water	Fruitful	4th
20 Sat	Pisces	Water	Fruitful	4th
21 Sun 6:10 am	Aries	Fire	Barren	4th
22 Mon	Aries	Fire	Barren	4th
23 Tue 8:33 am	Taurus	Earth	Semi-fruitful	4th
24 Wed	Taurus	Earth	Semi-fruitful	4th
25 Thu 8:15 am	Gemini	Air	Barren	New 3:44 pm
26 Fri	Gemini	Air	Barren	1st
27 Sat 7:25 am	Cancer	Water	Fruitful	1st
28 Sun	Cancer	Water	Fruitful	1st
29 Mon 8:12 am	Leo	Fire	Barren	1st
30 Tue	Leo	Fire	Barren	1st
31 Wed 12:16 pm	Virgo	Earth	Barren	1st

June Moon Table

Date	Sign	Element	Nature	Phase
1 Thu	Virgo	Earth	Barren	2nd 8:42 am
2 Fri 8:04 pm	Libra	Air	Semi-fruitful	2nd
3 Sat	Libra	Air	Semi-fruitful	2nd
4 Sun	Libra	Air	Semi-fruitful	2nd
5 Mon 6:46 am	Scorpio	Water	Fruitful	2nd
6 Tue	Scorpio	Water	Fruitful	2nd
7 Wed 6:59 pm	Sagittarius	Fire	Barren	2nd
8 Thu	Sagittarius	Fire	Barren	2nd
9 Fri	Sagittarius	Fire	Barren	Full 9:10 am
10 Sat 7:36 am	Capricorn	Earth	Semi-fruitful	3rd
11 Sun	Capricorn	Earth	Semi-fruitful	3rd
12 Mon 7:45 pm	Aquarius	Air	Barren	3rd
13 Tue	Aquarius	Air	Barren	3rd
14 Wed	Aquarius	Air	Barren	3rd
15 Thu 6:17 am	Pisces	Water	Fruitful	3rd
16 Fri	Pisces	Water	Fruitful	3rd
17 Sat 1:55 pm	Aries	Fire	Barren	4th 7:33 am
18 Sun	Aries	Fire	Barren	4th
19 Mon 5:53 pm	Taurus	Earth	Semi-fruitful	4th
20 Tue	Taurus	Earth	Semi-fruitful	4th
21 Wed 6:44 pm	Gemini	Air	Barren	4th
22 Thu	Gemini	Air	Barren	4th
23 Fri 6:07 pm	Cancer	Water	Fruitful	New 10:31 pm
24 Sat	Cancer	Water	Fruitful	1st
25 Sun 6:06 pm	Leo	Fire	Barren	1st
26 Mon	Leo	Fire	Barren	1st
27 Tue 8:41 pm	Virgo	Earth	Barren	1st
28 Wed	Virgo	Earth	Barren	1st
29 Thu	Virgo	Earth	Barren	1st
30 Fri 3:02 am	Libra	Air	Semi-fruitful	2nd 8:51 pm

Times are in Eastern Time.

July Moon Table

Date	Sign	Element	Nature	Phase
1 Sat	Libra	Air	Semi-fruitful	2nd
2 Sun 12:59 pm	Scorpio	Water	Fruitful	2nd
3 Mon	Scorpio	Water	Fruitful	2nd
4 Tue	Scorpio	Water	Fruitful	2nd
5 Wed 1:08 am	Sagittarius	Fire	Barren	2nd
6 Thu	Sagittarius	Fire	Barren	2nd
7 Fri 1:45 pm	Capricorn	Earth	Semi-fruitful	2nd
8 Sat	Capricorn	Earth	Semi-fruitful	2nd
9 Sun	Capricorn	Earth	Semi-fruitful	Full 12:07 am
10 Mon 1:35 am	Aquarius	Air	Barren	3rd
11 Tue	Aquarius	Air	Barren	3rd
12 Wed 11:51 am	Pisces	Water	Fruitful	3rd
13 Thu	Pisces	Water	Fruitful	3rd
14 Fri 7:52 pm	Aries	Fire	Barren	3rd
15 Sat	Aries	Fire	Barren	3rd
16 Sun	Aries	Fire	Barren	4th 3:26 pm
17 Mon 1:04 am	Taurus	Earth	Semi-fruitful	4th
18 Tue	Taurus	Earth	Semi-fruitful	4th
19 Wed 3:31 am	Gemini	Air	Barren	4th
20 Thu	Gemini	Air	Barren	4th
21 Fri 4:09 am	Cancer	Water	Fruitful	4th
22 Sat	Cancer	Water	Fruitful	4th
23 Sun 4:34 am	Leo	Fire	Barren	New 5:46 am
24 Mon	Leo	Fire	Barren	1st
25 Tue 6:32 am	Virgo	Earth	Barren	1st
26 Wed	Virgo	Earth	Barren	1st
27 Thu 11:37 am	Libra	Air	Semi-fruitful	1st
28 Fri	Libra	Air	Semi-fruitful	1st
29 Sat 8:23 pm	Scorpio	Water	Fruitful	1st
30 Sun	Scorpio	Water	Fruitful	2nd 11:23 am
31 Mon	Scorpio	Water	Fruitful	2nd

August Moon Table

Date	Sign	Element	Nature	Phase
1 Tue 8:01 am	Sagittarius	Fire	Barren	2nd
2 Wed	Sagittarius	Fire	Barren	2nd
3 Thu 8:37 pm	Capricorn	Earth	Semi-fruitful	2nd
4 Fri	Capricorn	Earth	Semi-fruitful	2nd
5 Sat	Capricorn	Earth	Semi-fruitful	2nd
6 Sun 8:15 am	Aquarius	Air	Barren	2nd
7 Mon	Aquarius	Air	Barren	Full 2:11 pm
8 Tue 5:56 pm	Pisces	Water	Fruitful	3rd
9 Wed	Pisces	Water	Fruitful	3rd
10 Thu	Pisces	Water	Fruitful	3rd
11 Fri 1:22 am	Aries	Fire	Barren	3rd
12 Sat	Aries	Fire	Barren	3rd
13 Sun 6:40 am	Taurus	Earth	Semi-fruitful	3rd
14 Mon	Taurus	Earth	Semi-fruitful	4th 9:15 pm
15 Tue 10:06 am	Gemini	Air	Barren	4th
16 Wed	Gemini	Air	Barren	4th
17 Thu 12:13 pm	Cancer	Water	Fruitful	4th
18 Fri	Cancer	Water	Fruitful	4th
19 Sat 1:55 pm	Leo	Fire	Barren	4th
20 Sun	Leo	Fire	Barren	4th
21 Mon 4:25 pm	Virgo	Earth	Barren	New 2:30 pm
22 Tue	Virgo	Earth	Barren	1st
23 Wed 9:05 pm	Libra	Air	Semi-fruitful	1st
24 Thu	Libra	Air	Semi-fruitful	1st
25 Fri	Libra	Air	Semi-fruitful	1st
26 Sat 4:53 am	Scorpio	Water	Fruitful	1st
27 Sun	Scorpio	Water	Fruitful	1st
28 Mon 3:48 pm	Sagittarius	Fire	Barren	1st
29 Tue	Sagittarius	Fire	Barren	2nd 4:13 am
30 Wed	Sagittarius	Fire	Barren	2nd
31 Thu 4:18 am	Capricorn	Earth	Semi-fruitful	2nd

Times are in Eastern Time.

September Moon Table

Date	Sign	Element	Nature	Phase
1 Fri	Capricorn	Earth	Semi-fruitful	2nd
2 Sat 4:06 pm	Aquarius	Air	Barren	2nd
3 Sun	Aquarius	Air	Barren	2nd
4 Mon	Aquarius	Air	Barren	2nd
5 Tue 1:28 am	Pisces	Water	Fruitful	2nd
6 Wed	Pisces	Water	Fruitful	Full 3:03 am
7 Thu 8:01 am	Aries	Fire	Barren	3rd
8 Fri	Aries	Fire	Barren	3rd
9 Sat 12:23 pm	Taurus	Earth	Semi-fruitful	3rd
10 Sun	Taurus	Earth	Semi-fruitful	3rd
11 Mon 3:29 pm	Gemini	Air	Barren	3rd
12 Tue	Gemini	Air	Barren	3rd
13 Wed 6:12 pm	Cancer	Water	Fruitful	4th 2:25 am
14 Thu	Cancer	Water	Fruitful	4th
15 Fri 9:09 pm	Leo	Fire	Barren	4th
16 Sat	Leo	Fire	Barren	4th
17 Sun	Leo	Fire	Barren	4th
18 Mon 12:52 am	Virgo	Earth	Barren	4th
19 Tue	Virgo	Earth	Barren	4th
20 Wed 6:06 am	Libra	Air	Semi-fruitful	New 1:30 am
21 Thu	Libra	Air	Semi-fruitful	1st
22 Fri 1:40 pm	Scorpio	Water	Fruitful	1st
23 Sat	Scorpio	Water	Fruitful	1st
24 Sun	Scorpio	Water	Fruitful	1st
25 Mon 12:01 am	Sagittarius	Fire	Barren	1st
26 Tue	Sagittarius	Fire	Barren	1st
27 Wed 12:24 pm	Capricorn	Earth	Semi-fruitful	2nd 10:54 pm
28 Thu	Capricorn	Earth	Semi-fruitful	2nd
29 Fri	Capricorn	Earth	Semi-fruitful	2nd
30 Sat 12:40 am	Aquarius	Air	Barren	2nd

October Moon Table

Date	Sign	Element	Nature	Phase
1 Sun	Aquarius	Air	Barren	2nd
2 Mon 10:26 am	Pisces	Water	Fruitful	2nd
3 Tue	Pisces	Water	Fruitful	2nd
4 Wed 4:40 pm	Aries	Fire	Barren	2nd
5 Thu	Aries	Fire	Barren	Full 2:40 pm
6 Fri 7:56 pm	Taurus	Earth	Semi-fruitful	3rd
7 Sat	Taurus	Earth	Semi-fruitful	3rd
8 Sun 9:44 pm	Gemini	Air	Barren	3rd
9 Mon	Gemini	Air	Barren	3rd
10 Tue 11:38 pm	Cancer	Water	Fruitful	3rd
11 Wed	Cancer	Water	Fruitful	3rd
12 Thu	Cancer	Water	Fruitful	4th 8:25 am
13 Fri 2:41 am	Leo	Fire	Barren	4th
14 Sat	Leo	Fire	Barren	4th
15 Sun 7:19 am	Virgo	Earth	Barren	4th
16 Mon	Virgo	Earth	Barren	4th
17 Tue 1:35 pm	Libra	Air	Semi-fruitful	4th
18 Wed	Libra	Air	Semi-fruitful	4th
19 Thu 9:41 pm	Scorpio	Water	Fruitful	New 3:12 pm
20 Fri	Scorpio	Water	Fruitful	1st
21 Sat	Scorpio	Water	Fruitful	1st
22 Sun 7:57 am	Sagittarius	Fire	Barren	1st
23 Mon	Sagittarius	Fire	Barren	1st
24 Tue 8:12 pm	Capricorn	Earth	Semi-fruitful	1st
25 Wed	Capricorn	Earth	Semi-fruitful	1st
26 Thu	Capricorn	Earth	Semi-fruitful	1st
27 Fri 8:59 am	Aquarius	Air	Barren	2nd 6:22 pm
28 Sat	Aquarius	Air	Barren	2nd
29 Sun 7:46 pm	Pisces	Water	Fruitful	2nd
30 Mon	Pisces	Water	Fruitful	2nd
31 Tue	Pisces	Water	Fruitful	2nd

Times are in Eastern Time.

November Moon Table

Date	Sign	Element	Nature	Phase
1 Wed 2:43 am	Aries	Fire	Barren	2nd
2 Thu	Aries	Fire	Barren	2nd
3 Fri 5:46 am	Taurus	Earth	Semi-fruitful	2nd
4 Sat	Taurus	Earth	Semi-fruitful	Full 1:23 am
5 Sun 5:26 am	Gemini	Air	Barren	3rd
6 Mon	Gemini	Air	Barren	3rd
7 Tue 5:45 am	Cancer	Water	Fruitful	3rd
8 Wed	Cancer	Water	Fruitful	3rd
9 Thu 7:29 am	Leo	Fire	Barren	3rd
10 Fri	Leo	Fire	Barren	4th 3:36 pm
11 Sat 11:41 am	Virgo	Earth	Barren	4th
12 Sun	Virgo	Earth	Barren	4th
13 Mon 6:26 pm	Libra	Air	Semi-fruitful	4th
14 Tue	Libra	Air	Semi-fruitful	4th
15 Wed	Libra	Air	Semi-fruitful	4th
16 Thu 3:19 am	Scorpio	Water	Fruitful	4th
17 Fri	Scorpio	Water	Fruitful	4th
18 Sat 1:59 pm	Sagittarius	Fire	Barren	New 6:42 am
19 Sun	Sagittarius	Fire	Barren	1st
20 Mon	Sagittarius	Fire	Barren	1st
21 Tue 2:14 am	Capricorn	Earth	Semi-fruitful	1st
22 Wed	Capricorn	Earth	Semi-fruitful	1st
23 Thu 3:14 pm	Aquarius	Air	Barren	1st
24 Fri	Aquarius	Air	Barren	1st
25 Sat	Aquarius	Air	Barren	1st
26 Sun 3:04 am	Pisces	Water	Fruitful	2nd 12:03 pm
27 Mon	Pisces	Water	Fruitful	2nd
28 Tue 11:30 am	Aries	Fire	Barren	2nd
29 Wed	Aries	Fire	Barren	2nd
30 Thu 3:38 pm	Taurus	Earth	Semi-fruitful	2nd

December Moon Table

Date	Sign	Element	Nature	Phase
1 Fri	Taurus	Earth	Semi-fruitful	2nd
2 Sat 4:21 pm	Gemini	Air	Barren	2nd
3 Sun	Gemini	Air	Barren	Full 10:47 am
4 Mon 3:37 pm	Cancer	Water	Fruitful	3rd
5 Tue	Cancer	Water	Fruitful	3rd
6 Wed 3:37 pm	Leo	Fire	Barren	3rd
7 Thu	Leo	Fire	Barren	3rd
8 Fri 6:09 pm	Virgo	Earth	Barren	3rd
9 Sat	Virgo	Earth	Barren	3rd
10 Sun	Virgo	Earth	Barren	4th 2:51 am
11 Mon 12:01 am	Libra	Air	Semi-fruitful	4th
12 Tue	Libra	Air	Semi-fruitful	4th
13 Wed 8:59 am	Scorpio	Water	Fruitful	4th
14 Thu	Scorpio	Water	Fruitful	4th
15 Fri 8:07 pm	Sagittarius	Fire	Barren	4th
16 Sat	Sagittarius	Fire	Barren	4th
17 Sun	Sagittarius	Fire	Barren	4th
18 Mon 8:33 am	Capricorn	Earth	Semi-fruitful	New 1:30 am
19 Tue	Capricorn	Earth	Semi-fruitful	1st
20 Wed 9:29 pm	Aquarius	Air	Barren	1st
21 Thu	Aquarius	Air	Barren	1st
22 Fri	Aquarius	Air	Barren	1st
23 Sat 9:42 am	Pisces	Water	Fruitful	1st
24 Sun	Pisces	Water	Fruitful	1st
25 Mon 7:27 pm	Aries	Fire	Barren	1st
26 Tue	Aries	Fire	Barren	2nd 4:20 am
27 Wed	Aries	Fire	Barren	2nd
28 Thu 1:23 am	Taurus	Earth	Semi-fruitful	2nd
29 Fri	Taurus	Earth	Semi-fruitful	2nd
30 Sat 3:31 am	Gemini	Air	Barren	2nd
31 Sun	Gemini	Air	Barren	2nd

Times are in Eastern Time.

Dates to Destroy Weeds and Pests

Dates	Sign	Quarter
Jan 12, 7:08 pm–Jan 14, 10:52 pm	Leo	3rd
Jan 14, 10:52 pm–Jan 17, 6:16 am	Virgo	3rd
Jan 22, 5:45 am–Jan 24, 5:43 pm	Sagittarius	4th
Jan 27, 3:37 am–Jan 27, 7:07 pm	Aquarius	4th
Feb 10, 7:33 pm–Feb 11, 8:52 am	Leo	3rd
Feb 11, 8:52 am–Feb 13, 3:43 pm	Virgo	3rd
Feb 18, 1:52 pm–Feb 18, 2:33 pm	Sagittarius	3rd
Feb 18, 2:33 pm–Feb 21, 2:08 am	Sagittarius	4th
Feb 23, 12:17 pm–Feb 25, 7:24 pm	Aquarius	4th
Mar 12, 10:54 am–Mar 13, 1:28 am	Virgo	3rd
Mar 17, 11:00 pm–Mar 20, 11:31 am	Sagittarius	3rd
Mar 22, 10:28 pm–Mar 25, 6:06 am	Aquarius	4th
Mar 27, 10:11 am–Mar 27, 10:57 pm	Aries	4th
Apr 14, 6:27 am–Apr 16, 7:05 pm	Sagittarius	3rd
Apr 19, 6:52 am–Apr 21, 3:43 pm	Aquarius	4th
Apr 23, 8:32 pm–Apr 25, 9:56 pm	Aries	4th
May 11, 12:59 pm–May, 14 1:37 am	Sagittarius	3rd
May 16, 1:50 pm–May, 18 8:33 pm	Aquarius	3rd
May 18, 8:33 pm–May, 18 11:52 pm	Aquarius	4th
May 21, 6:10 am–May, 238:33 am	Aries	4th
May 25, 8:15 am–May, 25 3:44 pm	Gemini	4th
Jun 9, 9:10 am–Jun 10, 7:36 am	Sagittarius	3rd
Jun 12, 7:45 pm–Jun 15, 6:17 am	Aquarius	3rd
Jun 17, 1:55 pm–Jun 19, 5:53 pm	Aries	4th
Jun 21, 6:44 pm–Jun 23, 6:07 pm	Gemini	4th
Jul 10, 1:35 am–Jul 12, 11:51 am	Aquarius	3rd
Jul 14, 7:52 pm–Jul 16, 3:26 pm	Aries	3rd

Dates to Destroy Weeds and Pests

Dates	Sign	Quarter
Jul 16, 3:26 pm–Jul 17, 1:04 am	Aries	4th
Jul 19, 3:31 am–Jul 21, 4:09 am	Gemini	4th
Jul 23, 4:34 am–Jul 23, 5:46 am	Leo	4th
Aug 7, 2:11 pm–Aug 8, 5:56 pm	Aquarius	3rd
Aug 11, 1:22 am–Aug 13, 6:40 am	Aries	3rd
Aug 15, 10:06 am–Aug 17, 12:13 pm	Gemini	4th
Aug 19, 1:55 pm–Aug 21, 2:30 pm	Leo	4th
Sep 7, 8:01 am–Sep 9, 12:23 pm	Aries	3rd
Sep 11, 3:29 pm–Sep 13, 2:25 am	Gemini	3rd
Sep 13, 2:25 am–Sep 13, 6:12 pm	Gemini	4th
Sep 15, 9:09 pm–Sep 18, 12:52 am	Leo	4th
Sep 18, 12:52 am–Sep 20, 1:30 am	Virgo	4th
Oct 5, 2:40 pm–Oct 6, 7:56 pm	Aries	3rd
Oct 8, 9:44 pm–Oct 10, 11:38 pm	Gemini	3rd
Oct 13, 2:41 am–Oct 15, 7:19 am	Leo	4th
Oct 15, 7:19 am–Oct 17, 1:35 pm	Virgo	4th
Nov 5, 5:26 am–Nov 7, 5:45 am	Gemini	3rd
Nov 9, 7:29 am–Nov 10, 3:36 pm	Leo	3rd
Nov 10, 3:36 pm–Nov 11, 11:41 am	Leo	4th
Nov 11, 11:41 am–Nov 13, 6:26 pm	Virgo	4th
Dec 3, 10:47 am–Dec 4, 3:37 pm	Gemini	3rd
Dec 6, 3:37 pm–Dec 8, 6:09 pm	Leo	3rd
Dec 8, 6:09 pm–Dec 10, 2:51 am	Virgo	3rd
Dec 10, 2:51 am–Dec 11, 12:01 am	Virgo	4th
Dec 15, 8:07 pm–Dec 18, 1:30 am	Sagittarius	4th

Times are in Eastern Time.